"*Revenge of the Com...* culture emerging from the technology revolution is evolving as quickly as the technology that drives it. As someone who has personally crossed 'the digital divide' career-wise, I wish this book had been available during my own transition. It is filled with fascinating stories of many of the landmark developments in computing history, punctuated with comments and observations from the survey respondents. What emerges from the survey results is sometimes surprising, insightful, occasionally disturbing, often funny, and always entertaining…
Where you are a novice or power-user, you will find *Revenge of the Computer Widow* a delightful read… not to mention, it is a great alternative to taking your laptop to bed…"
Greg Abrams, Director of Production, Sonoptic Technologies Inc.,
abrams@sonoptic.com

"“ *Revenge of the Computer Widow*” gives a glimpse into the sometimes strange workings of the computer geek ’s mind. Nattalia Lea has exhaustively documented the likes, dislikes, foods, drinks, prejudices, habits and innermost thoughts of those who work with computers, whether as practitioners or as victims. If you are a programmer, or user, analyst or tech writer, or merely a civilian who loves to hate Bill Gates, you & #8217'll find plenty of kindred spirits in Ms. Lea’s comprehensive analysis of the inhabitants of *Silicon Cowtown*. If you don’t recognize yourself, you’ll be sure to recognize your co-worker!"
Revett Eldred, founder of Minerva Technology Inc.,
(now part of xwave solutions.)

"*Revenge of the Computer Widow* mixes research and analysis with humor (sometimes sardonic) and techno-poignancy to create what I believe will become a watershed work. Nattalia Lea has an amazing capacity to inform you while you think you are just being entertained. Enjoy."
Jim Blasingame, The Small Business Advocate, www.smallbusinessadvocate.com

"You'll be :-D
You'll be :'-(
You'll be <:-0
Revenge of the Computer Widow reveals all, from abacus to sex to UNIX, everything you ever wanted to know about geeks, but were too afraid to ask!

So you don't feel like you're all alone in this world, as you look at the back of his head, hundreds of other computer widows are probably doing the same thing, this very second.

If you're looking for Mr. or Ms. Right, and you think the Internet would be a really neat place to meet someone, better read this book.

If you're Dilbert's boss, and you are too clued out to observe your employee geeks, get the book and have someone read it to you.

If your customers are geeks, you need this book.

Looking for Mister Good Geek? Need the true dirt on the geek's secret lives and desires? *Revenge of the Computer Widow* gives you the insight into the geek mystique that would normally take light-years to accumulate. Nattalia's own personal story brings the information to life, and offers an inspiring success story to computer challenged spouses! Jam-packed with true stories from hundreds of geeks and computer widows, it provides the definitive answer to that age-old question, What is a geek? The results may shock you!"

Liza Schmalcel, co-founder, www.geekculture.com

"*Revenge of the Computer Widow* provides a comprehensive review that discusses how the new Internet wealth has created a young upscale socio-economic elite and the impact of on-line relationships in our daily lives. Most important, the book outlines the significant impact of Cyber widows, or those who are not hooked on the Net live with a cyber-obsessed loved one. As Cyber affairs rapidly become a prominent issue in divorce cases, the book addresses how Cyber widows or those left in the aftermath of such an event will survive."
Dr. Kimberly S. Young, Founder and President of Center for On-Line Addiction and author of *Caught in the Net* e-mail:ksy@netaddiction.com

"Oh, dear, *Revenge of the Computer Widow* slam-dunks our Cyber generation with thoughtfulness, information and humor. Us geeks aren't all that bad, now are we? *Revenge of the Computer Widow* is another well-researched work by Nattalia Lea that bridges the gap between them and us. A must-read for anyone interested in people and computing."
Matthew Gray & Angelina, Love Life Radio Network, Honolulu
www.LoveLife.Com/menu.html

"If life has appeared to be treating you poorly in recent days, you need a good laugh. Try reading *Revenge of the Computer Widow* by Nattalia Lea. In the 11,820 seconds (that's 197 minutes for those weak in numeracy) it took me reading non-stop (except for bursts of laughter), Ms. Lea goes from 1800 BC (when the computer was in the mathematical womb) through the 14th Century Yuan Dynasty. Then creators of what was eventually the abacus, which even today in the right hands can equal many (most?) when it comes to totaling numbers on a modern computer. Lea also gets more modern explaining the now 37 year-old text-only Internet. The Internet was created and generously donated to the world I would point out by DARPA, the American military think-tank – that barely could walk until hackers showed it how, to the dynamic colorful 30 frames per second visual global fire hose (with T1 or fiber-optic line) it is today.

Lea built her access ramp of humor to the Information Highway everywhere. Her Mac fan versus Microsoft fan jokes for starters should be enshrined in the Apple Hall of Fame immediately.

Read this reasonably-priced book based on Lea's lifestyle survey of 800 widely and wildly-mixed computer users to see where you stand in the New 21st Century World. Astral signs, psychological, personality and computer types, family status and computer addiction, it's all there. Seek and thou shall find.

Don't just sit there in front of your computer, go out and BUY IT."

Frank Ogden, a.k.a. "Dr. Tomorrow"
e-mail:tomorrow@home.com

Revenge of the Computer Widow™

Also written by Nattalia Lea,

Miracles for the Entrepreneur –
A must have funny book for anyone in business

Platypus Publishers, June 1996

Revenge of the Computer Widow™

*How to Get What You Want in Life,
when Computers are Required*

For Computer Lovers and Luddites
Results of a lifestyle survey from over
800 computer users world-wide.
Now you can take charge of
running your life, instead
of the computer.

Nattalia Lea, P. Eng.

Platypus Publishers
Tel: (403) 283-0498
Fax: (403) 270-3023
E-mail: platypus@cadvision.com
Web: www.cadvision.com/eucalypt/platypus

Copyright © 1999 By Nattalia Lea
All rights reserved.
Cover Design - Alvin Choong Design Studio (403) 217-2908 e-mail:achoong@cadvision.com
Photography - Gerry Young Photography (403) 932-9279 e-mail:youngger@cadvision.com
First Printing, October 1999

Printed and Bound in Canada.

No part of this book may be used or reproduced in any manner whatsoever, without written consent from the publisher, with the exception of reprints in the context of reviews. For information, write to:
Platypus Publishers,
2323E 3rd Avenue N.W.,
Calgary, AB T2N 0K9 Canada
Tel: (403) 283-0498 Fax: (403) 270-3003 e-mail: platypus@cadvision.com
Internet: www.cadvision.com/eucalypt/platypus

This publication is designed to provide accurate and authoritative information in regard to the subject matter covered. It is sold with the understanding that the publisher is not engaged in rendering professional services. If legal, accounting, investment, business, marketing, sales, medical, psychological, information technology, computer services or any other expert assistance is required, the services of a competent professional person should be sought.

Care was taken to ensure technical accuracy of this book, but should there have been any bugs, please note any glitches and send them to the author c/o Platypus Publishers, and this data will be considered for future editions.

Author's Note

Names, places, occupations and other identifying information have been changed to protect the privacy and confidences of persons who were consulted with, or were interviewed by the author.

While this book has been written to assist those who may or may not be frustrated with living or working with computer users and computers, it is not intended to serve a replacement for professional medical or technical advice. The author/publisher disclaim any liability or loss arising directly or indirectly from the use or application of any information contained in this book.

Cataloguing in Publication Data

    Lea, Nattalia, 1953 -
    Revenge of the computer widow
    Includes bibliographical references and index.
    ISBN 0-9699864-1-6
1.computers and civilization. 2. Information technology—Social aspects. 3. Computer scientists—attitudes. I. Title.
QA76.9.C66L42 1999   303.48'33   C99-910675-9

To the GEEK of my life, Godfried —

our clones, daughter of a geek (DOAG) Alisse and,

son of a geek (SOAG) Cody —

for their love, humor and friendship.

About the Author

Nattalia Lea is an engineer, writer and entrepreneur, who is also a contributing editor to numerous trade publications, and has been an associate editor for *Alberta Business* magazine. Her articles have appeared in newspapers and magazines in Canada, United States, Malaysia and Singapore, such as – *The Globe and Mail, Profit, Marketing, Oilweek, Computing Canada, Chatelaine, Vancouver Sun*, etc., covering a breadth of topics ranging from small business to technological innovation; computers to the environment. In 1994, Cathay Pacific Airways and Singapore Airlines sponsored Lea to report on current affairs in South East Asia. Her article *Women Engineers: Dismantling the Myths* was chosen for inclusion in McGraw Hill Ryerson's book for high schools, *Gender Issues*. In 1996, Platypus Publishers released Lea's humorous business book, *Miracles for the Entrepreneur—a must have funny book for anyone in business*.

The first woman to have graduated from the University of British Columbia with a bio-resources engineering degree in 1978, Lea also holds a diploma of technology from the B.C. Institute of Technology. Upon graduation and up to 1986, she held numerous technical and engineering positions working for the government, consulting engineers and the petroleum industry. A popular public speaker and media personality who focuses on humor, entrepreneurship and technology, Lea has appeared on news broadcasts both regionally and nationally, including *CBC Newsworld*, CFCN News, CBC radio, and been quoted in *Fortune* magazine.

Lea is a member of Toastmasters International, and the Association of Professional Engineers, Geologists and Geophysicists of Alberta. Committed to the community, her extra-curricular activities have been recognized. She is listed in the *Who's Who of Canadian Women; Who's Who of International Women*; and *Canadian Who's Who*.

Acknowledgements

About seven years ago, Gloria and I were gawking at our then four-year-old daughters, as they pirouetted, jumped and sashayed across the gymnasium floor – in an optional modern dance class. While waiting for the lesson to finish, we compared notes of our spouses' nocturnal computing habits. She won out. Later, she dragged me to her condo to show me what disgusted her the most – the computer in the master bedroom. We joked, snickered and laughed about our situations. We went about our lives with our backs turned against our husbands', juggling career, family and leisure.

Before I knew it, I lost touch with Gloria. But if it wasn't for Gloria making such a big stink about being a computer widow, this book may not have been written.

Of more significant importance, I want to thank all those brave computer users and professionals and their families who willingly and openly shared with me their stories. It is your courage that has provided the basis for this book, which will help others understand how technology is impacting our personal lives and relationships.

Thanks to all the wonderful people who assisted with the production of this book, *Revenge of the Computer Widow*; graphic artist Alvin Choong, photographer Gerry Young, a shy desktop publisher and editorial "de-buggers" – Allan Bradshaw, Godfried Wasser, Doug Esson, Dave Morgan, and one shy friend. Thanks to Gary Freeman for designing the on-line survey and Liza and Bruce at geekculture.com for their unconditional support. Of course, thanks to all fans of my first book *Miracles for the Entrepreneur*, booksellers, distributors and the media who have been asking for this book since 1997. Procrastination has never been one of my redeeming qualities.

TABLE OF CONTENTS

Introduction		1
Level 1	Metamorphosis of the Magic Black Box	9
Level 2	Silicon Cowtown, how Digital Cowboys came of Age	15
Level 3	Meet the Nerd Next Door	21
Level 4	Sex, Computers or Chocolate	33
Level 5	Geek Consumerism	47
Level 6	Young, Hip and Now – A Career In Computers	63
Level 7	De-Coding the Geek Mystique	77
Level 8	Geek Girl Power	87
Level 9	Digital People and Techno-Cults	97
Level 10	Humor in Hyper-Drive, Boolean Logic and Binary Code	109
Level 11	Nerds in Love	117
Level 12	Forever On-Line	123
Level 13	Cruising Cyberspace for Sex, Money and Love	131
Level 14	Computer Widows Speak Geek-Free	143
Level 15	Crossing the Digital Divide – Overcoming Computer Phobia	149
Level 16	The Lego Effect – Raising Your Computer Quotient	157
Level 17	Games People Play	163
Level 18	Star-Gazing For Web Cruisers, Luddites and Super Geeks	167
Level 19	Revenge, Indictment and Black Widows	179
Level 20	Homo Geek – The Next Generation	187
Epilogue		193
Index		197
Bibliography		201
Appendices:		
Appendix I	Computer History 101 Time-Line	205
Appendix II	Revenge of the Computer Widow Survey	215
Appendix III	Salary Survey	219
Appendix IV	Glossary of Terms	221

Introduction

Sixteen years ago, I fell in love. The man of my infatuation was a Dutch-born petroleum geologist with the Pillsbury doughboy physique, cool wire rimmed glasses, a broad smile, broad shoulders and a very warped sense of humor. They say that opposites attract. If we were classified as pooches, I could be best described as one of those mouthy little Chihuahua types and he, the lovable quiet Saint Bernard.

When we married on March 1, 1985, his close friends giggled at me, "You know, you're marrying a computer geek." I was in a state of denial, until I witnessed computers take over our home. During our first year of marriage, I witnessed how strong the Force had to be – to keep my husband from touching those slippery keys of his Radio Shack Color Computer keyboard.

But the Dark Side beckoned and the honeymoon wore off. He sneaked back on the computer. At first, his after work activities seemed harmless. I thought to myself, "This will change after the birth of our first child." A beaming father, he stayed off the computer for the first six weeks and then crawled back on. So, I kept myself busy with two more babies – exposed to personal computers *in vitro*, a freelance writing business, teaching, public speaking and several whirlwind international journeys.

In 1992, my husband left the corporate rat race as a staff geologist to consult from home. More computers took up residency. At one point, our house contained in excess of one computer per capita. Were we becoming a little wired up? Were we the only ones with personal computers in every other room in the house? Did we have a problem?

Then I realized. We weren't employed in the computer/information technology (IT) world. What were the lifestyles of the computer professionals really like? Sure, manufacturers were producing computers with bigger hard drives, more memory and faster micro-processing speeds than ever. But what impact were personal computers having on people's lives, now that they had become ubiquitous, both in the workplace and at home. Curiosity got the better of me. So I decided to conduct a survey on the lifestyles of computer people.

Being the first woman engineer to graduate in Bio-Resources Engineering from the University of British Columbia, I recalled how first year peers were transformed into proverbial stereotypes by the time they graduated. Surely, computers were influencing our lives. Are we justified in saying that all computer geeks and nerds are a bland, boring, and anti-social lot? Are we running technology or is technology running us?

Why are so many people interested in what I have to say? There's no other study that I am aware of that has focussed on the impact of technology on our personal lives, especially after 5 p.m. The richest man in America, Bill Gates, C.E.O. of Microsoft, is undeniably a computer geek who exemplifies how much power technology has on the bank account. As America's middle class shrinks, we see an emerging and powerful techno-class. According to Statistics Canada, between 1989 and 1998, computer-related jobs grew at a whopping 100 per cent, the fastest growing job segment in Canada employing 326,000 persons in 1998. There appears to be no slowing down. Like in the United States, the average Canadian IT worker earns 64 per cent more than the average employed Canadian. Salaries south of the border are in fact even more lucrative than in Canada. So what do these jobs entail? How do IT professionals play and spend their money? What are their likes and dislikes and could you really become one of them?

Is it really that great to be a computer programmer? You will find out the pro's and con's of this profession and even read about burnt out computer professionals and why they left.

Then there's the issue of love. You will want to read this book, if your significant other is into computers. You could become another computer widow or widower and find out how couples have dealt with the computer at home. And you've probably heard the rumors that cyberspace has become a breeding ground for sex, love and passion. Is there something about your partner's cyberspace life you should know?

If you have never touched a computer keyboard or are thinking about buying your first computer, this book is for you. Maybe your children and grandchildren want you to buy a computer so you can play computer games, but you have no idea what welcomes you. If you are an educator and you want to help your students, you will want to read what parents have to say about fostering computer intelligence in children or how present computer professionals developed the skills they use in today's work environment. You may even be surprised by what today's computer professionals have to say about what they feel educators should be focusing on at school.

And if you fear technology, you will read this book and find out that you're not alone. For those of you who already thrive in the techie world, and are curious as to where you fit in amongst your peers, you'll enjoy this book. If you have a business that is looking to sell products and services to computer professionals and users, whether it be computer hardware, software, financial planning or insurance, read this book and find out who your customers are and what they want. You might find some of the insights in this book useful for your sales and marketing plan.

Over 800 individuals were directly contacted for this survey. Some 426 completed survey forms showed some interesting results:
1. A computer professional's age and education credentials had little to do with his or her annual salary. Individuals under 30 years are earning six-digit incomes, while several individuals over 50 years have never made six-digit incomes.
2. People who did not work 9 to 5 in the IT world were equally likely to spend time on the computer after 5 p.m.

3. Ten per cent of respondents slept in the same room as their computer. The highest number of personal computers per capita reported was 40. About 24 per cent of men and women surveyed have taken a laptop computer into bed with them. Forty per cent of computer professionals take their computers on their holidays with them.
4. Blue was reported to being the favorite color of computer users, followed by green, red and then purple.
5. There is a higher probability that a computer user lives in a household with a pet, rather than a child.
6. Even though some individuals had worked over 10 years in the computer industry, they strongly believed that computers were evil.
7. Not all computer professionals believed that putting children on computers at an early age was the best thing for them to develop the skills needed for the information age.
8. The extroverted personality types were more likely to succeed in the computer world than the introverted personality type.
9. Computer widows and widowers who were still married, often did little to change their home life situation.
10. Seventeen per cent of men and 20 per cent of women prefer spending time on their computers over indulging in sex or chocolate.

The Research

From January 1998 to June 1999, individuals were contacted directly by e-mail and telephone or interviewed in person. The ongoing survey is posted at www.geekculture.com/computerwidow. The 60 plus questions that make up this survey, were selected to determine people's comfort zones, why they liked computers, their perceptions of themselves and their peers, the personal relationships they sought and what they valued, their lifestyle, how they felt about using computers, success and their careers.

Conformity was not what I was looking for, so I sought out individuals who worked in the high-tech world under different circumstances, in different areas of specialization, at different times in history, at different levels within a corporation or organization or were self-employed and entrepreneurs. The questions on the survey were developed with help from friends, computer lovers, computer training instructors and the media.

I did not hesitate to e-mail Bill Gates at Microsoft. His e-mail, published in a weekly local newspaper column is askbill@microsoft.com. Gates did not respond. My ego was deflated, but my feelings weren't hurt. I didn't think it would be fair to exclude Steve Jobs. So I visited www.apple.com and sent an e-mail request directed towards management. They did not respond either.

They were other celebrity techies I tracked down. For aeons, IBM ran one-page ads profiling some of their brightest software stars. With job titles like *ethical hacker*, *three-dimensionalists*, or *digital conceptualist*, the temptation was too great. I picked up the phone and called that toll-free number, only to be intercepted by IBM's sales and marketing department. I explained my predicament to no avail and hung up. The question remains, "Are those people in the IBM ads real or virtual?"

I also sent Katrina Garnett, founder, President and CEO of CrossWorlds Software an e-mail message. She's the sultry brown-eyed brunette who in a revealing v-necked black dress, appeared in 1998 on the back covers of business magazines, like *Fortune*. Intelligent and married with children, Garnett has become a beacon for other women, initiating her own foundation to encourage girls to pursue technical careers. Still, there was no response.

While I did not ask respondents about their salaries, I can assure you that I did procure surveys from millionaires, and hope their insights on technology and life might assist you with your future business ventures. Luddites might be shocked by some of the money that's being made in this industry, although often it comes from hard work, personal sacrifice and luck.

For over a year, I attended evening and weekend computer classes to stuff my brains with all I could think of – everything from graphics programs to desktop publishing to accounting. The instructors proved to be very informative and insightful.

As various stories in the media arose about computers, I took note of the individuals being quoted and sent then personal e-mails. When one individual described himself as being "a life long nerd", I knew he was a perfect candidate.

About five months into the research, I became anxious about meeting my quota, until I visited local computer user/professional groups – Commodore users, SQL users, Corel Draw users, Mac users, Cal-PC's users, Unix users and so forth. With the exception of one computer user group, my presence was well received.

I checked out business cards of computer consultants, posted on public bulletin boards. I also attended high-tech career fairs, in a feeble attempt to find work for myself, as a technical writer. In the cluttered hotel hallways bombarded with banners and posters, while standing in line waiting to see recruiters, I commiserated with other job seekers – who, in the majority of cases, were gainfully employed but looking for ammunition for their next performance appraisal.

Many under-30 types, posing as serious job seekers in dark suits and white shirts, confessed that underneath their façade, they were empire builders of their own, but killing time working for someone else, until they felt ready to leave the corporate nest. For the record, I failed to find myself work as a technical writer after cruising two high-tech job fairs, but I'm happy to report that I did help one unexpectedly down-sized survey participant, find a new job.

International travel proved to be another great way to meet computer people. While waiting for baggage at Amsterdam's Schipol Airport, I chatted with an athletic young tanned woman sporting a backpack clanging with cowbells. She worked for Hewlett-Packard, Amsterdam in technical support, and had just returned from a Canadian Rocky Mountain hiking trip. People lugging their laptop computers around at airports, (assuming they had a sense of humor) were approachable for interviews, prior to boarding. During one line up, I interviewed two techie students en-route home to Canada from their European summer holidays.

It was on a train ride from east to central Holland that I interviewed a trio of computer lovers. They were the only ones speaking English on the train. With his wind-blown frazzled hair and horn-rimmed glasses, the pale-faced lanky Englishman had the absent-minded professorial look. It was with absolute confidence, even though I was suffering from a cold, that I asked him if he was a university professor. He used to be. The American, who worked in a daycare, was actually more of an after five p.m. computer user than the former mathematics professor who never touched the keyboard after work. Their third travelling companion, the Elton-John lookalike, once exposed, was actually the most passionate computer user of the travelling threesome.

It took over 18 months to collect the completed survey forms, the results of which form the basis for this book. Interviews occurred in person or by telephone interviews, and lasted anywhere from ten minutes to three hours, with an average duration of 25 to 35 minutes. With the assistance of my endearing webmaster Gary, my partners at Geek Culture and Rosie X at GeekGirl in Australia, we got the word out in cyberspace and collected another 72 completed surveys.

While the majority of persons interviewed reside in Calgary, Canada (which I proclaim to be *Silicon Cowtown*), others reside in Australia, Indonesia, United States, England, Norway and the Netherlands. A very shy software developer on a one-year contract in Indonesia agreed to participate. Getting information from him was like pulling teeth.

The survey has a very good cross-section of computer users, from high-tech rock stars to entry level programmers, from obsessive computer lovers who require to be within a ten-foot radius of a computer monitor 24 hours a day to users who fight with their computers daily. The majority of the people who participated claimed to be a combination introvert and extrovert personality type. Those who declined to participate may have been more introverted than the rest. Some interviewees spoke in highly measured sentences with soft raspy voices and I knew that completing the survey for them was not easy; and at times, greeted with suspicion. While some individuals fall into the category of Hollywood's version of the computer geek, others looked like they walked out of *GQ* or could pass as bionic Barbie dolls. Read on, about some of the findings and research, which even took me by surprise!

LEVEL 1

METAMORPHOSIS OF
THE MAGIC BLACK BOX

"I think computers are evil black boxes put on this planet to torment us."
38 year-old systems engineer

You would have to be hiding out in the tropical rain forest to have never heard of the computer. But even now, that unawareness may be history. Two years ago, on one sparkling afternoon in November, near the tiny village of Baina in Papua New Guinea, six petroleum geologists gathered in their makeshift canvas-walled huts. After a jungle expedition collecting data to map a potential oil field, the geologists were ready to turn on their computers.

A dozen barefoot natives, some dressed in grass skirts and loin cloths made from leaves, glanced over the foreigners or *waitpela's* shoulders. The whirling noises from the gas-fired electrical generator drowned the clickety-clack sounds coming from the laptop computers. The wide-eyed natives were intensively inquisitive. Until now, they had not seen, touched or heard a computer before. The bolder ones in their halting pidgin English and hand gestures questioned the geologists.

"A lot of times, they just saw us sitting in front of the computer," recalls the Canadian geologist in this group. "I don't think they were impressed."

The computer games stirred up some commotion. An animated outer space shooter game sent rockets and missiles in several trajectories simultaneously. But for the most part, the computer remained a magic black box – part of the *waitpela's* world.

Baina is as about as far away as you can get from the concrete jungle.

Harvested logs are carved into dug-out canoes and built into stilted huts with thatched roofs. The natives spend their days fishing, hunting with bows and arrows, gardening and preparing the edible starch of the Sago palm tree's pith. There is no running water, radio or telephone – only razor sharp human senses and instinct to reveal sleeping snakes or other life-threatening perils. Machetes and matches are the only icons of modern civilization.

If you were a Baina native, you probably do not understand why the pale-skinned *waitpela* are so wrapped up with their computers. Your most prized possession is *pik*, the rotund pigs roaming freely around in the village's backyard. Even so, there is a mystery on how they got the magic into their black boxes.

An explanation can not be revealed by the naked eye. The laptop's technical prowess is hidden beneath the plastic case that shrouds its private parts. By mid-1999, laptops were typically fitted with Pentium II chips – rated at 380 megahertz, 4.3 gigabyte hard drives, 32 to 64K random access memory (RAM), 32 speed compact disk (CD) drives and modems rated at 56K.

As the geologists keyed in mapping data, the computer zapped it over to the random access memory chip where the data was manipulated with amazing speed and accuracy. The microprocessor, a Pentium chip – the brain of the computer, which is comprised of millions of transistors on integrated circuits – on-off switches that direct the flow of electrons configured to carry out computational feats. Data can be stored on a hard diskette, or on the laptop's hard disk drive. The laptop's modem connection in the civilized world would be enough to transmit data via a public telephone system. But near Baina, the geologists had to set up their own satellite phone through which they send faxes weekly to Australia.

There is the question of how you get the computer to do what you want. The *waitpela* maneuver the computer mouse to point and click icons on the computer screen. But how did the computer know what to do? Computer software containing the instructions for personal computers are either installed right on the computer's hard drive or accessed externally from diskettes or CD's. Programs commonly installed into laptops include business applications, like spreadsheets, graphics or word processing programs. Just because computer games can be such memory hogs, users often keep such programs stored on CD's or diskettes, which can be inserted into the laptop's external disk drives for file transfer. Then an operating system acts like a messenger between the computer hardware and applications software.

If our geologist had a scanner and digital camera, he thinks the natives would have been more impressed by the computer. He could have demonstrated how pictures or photos could be made one with the computer. Or if they had a gutsy personal computer with a Digital Video Disc (DVD) drive, they could have shown them movies, too. Still, too far fetched for the Binai natives to contemplate are the factories where the computer's precious silicon chips are made under hypochondriac-clean conditions by a breed of dust bunny-suited workers. What is more amazing is that the silicon chips built by layering the silicon with metal, are often smaller than a quarter of an Aspirin – yet they contain millions of transistors.

The laptop computer has come a long way since 1833. That's when the world's first computer, the difference analytical machine was invented by England's Charles Babbage. Prior to that, slide rules were invented a century before – preceded by the abacus for mathematical computations, as early as 1800 BC in the ancient cradles of civilizations of Mesopotamia by the Babylonians. In antiquity, prior to 1800 BC, it is believed that the Greeks, Egyptians, Chinese and Russians used dust and pebble versions of the abacus as we know it. The slide rule survived well into 1970's, while the abacus is still customarily used in certain parts of the world, like China. Here, hawker sized shopkeepers shuffle the beads back and forth on an abacus, as quickly as any modern person would key in numbers into an electronic calculator.

Weighing in on scales under seven pounds, the laptop computer is a far cry from the earlier computers, which were realized decades ago. During World War II, the Electronic Numerical Integrator Analyzer and Computer (ENIAC), a first-generation computer was built at the University of Pennsylvania. It was characterized by 18,000 vacuum tubes that acted for its circuit elements.

This magic black box measured eight feet by 100 feet and weighed 80 tons. It could do 5,000 additions and 360 multiplications per second. Memory access time was 1 millisecond.

Impressive as the ENIAC was for its time, further advances in technology were substantive to eliminate the maddening difficulties arising from its operation and speed of computations. To leap from the ENIAC to the laptop, meant a series of radical transformations that would flex the brains of those individuals who challenged contemporary thinking of their time. In 1943, IBM chairman Thomas Watson said, "I think there is a world market for maybe five computers." *Popular Mechanics* magazine anticipated in 1949, computers in the future would weigh no more than 1.5 tons.

Since the 1940's, five generations of computers have evolved. Circuit elements of computers have progressed from vacuum tubes to solid-state transistors (1959) to integrated circuit silicon chip (1965) to Very Large Scale Integration (VLSI) technology in the late 1970's – each resulting in a dramatic reduction in the size and cost of circuit elements. In 1974, Intel Corp. introduced the 8080 chip, an 8-bit microprocessor that made personal computers a reality. With its 8-bit bus, 2 MHz processing speed, 6000 transistors, and 64 K address space, computers with that chip are Neanderthal by today's standards. By 1997, the Intel 200-MHz Pentium MMX was comprised of a 64-bit bus, 4.5 million transistors and 32 Kb on-board cache.

Likewise, data storage has been downsized drastically, as computers moved from paper and punched cards to magnetic tape to magnetic disk storage to compact disks (CD) and digital video disks (DVD). The CD at 640 meg of storage holds over 2300 times as much information as the 360k 5.25 inch floppy disks from the mid-1980's which are now extinct – as compared to 100 meg found in zippy disks or 640 megs in a CD.

Computer languages over the past five generations have shifted from machine and assembly code to high level languages like FORTRAN and COBOL, to structured languages like PASCAL and C, then to object-oriented languages like Visual Basic and C++. From the mid-1990's onwards, there's been a surge of languages like Java, PERL, HTML and XML from the great unwashed.

The first computers were dedicated to solving complex scientific equations. Then, commercial mainframe computers, super computers and mini-computers evolved to help corporations manage their research and development, business operations, accounting and databases of information. During the 1970's, mainframe computers got decentralized as Ethernet technology enabled computers to communicate with each other on Local Area Networks (LAN's). Today, monolithic mainframe computers are still kept in temperature and humidity controlled rooms with restricted access. But corporate employees from their desks can inter-act with the mainframe computer. Servers help manage the flow of data to and from the employees' workstations, which have more power than previous "dumb terminals".

The proliferation of personal computers since the 1970's, and the Internet since the late 1980's, has revolutionized the way people live, work and play. The downsizing of the computer's infrastructure took some time. In 1975, IBM's most portable computer was its 5100, that supported BASIC programs, 16KB RAM, five-inch screen and weighed a bulimic 55 pounds.

The power of the PC has exceeded everybody's expectations, in terms of widespread acceptance and computer capacity. In 1977, Ken Olson, president of Digital Equipment Corp. said, "There is no reason for anyone to have a computer at home." Four years later, Bill Gates said, "640,000 bytes of memory ought to be enough for any body."

Refinements in liquid crystal display technology spawned a breed of laptop computers during the late 1980's and more recently, a generation of personal digital assistants. With wireless telecommunications, laptops and personal digital assistants can be remotely linked up to corporate computers and their networks. The implications of such technology are phenomenal. It is magical that people can be physically connected around the world on the Internet – creating a global village that hums around the clock.

Still in Baini, the natives carry on living as they have since aeons ago. Their form of networking occurs without technology at annual festivities, where neighboring tribes gather in ceremonial costumes with wild bird feathered headdresses sharing a meal simmered in wood and stone. Perhaps by chance, one of the dozen Baina natives who met the geologists may have spoken about the *waitpela's* computers. The Canadian geologist, who reminisces about their idyllic lifestyle returned in 1999 to that part of the world. On discovering Internet access on one of the remote islands of Tonga, he realized how far the magic black boxes have spread. For a moment, the tropical air was unequivocally silenced.

LEVEL 2

SILICON COWTOWN
HOW DIGITAL COWBOYS CAME OF AGE

"I used to think that nothing happened in Calgary because when you're in Toronto, all the national news is about eastern Canada. Then I came to Calgary and walking around downtown, I can see a lot of things are happening. So in Calgary, I tuned into some national television and noticed that all the news here is about Toronto. Now, I understand why westerners resent Toronto. But I'm not exactly from Toronto. I'm from Hamilton..."

A visiting tradeshow exhibitor who works in Toronto, known as "the center of the Universe", telling me about her first trip to Calgary, May 1999.

CANADA'S LEADING TECHNOPOLISES:
- Ottawa
- Calgary
- Kitchener-Waterloo-Cambridge
- Halifax
- Montreal

SOME OF THE WORLD'S LEADING TECHNOPOLISES
- Silicon Valley, California
- Research Triangle Park, North Carolina
- Cambridge, United Kingdom
- Austin, Texas
- Singapore
- Hsinchu Science-based Industrial Park, Taiwan
- Bangalore, India

– Source: *The Globe and Mail*, Dec. 3, 1998

In April 1979, I left Vancouver for Calgary, a town that I knew nothing about, except that the unemployment rate was around four percent and my chances of finding work would be better than in Lotusland. I boarded an eastbound train, with a trunk full of my worldly possessions and engineering school textbooks and dressed in my one and only three-piece pin-striped interview suit. For $50, the trip was a bargain. I arrived to the land of rednecks without even a pair of decent blue jeans or cowboy boots, let alone ridden a horse. But my decision to move to Calgary was no different than that of the 12,000 others who came that year. I needed a job.

Twenty years ago, Calgary's dominant economy, the oil patch was booming. Those were the days when if you didn't like your boss, you could tell him to go to hell and walk across the street for a job that paid you 25 per cent more. Those were the days when noon hour lunches were accompanied by booze, people partied hard and locals felt invaded by *"eastern creeps and bums."* Restaurants, with minimal menus to choose from, were a bit crude and unrefined, along with the office politics and humor.

To truly understand Calgary's uniqueness, you've got to understand the oil patch, where a handshake consummates a deal and trust is not talk, but action. This industry sector is relationship oriented, where the old boys spend countless hours shooting the breeze after hours over steak and beer, delirious about their hopes and dreams. Close links to Denver and Houston give Calgary an American flair. Fiscally, the province of Alberta where Calgary resides, is the closest in economic mentality to an American state. At my second job, I worked for a Texan and petroleum geologists, geophysicists and engineers, think nothing of working on projects around the globe or studying a third or fourth language to get there.

For every boom, there's always a bust and the city has felt every blip in the oil patch since the 1950's. The National Energy Program of 1981 pummeled Calgary to a pulp, like a tornado with a vengeance, and stirred up political animosity with Ottawa. There was a dramatic exodus of petroleum personnel, as lay-offs could have been listed in the obituary section. Popular bumper sticks read, "Oh, please Lord, give me another boom. This time, I won't piss it away." In 1982, I left my second job as a scheduling engineer, under the knife of the second cut, after a Friday going away Mexican lunch celebrating four other departures and showered with "early retirement cards" and momentous for the occasion. The Monday after, my newly found unemployment status hit me like a real bad hangover. Emptiness sank at the bottom of my stomach, as I trudged down to the nearest Canada Manpower Center to stand in line to apply for some *pogey*, unemployment insurance.

Things in town got wicked. In 1983, 11,000 Calgarians left town; followed by 9,600, a year later. I stayed. There was no point in returning to Lotusland. I was hooked to Calgary's mountain air, cross-country skiing and sunny days. Besides, Albertans pay no provincial sales tax, maximum corporate tax is 44.62 per cent and maximum income tax is 45.60 per cent. Daunted but not downtrodden, I witnessed oil patch refugees take their severance packages and start up new companies.

The 1988 Winter Olympics brought glory for Calgary's open spaces, Rocky Mountain landscape and glowing sunrises. More importantly, it placed the city on the global map. Japanese tourists, who make pilgrimages to Banff via Calgary, are known to keep the city shopkeepers happy. The Olympics also left behind the legacy of fiber optic network at the Olympic Oval on the University of Calgary campus, where trade shows and exhibitions flourish regularly.

In March 1993, Premier Ralph Klein, offered tax incentives and shrunk bureaucratic barriers to encourage economic diversification, and outrageously slashed government spending, eventually eliminating a $3 billion provincial deficit. In 1994, manufacturing growth peaked at 20.4 per cent.

There were more oil patch booms and busts. The low oil prices of 1998 and the first part of 1999, have lingered like a *mononucleosis* virus. Even so, Calgary is growing and has been attracting 30,000 new persons for the past three consecutive years. Eastern Canadians move for a quality of life; Maritimers, out of an economic reality. Unlike previous years, where the migration was east to west, almost two-thirds of the newcomers nowadays are from British Columbia – disgruntled with the provincial government there, and morose economy. While apartment vacancy rates are tight and rents have spiraled up, Calgary is still more affordable than Toronto or Vancouver. With the average 1999 housing price hovering around $150,000, life here is still a bargain for young families.

So many oil patch geeks, including doodlebuggers, gears and rock hounds, having become accustomed to life in a commodity-based sector, focus on what's ahead. They keep their spirits up. Overheard at a luncheon conversation at a semi-private club, one man said, "What this economy needs is a bit of Viagra. That should keep things up."

Calgary is Canada's youngest major city, with one-third of its residents between 25 and 44 years of age and is second to Ottawa, in terms of the number university degrees per capita. While the oil patch has taken a back seat in Calgary's economy, its high-tech manufacturing sector is now the second leading employer, after retail and services.

Mogens Smed, the entrepreneur who just wouldn't be, has a high-tech custom-made furniture manufacturing plant in east Calgary. The company employs around 1700 persons and generates over $170 million in annual sales. Smed International has resurrected itself from an earlier fiasco that sent the banks after Smed, over a decade ago. I was told, "Mogens always says, please do not say it can't be done. It can be done. We just haven't figured a way to do it... yet."

The city is still growing. There are rumors that a major offshore semi-conductor manufacturer may set up shop here. While Toronto, holds the lion's share of corporate headquarters at 334, *The Globe and Mail* reported on November 2, 1998 that Calgary is in second spot with 194 corporate headquarters. Ninety-eight of the 194 Calgary corporate headquarters are in the oil and gas sector, but a significant and growing number of companies are in the high-tech sectors.

The Calgary Economic Development Authority estimates that upwards of 32,000 jobs are in the high-tech sector, out of a total of 496,000 jobs, a number that has more than doubled in the last

10 years. About 10,000 of these advanced technology jobs have roots in the oil and gas sector, while the remainder are in the following categories – telecommunications, electronics manufacturing, industrial instrumentation, computer hardware, computer software and services, life sciences and research and development. Growth in Calgary is by 10 to 20 percent annually and ten fired up high-tech companies here include Colt Engineering Corp., Computing Devices Canada Ltd., IBM, Kenonic Controls Ltd., MetroNet Communications Group, X-wave Solutions, Nortel Networks, QC Data, Telus and Shaw Communications.

Calgary exudes energy. People often start work at 7:00 am and leave at 6:00 p.m. When the Calgary Professional Club closed down its doors last year, I knew that a new city was emerging. Wired up, Calgarians don't need to congregate at private clubs to do business anymore. They can go to any of the excellent ethnic restaurants, from sushi to East Indian, Vietnamese to Australian. After 20 years of living here, my Vancouver sisters say I've become far too opinionated to exist on the West Coast. It's a great place to be, if you tend to bore easily. If you don't like the weather that's known to swing from 30 degrees below to 30 above, just wait five minutes and watch it change. In the middle of winter, it can snow one day and be sun-bathing weather the next. Calgary, I affectionately refer to as *Silicon Cowtown*, is in its infancy. It was just a few years ago, when a clerk from a Montreal-based company called me to check that Federal Express delivered to Calgary. But when people stop saying hi to you on the street, you'll know *Silicon Cowtown* has just grown up too fast.

> *"Calgary's got to have the highest number of computers per capita in the world, okay could be between Calgary and Houston because it's the center of the oil patch and companies replace their systems every two to three years. They have no choice because of Microsoft or Intel. So these computers have to go somewhere in the city. They end up in the employee's homes or computer geek's home or daycare. People still own Commodore 64K computers."*
> 25 year-old network administrator

L E V E L   3

MEET THE NERD NEXT DOOR

It was a fluke that I was invited to a party full of computer people. I accepted. The host was a high-level computer guy, who I knew was making a six-figure annual income. He was only 26 years old. He and his partner had just moved into this exquisite 3,500 sq.ft. house built to their whims, in an upscale neighborhood – five bedrooms, four bathrooms, three fire places and a kitchen filled with Jedi black appliances and cabinets. It's good thing that my husband didn't go to the party. Seeing their house would have depressed him. (We live in this modest 1000 sq.ft. 45-year old bungalow, complete with a leaky basement, no central vacuuming or kitchen garburator.) Their new furniture had not arrived yet, but the computer room on the lower level was already well worn. Not everything was wired, but out from an orifice in the wall, there cascaded a zillion cables and wires for future hook-ups.

Four couples, one single, DOAG and I showed up for the party. Upon arrival, cordial greetings were exchanged. Average age was 30 years. If the couples didn't own a house, they were having one built. The women were awfully quiet, although one gal griped her biological clock was ticking and her significant other hadn't proposed yet.

Last year's trip to Disneyland was the evening's entertainment. You have to understand that Disneyland, is a very popular place for computer geeks under 30 to visit. Nobody in this gang lived in geek flophouses, where small groups of 20 to 30'ish single computer geeks live in co-ed wired up houses. Santa Cruz in Silicon Valley claims to have one of the most evolved geek societies around with 27 geek flophouses identified by names like Antfarm, Marshmallow Peanut Circus or Hyperspace, with inhabitants known in cyberspace under aliases like *tapeworm* and *fleagirl*. *Silicon Cowtown* appears rather tame. The city is rumored to have a few geek flophouses. But for other geeks to publicly identify such co-ordinates to me, they felt would be like committing *hara-kiri*.

Do not assume that engineers and computer people are the same. True enough, there is that pervasive image that some engineers think that they're God's gift to the planet, marry nurses or teachers, drive Volvos, drink beer, have 2.1 children and live in middle-class neighborhoods with white picket fences. Pragmatic and proof-oriented, they adhere to engineering codes and standards of all sorts with tried and proven methods and keep an ultra-conservative outlook – shying away from public life and being queasy around abortion or gay and lesbian rights. Should engineers wish to enlighten themselves in management, they flock into night school masters of business administration programs, thriving on bureaucracy. Lawyers dread engineers who file for divorce – joint-custody schedules are proposed on spreadsheets down to 15-minute intervals.

On the other hand, the computer geek says, "I am a god." They nearly have to be. Their work environment is quite chaotic. Technical manuals are usually illegible and hard to read. By the time they open up the box of a new computer, it's already become obsolete. There are no standards, let alone regulations and licensing systems in place to drive down the digital highway. A brilliant computer geek needs to be creative in order to ensure the flow of information across various operating platforms and interfaces is seamless to the outsider.

For the most part, every day requires learning new things, mostly self-taught and at hyper speeds. The computer geek detests hierarchy in organizations, office politics, dress codes and other rigmarole that he or she must tolerate. The computer geek is a non-conformist and is always the first in a company to get away with going to work and trade shows in jeans, T-shirts, sneakers, shoulder length hair and pierced ears.

The rules by which computer geeks have to work and play haven't yet been set. There is no minimum age to start earning a six-figure annual income. While academic credentials don't hurt, they're not essential. More often than not, they're under 30 years of age, not over 50 years of age.

A 26 year-old lead programmer made this comment about formal training, "I have an AS – CIS. I learned nothing during the acquisition of it. College was an interruption to my normal learning process. I learned FAR more on my own than college ever taught me. I would never hire anyone I knew in college." And unlike other professional working classes, anybody can make it in the emerging unassuming techno-class, which I contend is rapidly becoming very influential.

If you live in *Silicon Cowtown*, you've probably met a lot of computer geeks. He could be that quiet bachelor next door who lives alone in a house all to himself with two cats, shops at discount stores and just quietly nods at you as you walk out the back door to dump your garbage. All you know about him is that he's on the computer a lot. Maybe you thought that he was still going to university. He could be rich, in fact, he could be really rich and maybe, obscenely rich, but you certainly can't tell from the unpretentious way he dresses or from that 15 year-old car he drives. You shake your head and ask yourself, what on earth does he spend his money on? Is he quietly socking it away for a rainy day or what?

So, now let's find out about some of the secrets of the nerd next door. Only 16 per cent of the survey responses came off-line from www.geekculture.com. The majority of the persons I contacted were through personal referrals. Where possible, interviews were held face-to-face. Due to time constraints and logistics, most people preferred to chat over the phone, although a handful insisted on e-mail communication only. A couple of glib engineers refused to co-operate unless they had the opportunity to review the survey first. In the end, they declined to participate.

"I know a lot of computer geeks with nice cars, nice wardrobes, pretty wives/girlfriends and good taste in music. They are far from being Nerds…"
26 year-old lead computer programmer

"Geeks vary more than perhaps any other stereotype out there. About the only things a person needs to be considered a geek, in my opinion, are the lust for technological advancement and love of acquiring information to better oneself."
22 year-old computer sciences student

"I am a god, confident and arrogant."
21 year-old biocomputational analyst

Some people will argue about the credibility of the information collected, that people made up things to create a better image of themselves. Even so, I will contend, this information is still valuable because it tells you what they aspire to be, their fantasies, their hopes and aspirations. The overwhelming majority of respondents were pretty honest about themselves. Their candor and frankness really surprised me. They volunteered information beyond my original expectations.

To begin with, it was not surprising that the proportion of male responses to females was about 3:1. In many instances, some survey responses were more gender-related than technology-related. Then people employed in the information technology (IT) area were found to have similar characteristics that singled them out from non-IT persons. That is not to say that the non-IT persons were less technologically astute. Their priorities were just different.

For comparative purposes, I assigned five major categories to put survey respondents in – IT males who worked from 9 to 5 p.m. in the high-tech/IT world, non-IT males who loved computers after 5 p.m., IT females, non-IT females and people from the Net. In the last category, Net people were the individuals who responded to the on-line survey at geekculture.com. Net people responded significantly different from the other four categories in that 63 per cent considered themselves to be geeks, while only 15 per cent of the other men and 19 per cent of the women would make such claims.

Nearly half of the responses came from males employed in the IT world. This category was further divided into two sub-categories – men who worked for corporations (Corporate IT-male) and men who were either consultants or entrepreneurs

(Self-Employed IT-male). The third largest response came from non-IT male computer users. The split between women employed in the IT world and those who were non-IT female computer users were nearly equal. IT females were also broken down further into two sub-categories – Corporate IT females and Self-Employed IT females. In the fifth category of Net people, there was an equal split between male and female computer users. Students comprised about 13 per cent of non-IT males, 10 per cent of non-IT females and 22 per cent of the Net people. Students from the Net were typically majoring in computer studies at college or university.

TABLE 3-1: AGE AND MARITAL STATUS OF RESPONDENTS

	IT MALES CORPORATE	IT MALES SELF-EMPLOYED	IT FEMALES CORPORATE	IT FEMALES SELF-EMPLOYED	NON-IT MALES	NON-IT FEMALES	NET PEOPLE
AVERAGE AGE (YRS)	34.8	44.5	32.7	39.6	39.7	36.4	30.7
SINGLE[1]	51 %	14 %	57 %	23 %	23 %	43 %	71 %
MARRIED WITH CHILDREN	29 %	83 %	11 %	54 %	56 %	34 %	29 %
MARRIED, NO CHILDREN	—	3 %	25 %	8 %	3 %	9 %	—
SINGLE PARENTS[2] GAY/LESBIAN	3 %	—	7 %	15 %	8 %	14 %	—

SINGLE[1] – ALSO INCLUDE DIVORCED PERSONS AND PERSONS IN COMMON-LAW RELATIONSHIPS
SINGLE PARENTS[2] – COULD BE DIVORCED OR NEVER MARRIED PERSONS WITH CHILDREN

People's marital status and the presence of children in their lives were influenced by two factors – their age and who their employer was. The younger respondents were more likely to be single and predominantly working for a corporation. About 51 per cent of corporate IT males (average age 34.8 years) were single, along with 58 per cent of corporate IT females (average age 32.7 years). The more mature self-employed IT males (average age 44.5 years) were more likely to have children than the corporate IT male. About 83 per cent of self-employed IT males were married men with children vs. 29 per cent of corporate IT males. The profile on the self-employed IT-male is on par with a recent study conducted by Kathryn Stafford, a professor at Ohio State

University in Columbia. She studied 899 households in nine states. She found the typical home-based worker was 44 years old, male, married and employed in marketing, sales or technology.

Both corporate IT males and IT females were respectively, younger than the self-employed IT males and IT females. They were also younger than the non-IT males and non-IT females, respectively.

The popularity of self-employment amongst IT professionals has rationale. In a recent survey conducted by American Express, 90 per cent of entrepreneurs interviewed are happy on their own, despite putting in 60-hour work weeks, with 30 per cent working more than 60 hours weekly. About 89 per cent enjoyed being their own boss and having control over business decisions.

Eighty-six per cent felt they made better use of their skills and knowledge and 70 per cent felt a strong reward financially, despite the stress, financial uncertainty and years required to build up a small business. Many computer consultants enjoyed their autonomy, saw greater opportunity for work and learning and excellent compensation. While men are more likely to become self-employed for financial reasons, women enjoy the flexibility and balance, especially, when raising a family.

At first glance, the low child bearing rates amongst computer people of any sort may be something to panic about. But it is a Canadian reality. It's been over a decade since the the average family was comprised of one man, one woman and two children. According to Statistics Canada, the average family means one man, one woman and one child.

COMPUTER PEOPLE PERSONALITY

"You can teach anybody computers, but you can't make them have a personality."
38 year-old computer training instructor

I pretended to tell the caller that I was expecting another call. A cramp in my neck seized up. Two hours later, the dissertation on why he is using the best operating system ever created since Adam and Eve, has only begun. Then after this verbal diarrhea, the caller tells me that he is an introvert. So is the shy respondent who wrote reams and reams of text, complete with emoticons and acronyms spewing out relentlessly across the computer screen. Still introverted, were individuals who talked loud on the phone with as much enunciation as a *Jeopardy* talk show host, knowing that we will never see each other face to face. Other introverts spoke in short measured sentences, separated by silent pregnant pauses. Talking on the phone was not easy for them.

TABLE 3-2: COMPUTER PEOPLE PERSONALITY

PERSONALITY TYPE	IT MALES CORPORATE	IT MALES SELF-EMPLOYED	IT FEMALES CORPORATE	IT FEMALES SELF-EMPLOYED	NON-IT MALES	NON-IT FEMALES	NET PEOPLE
INTROVERT-EXTROVERT	49 %	54 %	54 %	67 %	44 %	38 %	52 %
EXTROVERT	32 %	26 %	36 %	33 %	27 %	21 %	19 %
INTROVERT	19 %	20 %	10 %	—	29 %	21 %	29 %

Women surveyed claimed to be more outgoing than men. About 14 per cent of the women interviewed said they were introverted, 29 per cent were extroverted and 57 per cent were a combination introvert-extrovert. About 24 per cent of the men interviewed said they were introverted, 24.0 per cent were extroverted and 52.4 per cent were a combination introvert-extrovert. Extroverts were more likely to give me further referrals to interview, and were likely to hold the executive IT positions (managers, senior technical staff or project leaders) in an organization, be a consultant or entrepreneur. With the exception of one introvert amongst IT males, 42 per cent of the executive positions were held by extroverts, remainder were held by combination introvert-extroverts.

It was expected that asking somebody about their personality strengths and weaknesses would be the hardest question of the whole survey. Only about 60 per cent of interviewees chose to divulge their personality strengths and weaknesses, yet 90 per cent of those surveyed were willing to discuss their type of underwear style or if they wore underwear at all. While 4 per cent of men revealed that they do no wear any underwear at all, one female respondent volunteered to inform me that she did not bother with underwear, even though I assumed all women wear underwear.

Over 90 per cent of the individuals who declined to talk about their personality strengths and weaknesses were introverted.

> *"I don't need to relate to a celebrity. I'm already a household name."*
> 29 year-old computer guy

> *"I'm good at public speaking. So good looking. Very modest. Get me a 10 gigabyte drive to put all my strengths on and I need a back up to back my personality strengths."*
> 26 year-old president of a very successful computer services company

> *"My strengths? My ego (honestly). I use it largely to look optimistically on any situation. Honesty. My sense of humor, (I can find humor in almost anything.) My brains, I'm 'gifted' if you will. I tend to be very care-free. When I do worry it's not for myself. I'm not as self-centered as I suppose I sound. I have a natural ability to teach, and tutor. Energy, both physically and mentally. If I can find something that will get my attention you can be certain I will pursue it fiercely. Manual dexterity, I've worked with my hands all my life and I still love Lego…*
>
> *My weaknesses? Laziness coupled with being care free, the aforementioned energy I have and the ability to put things off leaves me with a great many projects on the go at any given time."*
> 22 year-old computer sciences student

Gender and workplace were the two major factors in determining how people described their personalities. Men were quick to talk *ad nauseum* about their personality strengths, but personality weaknesses were lacking. As one computer user candidly replied, "I used to be conceited, but now I am just perfect." Another 45 year-old computer user responded, "I have many personality strengths, but far too many to mention. But let me mention one – modesty." When it came to defining themselves, IT males who worked for high-tech corporations, tended to describe themselves from words off their resumes, "I'm organized, honest, have integrity, confident, strong team player, technically competent, good inter-personal skills, etc." They were motivated, aggressive, stubborn, easy to get along with, had a sense of humor and strong-willed, too. On the downside, men were willing to divulge their weaknesses – impatience, perfectionism, stubbornness, arrogance, procrastination, shyness, lack of focus, and so forth. A few cited being too emotional and being too sensitive as weaknesses. While a few males admitted feeling paranoid and distrustful, a few others cited gullibility. Amongst single IT males, shyness was a prevailing personality weakness.

> *"I can DO anything. I may not know how to do something at the MOMENT, but if need be, I will figure it out before deadline. I lie well. I am either clear or concise – never both. I laugh a lot. I handle frustration well. I respect other people. I try to fix something, build something, or think up something new every day. I have integrity. I never sacrifice my own credibility, and I know the difference between these things and honesty. I'm never cruel, stupid or careless, and I don't tolerate cruelty, stupidity or carelessness in others.*
>
> *I'm not a bigot. Bigots should be expunged from society like an unpleasant odor. I procrastinate sometimes. I don't save money. I don't tolerate silliness much. My sense of humor is bent the wrong way, forming a nasty barb if you should run into it coming from the wrong direction."*
> 26 year-old hardware designer

She was blonde, blue-eyed and immaculately dressed in a powder blue fitting suit. At first impression, I thought she was in public relations. She was poised, outgoing and laughed easily. She was a techie queen, an IT manager of some sort. Compared to their male counterparts, IT females exhibited a much broader range of personalities than their male counterparts. Women also emphasized their sense of humor and outgoing personalities as their strengths, but not to the extent of men and dwelled on weaknesses, like lack of confidence, being uptight, non-assertiveness and technical incompetence. Could these discrepancies be partially attributed to the age differences between the IT females and IT males? The women were younger and less established in their careers, than their male counterparts.

Teenagers and students described themselves with a different vocabulary than the adults, like "cool, awesome, neat, funky."

What They Did For Work

Individuals employed in the IT sector came from everywhere, at different levels within an organization – from programmers to team leaders and project managers to presidents, and had preferences for different operating platforms including IBM, Microsoft, Mac, UNIX, Linux, OS/2, NT, etc. Some worked for established Fortune 500 companies, others worked for more obscure emerging high-tech companies. They were employed in research and development, academia, IT training, sales and marketing, multi-media, programming, software development, network administration, systems analysis, hardware, systems integration, management, recruitment and so forth. They had different levels of formal computer education, but most claimed to be self-taught. Some were high school dropouts with a passion for computers, others had their doctorate degrees in mathematics or post-graduate degrees in computer science.

> *"We don't think computers are very funny. When you work with machines all day long, I pretty much laugh at myself."*
> 26 year-old IT executive

The self-employed/entrepreneurial IT workers, were typically one-person shops or small companies offering specialized computer services, often from their homes – web site design, Internet services, software development, training, sales, systems integration, systems analyst, management, virtual archeology, etc. Several individuals in this group became computer consultants, after working elsewhere in another profession or career. It was not unusual for them never to meet their clients face to face, conduct business off the Web or be part of an international virtual organization. Good programmers, said a *Silicon Cowtown* computer consultant, are few and far between. He claimed that there were clusters of programmers in Canada, the United States (in addition to Silicon Valley in cities like Boulder, Boston, and Chicago), France, Germany and Sweden. Some programmers were evolving from universities like Berkley, Harvard and Massachusetts Institute of Technology.

Among the passionate computer users, there were no responses from dentists, chiropractors, doctors, psychologists or massage therapists. There was the occasional nurse and teacher who responded, but most responses were from engineers, accountants, lawyers, stockbrokers, geologists, financial planners, entrepreneurs, geophysicists, writers, physically-challenged, students, photographers, graphic designers, homemakers, secretaries, realtors, retail staff, electricians, and burnt-out IT professionals.

"I swear that computers are out to get you. They act so flaky at times."
30 year-old computer guy

L E V E L 4

SEX, COMPUTERS OR CHOCOLATE

We've heard the myths about sex, computers and chocolate. One day, I logged on to the Internet and ran a search on sex, computers and chocolate, only to find the respective number of web sites – 10.68 million for sex, 9.69 million for computers and 0.944 million for chocolate. So what's really on people's minds?

TABLE 4·1: WHAT MADE RESPONDENTS TICK – SEX, COMPUTERS OR CHOCOLATE

PREFERENCE	IT MALES	NON-IT MALES	IT FEMALES	NON-IT FEMALES	NET PEOPLE
SEX	85 %	69 %	58 %	54 %	36 %
COMPUTERS	10 %	17 %	16 %	27 %	38 %
CHOCOLATE	5 %	14 %	26 %	19 %	26 %
THINKS OF SEX WHILE WORKING ON THE COMPUTER	67 %	56 %	40 %	48 %	83 %

Ah-huh, no surprises here. Gender, age and occupation were influential on how individuals responded. Seventy-five per cent of males preferred sex, 17 per cent preferred computers and 8 per cent preferred chocolate. Fifty-six per cent of females preferred sex, 24 per cent preferred chocolate and 20 per cent preferred computers. Net people at 38 per cent had a fetish for computers over sex or chocolate, "normal" considering that 22 per cent were computer science college and university students and 63 per cent self-prescribed being geeks.

However, lusty thoughts while working on the computer were highest for the Net people at 83 per cent; that was 90 per cent for

Net males and 73 per cent for Net females. Overall, 63 per cent of men and 44 per cent of women, said they thought of sex when working on the computer. About 67 per cent of IT males thought of sex when working on the computer, versus 56 per cent of non-IT males. Are women employed in the IT sector more conscientious on the job than men? Only 40 per cent of IT females said they thought of sex while working on the computer vs. 48 per cent of non-IT females.

There is some doubt how truthfully men were when they answered the question about their preference for sex, computers or chocolate. You never know if they just gave the answer that was expected of them. The same could be said of the women who preferred chocolate, quickly remarking how much more women normally enjoy chocolate over sex. There is some good news for chocoholics. A study of 7,841 male Harvard graduates, chocolate lovers were reported to live longer than non-chocolate lovers. Apparently, chocolate contains substances called phenols, which help reduce *arteriosclerosis*.

Not all males were spontaneous about answering the question regarding their preference towards sex, computer or chocolate. Often, there would be stone silence at the other of the telephone line. Then the male being questioned would re-gain his composure, push out his chest, take a deep breath and belch out the response that would be expected of any warm-blooded naked ape, "Of course I think of sex. I think of sex all the time, just like other men." One single 34 year-old programmer wrote, "If any guy says he prefers computers or chocolate over sex, he must be crazy." Another 34 year-old computer user who preferred computers said, "I bet it's the married guys who preferred computers over sex." One imaginative 19 year-old shared his sexual fantasy, "Chocolate syrup over my girlfriend and sex on a Californian beach."

Still, a 34 year-old programmer contends that my survey was incomplete. His logical mind pointed out that I forgot to ask, "Do we think of computers when we're having sex?"

TABLE 4-2: AFTER HOURS COMPUTER USAGE

PREFERENCE	IT MALES	IT FEMALES	NON-IT MALES	NON-IT FEMALES	NET PEOPLE
EXTRA-CURRICULAR HOURS	17.7	19.4	15.4	18.3	23.2
NUMBER OF MEALS EATEN WEEKLY IN FRONT OF A COMPUTER	4.7	3.4	2.4	3.7	6.0
PLAYS COMPUTER GAMES	71 %	38 %	71 %	51 %	79 %
ON CHAT GROUPS	23 %	15 %	21 %	44 %	60 %
ON COMPUTER USER GROUPS	12 %	13 %	13 %	5 %	43 %
PREFERS COMPUTER OVER SOCIALIZING	36 %	31 %	29 %	27 %	49 %
TAKES COMPUTER ON HOLIDAYS	38 %	39 %	23 %	9 %	47 %
NUMBER OF COMPUTERS AT HOME	3.1	2.2	1.7	1.7	3.2

When it came to working or playing on their computers after hours, the Net people spent the most time on the computer after 5 p.m. – on average 23.2 hours weekly. One blue-collar worker by day, spent every waking moment on the computer to teach himself everything he needed to know about computers for a computer college diploma. That meant nine hours each weekday night plus weekends with time off only for grocery shopping and laundry. Another Net person wrote, "I just can't get enough of the computer. I'm looking forward to the day when they can hook me up to the computer, like a peripheral!"

> *"Computers have this f—king addictive screen. So much time is spent working on purely elementary stuff and not working on the next great painting or novel!"*
> 34 year-old computer user

Only a handful of survey respondents were computer celibate, as rare as bug-free software. On the other end of the spectrum, others spent every waking moment. One female techie wailed at me about her male co-workers, "I never see them leave the computer. They don't take lunch breaks or coffee breaks. They don't seem to even get up to go to the bathroom. I wonder what their bladders are made of." Women spent on average two more hours per week on the computer after 5 p.m. than men. IT males spent about 15 per cent more time on the computer after 5 p.m. than non-IT males; IT females spent 5 per cent more time than non-IT females. While single individuals typically spent a little more time on the computer than others, it was the married women with children who also spent a little more time on the computer than married women without children.

> *"The problem is not that you are on the computer at 6:00 am. The problem is that you have logged off the computer at 6:00 am."*
> 50 year-old network guy

Generally speaking, gender played a big role in who played computer games or spent time in chat rooms. Men played more games than women, while more women were in chat rooms than men. Net people whom were comprised of the highest proportion of teenagers and introverts had the highest number of chat room participants at 60 per cent.

When it came to choosing between a social invitation to go out with friends or spending time on the computer, not everybody was inclined to leave the PC behind. (Some single IT males just muttered under their breath something about never receiving social invitations.) Forty-nine per cent of Net people would turn down a social invitation to spend time on the computer; another 5 per cent would consider doing such a thing. Thirty-three per cent of males said they preferred to work or play on the computer than socialize, versus 29 per cent for women. Both IT males and IT females cited that meeting a deadline was the reason for turning down a social invitation.

About one in ten persons were workaholics and abstained from taking holidays. However, Net people who did not take holidays reported doing so, because their life is just the way they like it – in front of the computer. While travel, camping and visiting family were the top holiday activities, others who stayed in town reserved their time for sleeping, doing housework and vegetating. Relaxation seemed to have been deleted from many respondents' lives. While waiting to download, most persons were doing some other computer-related activity besides eating, napping, smoking, sipping coffee, going to the bathroom or "picking lint from my navel."

For those persons indulgent enough to get away for holidays, bandwidth anxiety was problematic for some. About 47 per cent of the Net people, followed by 38 per cent IT males and 39 per cent of IT women took their laptop computers on their holidays, as compared to 23 per cent of non-IT males and 9 per cent of non-IT females. One reason for this discrepancy is that IT professionals are often provided laptops by their employers.

The year in which people learned how to use a computer mouse indicated how long they've been using computers. Here is another correlation among IT professionals, where the year that IT males learned to use the mouse was 1987; IT females, 1986. Amongst non-IT males, the year for learning to use a computer mouse was 1988; for non-IT females and Net people was 1990.

TABLE 4·3: MORE ABOUT COMPUTER USAGE

PREFERENCE	IT MALES	IT FEMALES	NON-IT MALES	NON-IT FEMALES	NET PEOPLE
PREFERS KEYBOARD COMMANDS	25 %	16 %	20 %	23 %	35 %
YEAR LEARNED TO USE A MOUSE	1987	1986	1988	1990	1990
SPENDS 5 OR MORE HOURS WEEKLY COMPUTER SHOPPING	95 %	72 %	98 %	65 %	69 %
SPEND LOTTERY MONEY ON COMPUTERS	27 %	33 %	39 %	25 %	39 %
USES ELECTRONIC ORGANIZERS	30 %	35 %	29 %	14 %	39 %
TAKEN A LAPTOP COMPUTER TO BED WITH THEM	30 %	33 %	16 %	18 %	43 %

About 24 per cent of IT males preferred using keyboard commands, 39 per cent preferred the mouse and the rest had no preference. Among IT females, 16 per cent preferred keyboard commands, 46 per cent preferred the mouse and 35 per cent had no preference. The preference to use the mouse was significantly higher among non-IT persons, who were originally taught on PC's equipped with mice. About 53 per cent of non-IT males and 51 per cent of non-IT females favored the computer mouse. Speed was the main reason why some individuals preferred keyboard commands, while others thought the mouse was more convenient to use.

Thirty-five per cent of Net people, preferred keyboard commands – a phenomena possibly related to the young age of starting to use a computer. Net people, on average, began using a computer at 13.5 years. Thirty-five per cent of Net people started on a computer at 8 years or younger. Seventy per cent of Net people who were 9 years or younger when they started to use a computer preferred keyboard commands.

Despite saged advice to keep your computer away from dirt and dust, nothing stopped computer lovers from eating in front of the computer. Crumbs, smoke and greasy fingers are all hazardous for the personal computer. Your computer mouse is a haven for lint, cat hair and other disgusting grime. Even electronic components can suffer from second hand cigarette smoke. Net people led the pack eating 6.0 meals weekly in front of the computer, IT males – 4.7 meals weekly, IT females – 3.4 meals, non-IT males – 2.4 meals and non-IT females – 3.7 meals. Non-IT males reported with snide comments, "I would if I could, but I'm not allowed to." Several individuals off the Net, single men and even one married man with children, ate all of their meals in front of the computer. Lunch was cited as the most common meal eaten in front of the computer, followed by breakfast.

Computers, Computers and More Computers

Do you want to hit it off with a computer lover? Then ask him or her about their first encounter with a computer. Interviewees spoke of their first computer with great affection, down to the exact model number, microprocessor chip and monitor size. Just like my transformation going from a slide rule to calculator geek.

During the 1970's, several generations of Hewlett-Packard calculators, which were conceived a decade earlier, eased into the hands of slide rule geeks. In 1976, the hand-held HP-67 and Hp-97 programmable calculators with magnetic cards really hit engineering school big-time. Three months of hard-earned summer job salary was advertised on the hip pockets of the third year electrical engineering students. Yeah, right, I wasn't going to give in yet. Fourth year engineering rolled around and I yielded to the technological revolution of the time, took a 90-minute bus ride to the other side of Vancouver to purchase a Melcor calculator for the price of one-month's rent. My first hand-held calculator could add, subject, multiply, divide, carry out logarithmic functions, store, compute square roots and a few extras. It had to be plugged in virtually at all times but had enough juice inside to operate for about two hours plug-free before going on the fritz. My Melcor lasted about a year, as one accidental fall from my backpack after my last exam, killed it. About the same time, the company that made my first hand-held calculator went belly up. The timing could not have been more perfect.

Isn't it enough that the average respondent spends up to 77 hours weekly in front of a computer? Have they become so attached, that they are almost peripherals? Do they think of anything else?

> *"I'm peeved by that never ending black hole in which you throw buckets of money to fund a lifestyle that Bill Gates has grown accustomed to."*
> 37 year-old computer user

Of course, they think of something else. They think of what they would like in their next computer. On a weekly basis, individuals were asked if they spent any time cruising for new hardware and software. How anxious were they to keep up with the latest technology, whiz-bang gizmo and other digital toys to play with?

Now, we're talking about people who read *PCWeek* and other computer magazines before they go to bed. We're talking about people who gossip about which high-tech company is taking over so-and-so and for how much, while the rest of the world is still talking about Martha Stewart's latest pumpkin pie or Monica Lewinsky's lip color. So, it's no surprise that on a weekly basis, that 96 per cent of males and 69 per cent of females spend up to five or more hours weekly browsing on-line, hanging out a computer stores or reading computer magazines during their leisure hours. While the rest of us may be grocery shopping on weekends, computer people who are free of family obligations or significant others, have already hit the local computer store or are on-line in search of their next up-grade.

While car enthusiasts talk about engine size, number of cylinders and miles per gallon, computer people are talking about microprocessor speed, hard drive size, firewall protection, their personal web sites for pets, bandwidth for modem transmission and Internet access. At our daughter's 11th birthday party, a very bright computer savvy boy came to her party.

She lamented, "He never gets invited to parties." Since he liked computers, I asked him, "So, what kind of operating system are you working on? MS-DOS?" He shot back at me, "Come on. Nobody nowadays works on something less than 330." I was stunned by his assertiveness. "What do you mean 330?" I asked. Then I realized he meant 330 megahertz micro-processor speed. So I asked him, "So you must have a Pentium at home?" He replied, "Which one are we talking about, Pentium I or II? We got Pentium II and we're getting another one." So I thought I would carry out this conversation one step further, despite our daughter's pleas. "So how big is your hard drive?" He replied, "Six gigabytes, but we're going to up-grade soon." I was impressed.

Sixty-seven per cent of males and sixty-three per cent of females interviewed spend up to five hours weekly, checking out computer hardware and software. Some 29 per cent of males and 16 per cent of females spend more than five hours weekly in search of new technology.

"After working with computers for years, I have computer phobia. But I'm okay with that!"
25 year-old computer user

Assuming that an individual had won a few thousand dollars and had no outstanding debts, they were asked what would they spend their money on. Thirty-one per cent of the men versus 39 per cent of the women wanted to take a holiday. The desire to take a holiday and go travelling was strongest among IT-females at 42 per cent, followed by IT males at 36 per cent. The next popular response was the urge to accumulate more high-tech gadgetry, ranging from more powerful computers to DVD disk drives, etc. About 32 per cent of men and 29 per cent of women wanted to buy more computer stuff. The group most likely to buy computer stuff were Net people and non-IT males at 39 per cent. Nine per cent of men and women surveyed would spend the extra money on home renovations or good quality furniture. Other desirable items mentioned by respondents included new cars, investments in high-tech stocks, motorbikes, clothes, books, CD's, and by three men, donations to charitable causes.

From this survey, it was not unusual for computer lovers to tell me how much they enjoyed ADSL, ISDN or Ethernet technology in their houses. Such high-speed access was found typically in the homes of IT professionals, who didn't wanted to slow down on the digital highway after work.

> *"A geek is a person who up-grades as often as possible, not because of a need for faster or better equipment, but because of the 'coolness' factor."*
> 21 year-old computer user

The highest number of personal computers people in a home was 40, owned by a single 40 year-old computer guy who just kept every single computer he had purchased over the past 25 years. Still, there were three other men who owned 18 to 20 computers, all very functional, but not necessarily turned on. One computer programmer had 18 computers on a local area network in his main floor living room. One major drawback of his expanded home office was that the thermostat was located in the same room and caused domestic heating problems. A number of computer lovers installed computers in every second room of their houses, so families could play inter-active computer games together.

The highest number of computers per household were reported by Net people at 3.2 computers per household, followed by IT males at 3.1 computers per household. Women employed in the IT sector reported 2.2 computers per household. Non-IT males and non-IT females averaged 1.7 computers per household.

If there was one electronic advice, which received a fair rating among computer people, it was the electronic organizer. Countless respondents griped about batteries going dead during crisis moments, and losing the darned things. Thirty-nine per cent of Net people, 35 per cent of IT females and 30 per cent of IT males used electronic organizers. The GEEK who got fed up with his electronic organizer reverted back to paper day timer. Now his main contention is that he's missing meetings because the day-timer doesn't beep at him. There were no complaints about the palm pilots – a definite status symbol among high-level computer geeks.

Likewise, phones per household correlated well to number of computers per household. Men reported 2.4 phones per household vs. 1.7 phones for women. One Internet service provider had 52 phone lines – the highest number of phones reported in one household. The average number of phones per household: IT males had 3.2 phones, IT females had 1.9 phones, and non-IT males and non-IT females – 1.6 phones.

> *"Using the computer in the bathroom goes beyond the realm of pathetic. It's disturbing. Is this crap on-line? Can you imagine being on e-mail to Fabio who says he's driving in his Lexus with his laptop when instead, he's really sitting on the toilet at home?"*
> 26 year-old computer user

The most likely location to find computers at home is in the home office or den for 47 per cent of all persons surveyed, followed by the basement for 24 per cent of IT males and non-IT males. Only 13 per cent of women kept their computers in the basement, with 18 per cent of them preferring to use a spare bedroom. Ten per cent of men and women surveyed slept in the same bedroom as their computer. Twelve per cent of men and 28 per cent of women reported keeping their computer in their living room. Six per cent of men and only 1 per cent of women reported keeping a computer in the kitchen.

One fellow kept six computers in his two-bedroom apartment, strewn in every room except the bedroom. "That's off limits," he said. Keeping a computer in the kitchen was practical. He could work on it and eat freshly prepared blue box macaroni and cheese from the pot quickly before it developed *rigor mortis*.

Several programmers swore by sleeping in the same room as the computer – just in case they wake up in the middle of the night and have to get on the computer right away. An English programmer said that the bedroom was the most comfortable place for him to work, often going 21 hours at a time, and sometimes keeping his television going in the background for entertainment. Several individuals not only slept in the same room as their computer, but kept the computer on all time. The English programmer found sleeping in the same room with a turned on computer rather disturbing.

"Having the computer in the master bedroom was an ongoing concern. After nine months of marriage, my wife said, 'Get rid of it.' I did because I realized that I cared more for her, than the computer."
26 year-old newly-wed computer guy

I never thought of asking people if they had a computer in their bathrooms. But no doubt some people have thought of having one with them there. One computer consultant who had been in business for about five years, noted that two customers have requested him to install computer hook-ups in their bathrooms. He refused.

Dream on. There's more to computers in the bedroom. There is the trend of people taking laptops into bed with them, led by 43 per cent of the Net people.

Twenty-four per cent of men and women surveyed have taken a laptop computer to bed with them. Here, was an item that brought IT professionals together. About 30 per cent of IT males and 33 per cent of IT females confessed to bringing the laptop computer to bed with them, with comments, like, "I was sick and I had to get this project done, so I took the laptop to bed with me." Only 16 per cent of male computer users and 18 per cent of female computer users reported taking a laptop computer to bed, but this group was also the group least likely to own a laptop computer, too. Slightly embarrassed by his admission, one computer professional remarked, "Hey, you didn't ask me if I kept the laptop on top of the covers or under the covers. Well, at least, it's above the covers."

For some highly-computer literate couples, one woman candidly said, "I said, no, to keeping the computer in the master bedroom. So we comprised, I allow him to bring the laptop into bed." Incidentally, one advantage cited by computer lovers to being so intimate with their machines – computers generate so much heat, that if you had problems with your furnace, you needn't worry about being cold.

On hearing about the presence of computers in the bedroom, one anxious respondent asked me, "Don't you think the computer in the bed room is going to ruin their sex life?" I corrected him, "Well, I wouldn't know. I didn't ask if they had a sex life!"

There's been ongoing controversy whether you should keep your computer turned on or off, when not in use. For small business owners, where the computer also served as a fax machine or answering machine, it was necessary to keep at least one computer on all the time. About 39 per cent of men and 38 per cent of women kept their computer on all the time. Many contend that by turning your computer on and off all the time, you will cause damage to the computer's hardware components which are sensitive to internal temperature changes, in the way a light bulb is affected by the constant switching on and off.

One computer person simply stated the facts, "Your computer could fail either mechanically or electrically. If you keep it on all the time, it only has a chance of failing mechanically." Still, others will argue that the life span of a computer is contingent on the hard drive, often rated for 100,000 hours.

> *"I'm always on my computer. I only turn it off if I'm going to be gone overnight somewhere."*
> 24 year-old techie, who lives with a cat name called Isosceles Scrossle Triangle or Sasha for short.

But from a security perspective, Kim Greenizan, an Airdrie, Alberta-based security consultant, suggests that people turn their computers off, when not in use. Not only do you save electricity, you reduce your exposure to unwarranted power surges entering your computer and causing severe damage. Power bars, are supposed to offer some protection from power surges, but most people don't know that most power bars do not offer strong enough protection, and fail to read the fine print on the product specifications, says Greenizan. Even if your computer is turned off and you're planning to go away or not use your computer for awhile, Greenizan strongly recommends that you unplug your computer. Even if the computer is turned off, some power surges can be problematic. A five-year study conducted by the National Power Laboratory conceded that the average power site is subjected to 443 disruptive power disturbances annually.

"I firmly believe computers are in fact mechanisms created by Satan to cut years off my life through the 'Blue Screen' effect. Life in general also seems to have this, although someone recently remarked that that was actually just the 'sky...' Go figure."
25 year-old computer user

"People who don't like computers, just haven't tried them yet. Once they do, they're hooked."
36 year-old female computer user

LEVEL 5

GEEK CONSUMERISM

"Come on, look at the richest man in the world. And he can't even get a decent hair cut."
29 year-old software programmer

Do you know a computer geek when you see one? What is geek chic? Can you tell a geek from what he eats? Read on. You may be surprised.

When it comes to home ownership, 73 per cent of the men and 52 per cent of the women surveyed owned their own homes or lived in a house owned by their parents. Home ownership was highest among non-IT males at 79 per cent, followed by IT males at 67 per cent, non-IT females and 54 per cent and IT females at 50 per cent. Net people, being young and restless (only 29 per cent were married with children) had the lowest percentage of home ownership at 38 per cent. Their home ownership and rental patterns were not unusual for *Silicon Cowtown* where the majority of survey respondents lived. For comparative sake, 37 per cent of *Silicon Cowtown's* residents rent, while 63 per cent own their own homes.

Contrary to rumors that single computer people live at home, only 6 per cent of respondents did so – the majority being high school and university students. Just one 30 year-old IT male, reported living at home. Respondents lived in structures no different than you and I, whether it be owning or renting a house, condo or apartment. Bruce Campbell, a Portland, Oregon-based engineer takes exception. He had no qualms about salvaging a well-used Grecian 727 jet to create his dream home. Progress on his home renovation is documented at www.airplane.com. He has no interest in replacing the exterior of his aircraft, as aluminum is a much better housing material than wood, which he eschews as "termite chow." He intends to keep the original shape of the plane. "I want it to look like a fully operational aircraft... They look so sexy when they're complete and clean." Campbell plans to keep the main cabin undivided, leaving him with one super-long studio apartment, which will be the saloon for his 12-computer collection. A bachelor, he hopes to meet his "soul mate" and thinks of buying a 747 for them to settle down in on his 10-acre property.

TABLE 5·1: HOME AND GOING TO WORK

	IT MALES	IT FEMALES	NON-IT MALES	NON-IT FEMALES	NET PEOPLE
HOUSE OR CONDO	73 %	81 %	52 %	54 %	37 %
LIVES AT HOME	1 %	3 %	0 %	7 %	11 %
RENTS HOUSE	15 %	1 %	30 %	24 %	31 %
RENTS APARTMENT	6 %	7 %	13 %	11 %	21 %
RENTS CONDO	5 %	8 %	5 %	4 %	0 %
DRIVES OR CARPOOLS TO WORK	71 %	82 %	59 %	65 %	53 %
WALKS TO WORK	8 %	8 %	9 %	9 %	16 %
CYCLES TO WORK	4 %	5 %	6 %	17 %	15 %
TAKES PUBLIC TRANSIT TO WORK	17 %	5 %	26 %	9 %	16 %

If cars can say anything about people's personalities, then do we have a story for you here. While describing personality strengths and weaknesses was a sore point of the survey, people took time to tell me things about their car I didn't ask – their car's age and mileage. Status-oriented cars, with the exception of one BMW, one Mercedes Benz and one Jaguar, were definitely the anomaly, not the rule. While computers are known to come in and out of their lives, computer people wanted cars that you could count on. In terms of popularity, car manufacturers ranked as follows – GM, Ford, Honda, Toyota and other Japanese cars. However, in *Silicon Cowtown*, the most popularly mentioned car manufacturer and model by IT males and females were Honda Accords/Civics and Toyota Corollas – the geekmobiles in town. The Net people were similar. They repeatedly mentioned Honda Prelude and Acura. Proud were these Japanese car owners that their car was over 10 years old and had six-digit odometer records. Senior citizens stuck to driving the gas–guzzling big American cars, like Cadillac and Buick. It's ironic that the Net people had the highest number of computers per household, yet they outdid everybody when it came to mentioning the age of the 30-plus year-old cars they drove – 1969 Volkswagen bug, 1963 Chevy Impala or 1968 Plymouth Valiant.

Seventy-five per cent of the men reported driving to work vs. 62 per cent of the women. Among the Net people, just 53 per cent of the respondents drove to work. There was an equal split between men and women choosing to take public transit to work or walk and cycle.

NUTRITION AND THE NERD

"Coke is the elixir of the gods."
34 year-old programmer

TABLE 5-2: **BEVERAGES AND THE NERD**

	IT MALES	IT FEMALES	NON-IT MALES	NON-IT FEMALES	NET PEOPLE
DRINKS COKE	43 %	47 %	40 %	38 %	34 %
DRINKS PEPSI	13 %	11 %	8 %	10 %	7 %
DOES NOT DRINK POP	25 %	11 %	25 %	44 %	17 %
DRINKS REGULAR COFFEE[1]	37 %	45 %	13 %	24 %	34 %
DRINKS LATTE	13 %	11 %	26 %	14 %	25 %
DRINKS CAPPUCCINO	14 %	15 %	29 %	25 %	25 %
DOES NOT DRINK COFFEE	27 %	16 %	18 %	19 %	30 %
DRINKS BEER[2]	43 %	44 %	39 %	19 %	35 %
DRINKS WINE	9 %	12 %	23 %	24 %	18 %
DOES NOT DRINK LIQUOR	18 %	17 %	15 %	33 %	31 %

COFFEE[1] – RESPONDENTS WERE ASKED WHAT THEY WOULD ORDER IF THEY WENT OUT TO A COFFEE HOUSE, LIKE STARBUCKS OR SECOND CUP.

BEER[2] – RESPONDENTS WERE ASKED WHAT THEY WOULD DRINK IF THEY WENT OUT FOR AN EVENING WITH THEIR FRIENDS.

When it came drinking pop, Coke was the first place choice for 44 per cent of the men and 39 per cent of the women. It is amazing that this fizzy beverage invented in 1886 could have so much staying power. Coke consumption defies the fact that in 1996, more Pepsi was sold in Canadian national grocery stores. Coke consumption amongst IT professionals was the strongest. Forty-three percent of IT males and 39 per cent of IT females said Coke was their favorite pop. Pepsi was second for 12 per cent of men and 9 per cent of women. Amongst IT professionals, root beer was their favorite drink for 5 per cent of them. Ginger ale at 4 per cent beat out 7-Up and Sprite, at 3 per cent. Ginger ale and Pepsi were each favored by 8 per cent of IT females. Mountain Dew is also worthy mentioning at 3 per cent of all interviewees, along with Dr. Pepper and cherry cola combined at 2 per cent of all responses.

Still, abstaining from pop consumption was significant. Twenty-one per cent of men and thirty-four per cent of women do not drink pop, preferring to drink plain water, juice or nothing at all. Pop consumption at 89 per cent was highest among non-IT males and lowest among non-IT females at 56 per cent. Only one IT male and one Net person imbibed Jolt, but did mention its jittery side effects. Some pop drinkers did mention that pop consumption had to be reduced due to the effect on upsetting their stomachs.

What do you expect from no-frills people? Thirty-nine per cent of men and 18 per cent of women would order a regular cup of coffee from a specialty coffee house, despite the enticing selections available. While IT females were least likely to just order a regular cup of coffee at 13 per cent, non-IT males at 45 per cent were the most likely to order a regular cup of coffee. Gender was a definite contributing factor to consumer choice. Fourteen per cent of men and 28 per cent of women would order cappuccino, 12 per cent of men and 21 per cent of women would order latte, followed by expresso at 5 per cent for men and women who responded to this survey. Other coffee beverages, individuals mentioned drinking included mocacino, frappacino and specialty flavored coffees. Still, a very significant number of computer users can't be bothered with drinking coffee, some preferring tea, juice or pop. About 23 per cent of men and 19 per cent of women do not drink coffee.

Considering liquor consumption, IT professionals were linked by drinking beer, 39 per cent for IT females and 43 per cent of IT ales preferred drinking beer when out with friends. Thirty-five per cent of Net people also preferred drinking beer. About 44 per cent of non-IT males also ordered a beer, when dining out, too. For non-IT females, wine was ordered by 24 per cent. Hard liquor was favored by 18 per cent of IT females, 21 per cent of non-IT females, 16 per cent of IT males and 19 per cent of non-IT males. Abstinence of alcohol was highest among non-IT females at 33 per cent, followed by 31 per cent of Net people and 18 per cent for IT males.

With the strong image of Californian computer geeks, outsiders are certain that computer people are vegetarian. In *Silicon Cowtown* – the heart of Canada's beef country, it's pretty tough being a vegetarian. Just 3 per cent of men and 14 per cent of women in this survey claimed to be vegetarians. There were no vegetarians among non-IT males and vegetarianism was highest among non-IT females at 22 per cent. Net people reported a 10 per cent vegetarianism rate.

TABLE 5-3: DIET AND THE NERD

	IT MALES	NON-IT MALES	IT FEMALES	NON-IT FEMALES	NET PEOPLE
IS VEGETARIAN	4 %	0 %	5 %	22 %	10 %
TAKES OUT[1] CHINESE FOOD	33 %	40 %	53 %	30 %	46 %
TAKES OUT PIZZA	29 %	32 %	18 %	38 %	20 %
TAKES OUT HAMBURGERS	13 %	12 %	3 %	12 %	11 %
SNACKS[2] ON CHIPS	34 %	23 %	30 %	28 %	18 %
SNACKS ON POPCORN	12 %	3 %	13 %	3 %	3 %
SNACKS ON CHOCOLATE	10 %	14 %	10 %	15 %	15 %

TAKES OUT[1] – RESPONDENTS WERE ASKED FOR THEIR FAVORITE TAKE OUT FOOD.

SNACKS[2] – RESPONDENTS WERE ASKED FOR THEIR FAVORITE SNACK FOOD.

Vegetarians among IT professionals were pretty close at 4 per cent and 5 per cent, for IT males and IT females, respectively. People who had an Asian influence in their upbringing or had lived on the west coast of North America, were more likely to be vegetarians.

"Pizza is the national geek food."
56 year-old retired IT executive

Yes, pizza is popular among computer geeks, but there is something they like better and their food tastes are not so deviant from the Canadian palate. The 1997 Canadian and American food industry report published by the Canadian Council of Grocery Distributors reported that Canadian consumer interest in ethnic foods was led by Chinese food – favored by 56 per cent of respondents, followed by Italian at 51 per cent and Mexican with 35 per cent.

Chinese food (including Thai and Vietnamese), were cited by 36 percent of the men and 40 percent of the women as their most popular take-out dish. Even some vegetarians contradicted themselves, when they mentioned their favorite take-out dish was ginger beef. Chinese food take-out was highest among IT females at 53 per cent, while the lowest among non-IT females at 30 per cent. One IT female told me, "Heck, I can make pizza at home any day of the week, but I can't make Chinese food as good as in the restaurants."

Pizza, which is the only third most popular food item ordered at restaurants by Canadians, after French fries and salad, was the second favorite take-out meal for 31 percent of the men and 28 per cent of the women. Still, 13 per cent of men and 8 per cent of women cited the good old burger, often from the Golden Arches, as their favorite take-out food.

Six per cent of men and five per cent of women ordered fried or barbecued chicken. Sandwich and submarine sandwiches were ordered by four percent of all survey respondents. Sushi was only mentioned as being a favorite take-out food for IT males. But East Indian food, was more popular than Japanese food, seducing two per cent of the men and three per cent of the women. Fish and chips and Lebanese food, each gained 1 per cent of the respondents' approval. Surprise? But tacos were more popular amongst the women than the men by four to one, at 4 per cent and 1 per cent, respectively. Women ordered more salads and Greek food than men.

"What is a computer's favorite snack food?" — *"Chips."*
10 year-old kid

When it comes to snacking, both gender and occupation, seemed to influence people's choices. The most popular snack food cited by respondents was chips. While potato chips led the way – cheezies, nachos and taco chips, were fondly mentioned. About 29 per cent of men and women snack on chips. Chip consumption is highest among IT professionals, 34 per cent for IT males and 30 per cent for IT females. Another food item that linked the IT professionals together was popcorn, the second most popular snack for 12 per cent of IT males and 13 per cent for IT females. The third food item that also linked IT professionals together was chocolate, which was lower among IT professionals than non-IT persons. Ten per cent of IT males and IT females mentioned chocolate as their favorite snack vs. 14 per cent of non-IT males, 15 per cent of non-IT females and Net people. Lastly, ice-cream linked IT people together, with 4 per cent of IT males and 5 percent of IT females heading for the freezer between meal times. Candy accounted for 7 per cent of men and 5 per cent of women's responses, while cookies were mentioned as being popular for 6 per cent of men and women.

When it comes to dental care or weight control or perhaps, a sign of youth, the IT females were sticklers for eating fruit and raw vegetables in between meals, at 19 per cent. Women outnumbered men about 3:1 in this category, with 16 per cent of women and only 5 per cent of men, indulging in some rabbit food snacking. Conscious about the fat content in snacks, 3 per cent of women and 1 per cent of men, ate bagels in between meals.

Pretzels were enjoyed by 1 per cent of men and sunflower seeds, (which are a good source of calcium and various vitamins) were enjoyed by 3 per cent of persons surveyed, regardless of occupation or gender.

In terms of other snack food choices, men were definitely more creative, cleaning out the refrigerator for leftovers. Some IT males had fairly exotic snacking specifications, like salmon mousse on crackers or ultra healthy tastes, like tofu or beans and rice.

Color My Computer Blue

Table 5·4: More About Respondent Preferences

	IT MALES	NON-IT MALES	IT FEMALES	NON-IT FEMALES	NET PEOPLE
Likes Blue	59 %	39 %	35 %	46 %	21 %
Likes Green	18 %	22 %	22 %	8 %	29 %
Likes Black	—	—	—	—	24 %
Likes Red	13 %	24 %	8 %	8 %	10 %
Likes Purple	5 %	3 %	8 %	19 %	10 %
Shops for Clothes at One Store	19 %	15 %	21 %	17 %	7 %
Has Pierced Ears	9 %	15 %	82 %	74 %	34 %
Has Pierced Body Parts	1 %	0 %	3 %	12 %	14 %
Has Tattoos	8 %	4 %	8 %	11 %	20 %

Do boys prefer blue because they were dressed in blue sleepers as infants and everybody gave them blue clothing? In the same manner that Coke was the nectar for computer people, blue was the most popular color for 48 per cent of the men and 40 per cent of the women. It was highest for IT males at 54 per cent, with favorite shades of blue ranging from baby blue to navy blue. Under 30 computer people really liked black, but green, especially forest green, was the favored color for Net people.

Overall, the second most popular color was green, for 19 per cent of men and 15 per cent of women. Green lovers also expressed an interest towards the dark conservative green colors, like forest and hunter green or teal. Eighteen per cent of men liked red vs. 8 per cent of women. At four per cent of responses, the next favorite colors for men were purple and yellow.

Overall, women, responded with more sensitivity defining a larger color palette from cream to fuschia to burgundy. After blue, followed by green, purple was the most popular for women in general – although a number of female computer users preferred purple over green. After blue and green, pink was cited as the most popular color by 10 per cent of IT females.

So How Do They Shop

About 18 per cent of men and 19 per cent of women shop for clothes at one type of store. Everybody else shops where they pretty damned well pleased. Reasons for shopping at one store, include getting the cheapest prices by men, proper sizing in the case of petite women, value in the case of *Winners* (discount designer store) and for time-pressed women, close proximity to home. In terms of style that emanates the right type of image, Eddie Bauer and Mountain Equipment Co-op, were named as the two places most computer professionals (especially, those employed in the oil and gas sector) shopped at in *Silicon Cowtown*. The under-30 crowd, were the most fashion-conscious, with a few men shopping at the GAP. One man told me that you couldn't get any decent clothes in Canada. Once a year, he flew to San Francisco to shop.

Twelve per cent of men and three per cent of women reported that either their spouses or mothers purchased their clothes for them. In the case of married men, often their wives would select upscale suits, like Hugo Boss.

An eastern-based female computer consultant e-mailed me, "Forty per cent of the time I am sitting in front of the computer naked." She sits in a room with six computers. No wonder. The rest of the time, she just wears T-shirts and jeans. She astutely pointed out that I forgot to ask everybody if they have ever sat naked in front of the computer. For a fact, the GEEK has dashed out of the morning shower to run into his home office and key in something that has crossed his mind.

So where are all those funny looking guys wearing cartoon ties? Well, IT males detest ties and only 44 per cent own cartoon ties. Most don't wear them. About one in four male computer users had in their possession cartoon ties, typically a gift from their kids.

When it came to piercing body parts, the Net people were in the lead at 14 per cent, followed by non-IT females at 12 per cent. Ears were cited as the most commonly pierced body part by 82 per cent of IT females, 74 per cent of non-IT females, 34 per cent of Net people, 9 per cent of IT males and 12 per cent of non-IT males. Beyond ears, the other strategic body locations included 3 per cent of the navels for IT females and 5 per cent of non-IT females, the nipple for 5 per cent of non-IT females and nose for 2 per cent of non-IT females. One daring IT female reported that her clitoral hood was pierced. Many IT males made comments that they removed their earrings when going to the office.

Net people led the trend of tattoos at 20 per cent, followed by non-IT females at 11 percent, then IT males and IT females at 8 per cent. With respect to tattoos, women felt if they would decorate their bodies, why settle for just one? Eight per cent of IT females and 11 per cent of non-IT females had one tattoo, with 5 per cent and 9 per cent respectively, having more than one. Ten per cent of the Net people had more than one tattoo, too. The IT males were more tattooed than non-IT males. Six per cent of IT males sported tattoos vs. 4 per cent of male computer users, while 2 per cent of IT males had more than one tattoo. Tattoos were popular among individuals with military service.

Entertainment and Computer People

"Science fiction is reality"
Frank Ogden, a.k.a. Dr. Tomorrow

Star Trek, Star Wars and Phantom Menace. Doesn't matter if Captain Picard, Luke Skywalker or Darth Vader stroll on topsy turf in their inter-galactic pursuits. Doesn't matter if weird and incomprehensible species, like *Jawas* and *Wookies* grunt across the screen. So what if the 50th episode of Star Trek's script appears to be the same, one battle after the next in a universe with Klingons. So what if it took a whole movie to insinuate whom Luke Skywalker's father really was. Science-fiction at its finest, the kind that makes some computer people drool for more. "It's that what if case scenario that turns me on," says the GEEK, who for over a decade religiously escaped computer terminal illness every Saturday night to watch Star Trek.

TABLE 5·5: ENTERTAINMENT AND COMPUTER PEOPLE

	IT MALES	NON-IT MALES	IT FEMALES	NON-IT FEMALES	NET PEOPLE
IS A TREKKIE	60 %	66 %	43 %	32 %	37 %
READS SCIENCE-FICTION BOOKS	36 %	40 %	14 %	30 %	47 %
LISTENS TO A VARIETY OF MUSIC	19 %	20 %	18 %	21 %	46 %
LISTENS TO ROCK	23 %	19 %	33 %	21 %	5 %
LISTENS TO CLASSICAL MUSIC	11 %	21 %	3 %	15 %	6 %
WATCHES TV SITCOMS	87 %	94 %	85 %	67 %	83 %
LIVES WITH PETS	53 %	58 %	70 %	61 %	56 %

About 64 per cent of men and 37 per cent of women were Star Trek devotees. Many explained how they worshipped the old series, carefully video-taping each episode. Trekkie purists were deeply offended by newer renditions of Star Trek and newer series, like *Deep Space Nine*, which had weak plots and too many offensive-looking aliens.

Ever since Arthur C. Clarke's movie *2001:A Space Odyssey* in 1968, bystanders have been fascinated by what our future holds from science-fiction plots. Clarke's talking computer, HAL, with artificial intelligence was not out to lunch. All trekkies know that the Altair computer built in 1975, was named appropriately after a Star Trek episode – *A Voyage to Altair*.

Science-fiction fantasy books were the favorites for all computer persons, regardless of gender or occupation. However, the preference for such books was strongest among the male users, namely 40 per cent of non-IT males, followed by 36 per cent of IT males, 30 per cent of non-IT females, and 14 per cent of IT females. Murder mystery suspense, at 24 per cent, was the leading book category for IT females.

Both male and female IT professionals whined about the lack of time they have to read books for pleasure. Reading computer books recreationally was highest among IT professionals, for 10 per cent of IT males and 5 per cent of IT females. IT professionals also mentioned reading adventure and philosophy books, which male and female computer users did not express as much interest in.

While some individuals in all categories read self-help books, this category was definitely more popular among women. Twice as many women as men reported reading self-help books. Six times as many women as men read romance novels.

At 23 per cent, non-IT females read the most number of novels, followed by non-IT males at 12 per cent. About 5 per cent of IT males and females reported reading novels.

IT males also were the most likely to enjoy horror books, followed by IT females and non-IT males. Men over women, reported favoring humor, comic, science, and car books. History was most popular among IT males and business books were more likely to be read by IT females.

Music & Television

When it came to music, there was a range of responses and preferences, including rap, alternative and techno for the under 35 crowd; Celtic, folk, contemporary, dance, jazz and new age for others. With the exception of 47 per cent of Net people, about one in five persons surveyed enjoyed a variety of music to listen to. Rock music was the most favorite music for 27 per cent of the women and 22 per cent of men, but only 5 per cent of Net people. While 15 per cent of IT females found country music singing in their ears, classical music was preferred by 15 per cent of men and female computer users. Several men remarked that they will listen to a variety of music, with the exception of country music. In *Silicon Cowtown*, country music lovers insisted on listening to their one and only category.

Classical music made its way to the top 10 of computer people. That's not surprising considering that there were quite a few responses from musicians in the survey. About 47 per cent of women and 44 per cent of men reported playing a musical instrument. A handful of persons interviewed played in bands or were former concert pianists.

When it came to television sitcoms, about one in seven persons surveyed did not watch them. Are women less humorous, do they take themselves more seriously or do they have less time to watch television than men? Some 24 per cent of women and 11 per cent of men do not watch sitcoms.

Sixteen per cent of women and only 7 per cent of men liked *Frasier*. The now defunct *Seinfeld* left an indelible impression on 7 per cent of women and one in five men. For the under-30 crowd, *The Simpson's* drew some rave reviews, along with *South Park*.

PETS GET REAL

So true about the cliché that a man's best friend is his dog. In the household of the average computer user, there's a higher probability that he or she lives with a pet than a child. Sixty-five per cent of the women surveyed lived in a house with at least one pet, while 34 per cent had children. Fifty-four per cent of men surveyed lived in a house with at least one pet, while 49 per cent had children. There were no significant differences among the four groups studied, in terms of pet ownership. About one in four persons lived with a dog and about one in three persons lived with a cat. Amongst women, cats was the preferred over dogs, but only by a few percentage points. About one in ten persons kept more than one pet at home. After cats and dogs, fish was the popular pet for computer people, although they did mention gerbils, rabbits, and lizards, too.

People did not name their pets after computers, but the occasional user gave their computer a name. Computer people had a tendency to name their pets after franchised foods or national brand names. Netscape named its internal departments after fast-food franchises, like Burger Kings, Crispy-Crème Do'Nuts and so forth. One programmer called her budgie, Jell-O. Another guy named his two dogs after Kentucky Fried Chicken. He explained, "One's called Kentuck and the other is Chick-Free". Still, a third person named his three fish after the Golden Arches, "Big Mac, Quarterpounder and French fry." His fish were lucky. The lower on the food chain the pet was, the least likely it got a name at all. Single under 30 computer professionals, kept the more unusual pets, like pythons, boa constrictors, iguanas, skunks, newts and ant farms.

Let there be Light

What did time-pressed computer people do for recreation? Gender was the deciding factor what computer people did in their spare time. About 56 per cent of IT males preferred seeing some sunlight, whether they be walking, hiking, skiing, snowboarding, fishing or golfing. Another 29 per cent enjoyed reading while one in five participated in sports, like tennis, basketball, soccer or working out and lifting weights. For 16 per cent of Net people and 12 per cent of IT males, spending more time on the computer was just fine. Playing musical instruments, going to movies, fixing cars and spending time with their family were also commonly mentioned. Non-IT males were into the same things as IT males, except more were into sports and fewer were into reading books.

Popular pastimes for women were first reading books, followed by sports and outdoors activities. While men expressed interest in woodworking and home renovations, women expressed interest in crafts, especially cross-stitching and cooking and gardening.

About 10 per cent of those surveyed did not take holidays at all. For those who did, travel was the number one priority, followed by spending time with their families and camping. Stressed out men and women just reported using the time to relax.

Table 5-6: Spare Time and the Meaning of Success

	IT MALES	NON-IT MALES	IT FEMALES	NON-IT FEMALES	NET PEOPLE
Spare Time Activities:					
Reads	29 %	9 %	19 %	33 %	42 %
Outdoor Activities	35 %	14 %	15 %	8 %	21 %
Sports	21 %	29 %	16 %	8 %	21 %
Crafts	0 %	2 %	12 %	13 %	10 %
Meaning of Success:					
Being Happy	25 %	31 %	44 %	42 %	33 %
Being Wealthy	12 %	15 %	10 %	13 %	31 %
Being Loved	7 %	11 %	2 %	0 %	19 %
Gives to Charity	87 %	90 %	87 %	88 %	75 %
Believes in God	58 %	61 %	85 %	60 %	44 %

Success, Happiness and Love

When it came to defining success in their lives, women and men were on different wavelengths. Forty-three per cent of women just want to be happy vs. 27 per cent of the men. Except for 31 per cent of Net people, about one in ten persons, male or female, defined success as having oodles of money. Women couldn't care less about family or close relationships, while almost one in five Net people and almost one in ten men highly valued success by their family, their wife and close friends. IT females stood out like a sore thumb in that 18 per cent wanted balance between work, career and family in their lives. For 8 per cent of IT males and IT females, success was having freedom to do what you want. More men than women defined success as being of service to others. Such a philanthropic goal was more prevailing among the mature IT professionals who had already attained financial security in their lives, although several Net persons just starting out in their careers shared the same vision, too.

Ninety-seven per cent of those surveyed answered questions about God and charity. Seventy-four per cent of women and 59 per cent of men believed in God in the Judeo-Christian sense. Eighty-six per cent of men and women gave to charity, regardless of their vocation. Some 44 per cent of Net people believed in God, several reported being Wicca and pagan practitioners instead. Just 75 per cent of Net people gave to charities. Individuals least likely to be charitable include those who believed that success is about making money, or were Y2K consultants, students or retired persons. Sixty-eight per cent of those who declined to give to charity did not believe in God.

> *"That's not a wish when you want something to happen to yourself. It's not a wish if you want something to happen to this world. I wish that something could happen for the whole wide Universe. Now that's what I call a wish."*
> 7 year-old DOAG

> *"Don't think of being rich. Don't dream of being rich. Be rich. Don't think of the money you have. Think of money you could have."*
> 11 year-old DOAG

LEVEL 6

YOUNG, HIP AND NOW
A CAREER IN COMPUTERS

"This (computer) profession is the only industry I know where you can triple or even quadruple your salary in a year."

"It's not what you know, but who you know."
35 year-old systems analyst

HIGH-TECH HYSTERIA

The demand for computer and high-tech professionals seems too good to be true. The Canadian information technology sector, a $73-billion industry comprised of software developers, telecommunications companies and multi-media firms, is stressed trying to find suitable job candidates. Industry sources claim that there's a 4.0 per cent vacancy rate in Canada's high-tech industry, which employs 400,000 persons and is growing between 15 to 20 per cent annually. Such hype has hit the media with a vengeance and computer training schools have appeared out of higher altitudes. The Software Human Resource Council, an Ottawa-based organization, estimates that there will be 20,000 new jobs available in the year 2000.

In another study conducted by International Data Corp., a Toronto, Ontario-based research firm revealed that software developers and computer programmers continue to be in highest demand across the IT sectors, particularly, in telecommunications. IDC also reported that 7 per cent of the large companies allowed technology staff to work from home and 70 per cent of the 200 companies surveyed were hiring in 1999.

"If a person doesn't like change, they shouldn't study computers."
40 year-old computer training instructor

High-tech job fairs are routinely held in Canada's high-tech centers of Ottawa, Montreal, Toronto, Vancouver and Calgary, with stiff competition from American companies that frequently come north for techie talent. It is estimated that there are 191,000 unfilled IT jobs in the U.S. today. According to the American Electronics Association, there were 152,203 technology companies in the U.S. (April 1999) – that was 74 per cent more than in 1990; and creating 617,000 new jobs since 1994. So critical is this shortage of manpower that it's not uncommon for staff to be hired un-seen or via e-mail. *Htc: High-Tech Career Journal* estimates that 73 per cent of IT professionals seek work on-line.

In Canada, high-tech jobs account for 5.7 per cent of jobs. But in the Ottawa-Hull area, computer jobs account for 11 per cent of the work; Calgary, 9 per cent. In 1998, computer jobs paid a weekly average of $842 per week, a notch below managers who on average, earned $871 weekly. According to Statistics Canada, the hottest jobs are for systems analysts who can design computer systems and software, software programmers and service technicians who can maintain computer hardware. Systems analysts and computer programmers account for more than 80 per cent of the computer-related high-tech jobs in Canada. In 1998, IBM Canada Ltd. hired more than 3,000 high-tech workers.

Beneath this high-tech hysteria, computer cowpokes ought to check out how big those saddle sores are going to be once they hop into the saddle. Two years ago, Northern Telecom Ltd. announced a four-year, $250-million expansion to its research and development operations in the Ottawa area, creating 5,000 new jobs. To fill 50 to 70 per cent of these new openings, Nortel is looking to hire entry-level positions in computer sciences, computer engineering and electrical engineering. The average employee age at Nortel is 30 years. That's old. The average age at American-based CNET, a burgeoning on-line communications empire growing like a fungus, is 27 years.

Hey, what about those big, bold and beautiful career ads by computer training institutes that promise techie nirvana, once you've procured your computer diploma? They say you will get a job with money to boot, when you graduate. But we all know, that life offers no guarantees.

> *"It's a paradox. There's a shortage of workers but there's not. There's a ton of people who are willing to work in high-tech and could be a good at it. Employers are screaming about a shortage of high-tech workers, but they're unwilling to train. They will hire you, if you're fresh out of university or from college with the skills they want. I have a brother who has a good background in math and science. He took a 6-month course computer course by a company that claimed there would be a 95 percent job placement rate. In the end, he didn't get any job."*
> 45 year-old software programmer

If you're going to chain yourself to computer studies for half a year to two years and spend in the order of $8,000 to $30,000, you should really investigate what you will be getting. Look for on-the-job practicum experience and check the extent of hands-on learning. Get on your high horse, barge in and ask to speak to previous graduates. Just because you've got the right credentials on paper doesn't mean the world is going to beat a path to your door.

Gung-ho Geeks

Now the show down begins. How hard are you going to work? Your competition for that entry level techie position could very well be that effervescent punk next door who can shoot you down, when it comes to time and energy. Probably single, he or she is willing to work up to 20 hours a day behind the computer, even seven days a week. This generation has seen their parents get laid off and lived through their divorces. Do you want some advice for success from one? "Exploit every opportunity you can. Be prepared to shift direction at any moment. Squash your competition, even if it means screwing your mother or significant other." It's survival of the fittest in the silicon jungle and you ain't seen nothing yet.

One 20 year-old entrepreneur attends university full-time and manages a computer consulting company that he and a few high school buddies had established when he was 16 years old. Their first business venture lost $5,000. For that, he just shrugs his shoulders. "Girlfriends are too demanding time-wise," he snaps. He rises at dawn to attend breakfast clubs before school and skips classes at noon to network at luncheon meetings. Nobody would guess he's a full-time student, dressed in a dark conservative suit. His company, which employs over 10 persons, keeps a futon in the reception area for overnighters.

A 16 year-old website designer, still in grade 10, told me, "I started my own computer business. It's not fun. It's really fun. I'm already certified as a computer technician and next summer I will be a certified Microsoft Systems Engineer. When you're in business for yourself, you get up and you curse your clock. When you're in business for yourself, you work whenever you want and that's usually weekends and vacation."

Adam MacLean is 18 years old. He is the Vancouver-based sole proprietor of Nautulus Systems, a computer maintenance and consulting company. During the first four months of 1999, his company grossed $120,000 in revenues despite the fact that he is attending Simon Fraser University full-time studying computer science.

One third-year honors university student IT consulted downtown for 40 hours weekly, literally raking in a minimum of $2,000. Most of his classes were held after 5 p.m. Quite frankly, he was smug enough to keep his mouth shut, making more than what the people who worked in that IT department were earning. Looks can be deceiving. If you met him in person and saw the beater he drove, you'd swear that he was trying to make ends meet.

A former 40 year-old civil servant, who made the career switch into computer consulting teamed up with two much younger partners, including a 25 year-old. With envy, he spoke of his younger partner. "He goes for an interview and they want to know if he can program in C++. He says yes. On Friday, he picks up a copy of the C++ training manual and reads it all Friday night and all weekend. By Monday, he starts the contract and is programming in C++. This guy's been programming computers since he was five years old and ran a bulletin board at 10 years of age. Writing in code is so assimilated into his being."

DIVING INTO THE DIGITAL ABYSS

Fortune columnist Annie Fisher suggests mid-life career switchers consider sales and marketing jobs at high-tech organizations, where experience would be considered an asset. You could acquire a good understanding of computers by taking computer courses and subscribing to computer magazines like *PC Week*. Your passport into the IT world commands that you know what's happening, and you can speak their talk. If your children are computer-literate, you could pick up a few cues from them. William Schafer's book *High-Tech Careers for Low-Tech People* at www.hightechcareers.net offers advice on how to make the career transition without blowing it.

> *"It's 2:00 a.m. in the morning. Somebody is yelling at you. You have crashed into somebody's system. You tend to be superhuman."*
> Former corporate IT professional

Big corporations have pretty standard criteria for hiring techies. After attending two high-tech job fairs, the game strategy is simply put, you're being hired for your potential, not your past performance. A popular question they ask, "Tell us what you want to do with your life for the next five years." One recruiter replied, "Fine, that's nice. We'll get back to you if you fit in with our plan." Working after 5 p.m. or pulling all-nighters is not out of the norm. Your best bet for the mature worker may be targeting smaller and entrepreneurial companies, although the workload will be equally heavy. Several outgoing interviewees who made a mid-life career switch armed with a rolodex of contacts, set up their own computer consulting companies, catering to clients their own age.

> *"We hire on skills and attitude. We look for people who have a love for learning and have no difficulty in putting in extra hours when we need to. We have one employee who made a mid-life career switch into the technical area at 48 or 49 years of age. He was willing to re-establish himself and start at the bottom and then prove himself to us."*
> Nancy Knowlton, president and C.E.O. of Smart Technologies Ltd.

Nobody I spoke to thought there was a stigma about being a mature techie. In theory, everybody said that being over 40 years of age and married with children, should not be viewed as a barrier into entering the IT profession. As long as you can keep up with the hyper kinetic workplace. Recruiters do whine about mid-life career switchers who during interviews tell them how they've fallen in love with computers and want to be a techie for all the opportunities the industry offers. Instead, they would prefer to find individuals, who thrive in adversity, love a challenge and are passionate about problem solving.

Harvey Peters, an instructor with The Institute for Computer Studies in Calgary notes that organizations have two philosophies when hiring, "There are those who want the young, single portable people who they could send around where they want. Then, there are those who want staff with some sort of business-related experience, whether it be oil and gas, manufacturing, engineering, retail or consulting. Consulting companies want people with more experience."

Large corporations with in-house software development departments typically are hungry for junior staff. SAP and ERP (Enterprise Resource Planning) job candidates require a combination of business and technical skills, so creative solutions can be derived. The bottom line, Peters concedes as who gets the job, "Whether you get the job or not, depends on your personality and that of the organization that's doing the hiring."

Dave Brown, a recruiter with Saber, a CNC Global Company in Calgary, agrees with Peters. But he notes the main reason why people can't get jobs is that they don't have any experience. He suggests job seekers not sit around for six months and wait for a job, but go out and do something instead. "They've gone to school for technical training, like a Microsoft Certified Software engineering course. Now they can apply what they have learned. They can go develop web pages for small business owners or volunteer or train seniors on how to use computers," says Brown. "Certification is not the key, experience is. Let's say given two candidates, one with five years of experience and another with five years of experience plus a certificate, the job goes to the person with the certificate. However, given two candidates, one with five years of experience and one with the certificate, the job goes to the one with the five years of experience."

Concedes Brown, "IT companies, if they want you, they can be very flexible. If they don't want you, they're not flexible at all."

But if temporary contract work is what you after, why not consider the premier temp-work site recommended by a geek named "Skywalker" – www.dice.com. Contractors typically earn 20 to 30 per cent more than staff, but have to pay for their own medical and dental benefits.

Baby, It's a Wild World

Who said life was fair? Compensation in the IT world has nothing to do with years of experience or age. Roping a job has to do with what value you're going to be to the company.

> *"Managing programmers is like herding cats. Too many egos."*
> 32 year-old programmer

It's not uncommon for certain computer professionals (even those under 30 years) to make $20,000 monthly or over $100,000 a year. Appendix III in this book, lists results of salary surveys conducted by Personnel Systems of Ottawa, Ontario.

To make big money, many survey respondents suggested moving to Silicon Valley, where part-time jobs could pay U.S. $85,000 per year. A December 1998 survey conducted by Ottawa-based Personnel Consultants, reported that 78 percent of 500 students from 30 Canadian campuses, 1999 computer science and engineering graduates were willing to move to the U.S. to find work. The reasons for heading south included higher salaries, prognosis for long-term earnings, greater career opportunities, lower taxes and overall, a more vibrant economy.

A Calgary computer cowboy, one year out of computer school, was making a mere $50,000. He left for Chicago when they offered him U.S. $180,000. Another individual, a 26 year-old electrical engineer moved to South Carolina for a U.S. $270,000 annual salary. Now that's something to write home about!

> *"Sure you can make double the money in the United States, as in Canada. But you've got to be careful, too. A house in Silicon Valley starts at $300,000 U.S., about twice as much as here. The traffic jams are much worse for getting to work. And you receive health insurance only when you're being employed. If you get laid off or decide you want to do contract work, you're not covered for any health insurance, so you have to return to Canada, any ways."*
> Programmer living happily ever after in Silicon Cowtown.

The prodigies who are programming computers by 10 years of age are the stuff that Silicon civilizations stalk. No training manuals, no computer courses, no help desk support. It's as if Mother Nature implanted RAM in their DNA. When James Gosling, the creator of Java was 12 years old, he invented an electronic version of tic-tac-toe using a phone switch and an old television.

> *"I've been programming since I was 9 years old and sold my first commercial software package at 13 years of age. You go inside the computer figuratively. You explore and create worlds within the computer. It's a creative process and so I practically become part of the computer. I block everything else out. So when I'm working, it can be more like going into a trance state and shut off all other parts of the world. I only program in the dark and only at night. I close all drapes and blinds and turn off all the lights. The only light in the room is from my computer monitor. This allows me to get in the mode of it. I forget to eat and lose aspect of time. On one project, I worked for eight hours and slept for three hours. Then I decided it was time to eat. I was famished. I hadn't eaten anything for 40 hours. For me, there is no difference between work and play. I'm on the computer all the time."*
>
> *"I don't work for a corporation because they always want to pigeonhole employees. You get stuck in a role that you don't want to be in. They focus on the minimum, not the maximum and when they promote you, you get in a level of incompetence."*
> 29 year-old independent software programmer

Yes, the young techie prima donnas, established by their mid-20's can be somewhat arrogant, conceited and cocky. "Hey, I worked hard at computer school. I've got a good job. I get paid well and I've got a future," says one 24 year-old analyst defensively.

But for how long? Technology trends hit the streets like a bat out of hell and then fade as quickly as Cinderella switches from princess to pauper. Y2K consultants, once the high-paid vigilantes on re-configuring COBOL source codes are now weeping wallflowers.

The madness keeps everyone on edge. Some individuals consume up to 25 per cent of their time, just trying to stay in the fast lane. A 29 year-old computer programmer, seven years out of university with a computer science degree, was already feeling abandoned. Still another, one 37 year-old computer technologist graduate is sleepless at nights, "You never know when they're going to lay you off. They could hire somebody out from school to replace you and pay them $2,000 less per month than you."

New graduates are like young race horses with the propensity for burning out within six years. But with the switch from corporate mainframe to networked desktop computing work environments, employers seek techies with inter-personal and team-playing skills. Graduates rarely over-extend their stay at any one organization and focus on getting a wide range of experience. A typical career path is to enter the IT pyramid as a programmer and progress up the organization in database administration and design, become a team leader and project manager.

In the past, employers have tolerated a certain level of geekiness amongst programmers and analysts when hiring. But the truth is that the introverts do not fair as well in corporate America as the extroverts. Survey respondents who held senior executive or managerial positions or were self-employed consultants, were either extroverted or a combination introvert-extrovert personality type. Only one of the 12 IT executives (i.e. presidents, vice-presidents and managers) interviewed, was introverted. Most of the introverts, despite their years of experience settled for junior to mid-level corporate positions. And women working in a male-dominated profession have to be twice as good, contends a male observer.

"I would advise people to get an education which combines people, business and computer skills. They should be selective where they want to go. Right now, some trends indicate training has become a big issue. People who have business and computer skills do well with SAP," says Peters.

Today's IT recruiters look for aptitude, attitude, and communication and technological skills. But if you're going to be spending one-third of your day or more doing something with your life, be sure it's some occupation that you enjoy. IT professionals who responded to the survey, often yearned for more freedom in their life, more holidays and more balance.

Still, compared to other jobs available, high-tech jobs are the best you can get according to income, stress, physical demand, potential growth, job security and work environment. *The Jobs Rated Almanac* by Les Krantz, lists nine of the top ten jobs in the computer or math-related fields, with web site managers being King Kong of the workplace. Both systems analysts and software engineers were also in the top 10 best jobs category.

How Computer People Work

"Being a network analyst, it's high stress and no appreciation. They think anybody can fix a computer. Try make them work in a corporate environment. You get to hate Mr. Gates real fast. The computer industry is tough on people."
38 year-old network analyst.

"Since grade 10, I've enjoyed computer programming. It's kind of artistic. You tell a machine what to do and you think I made it do this. It's kind of fun most of the time. But typically, in this field, the longer you work in computers, you get less and less of the hands on stuff because you work your way up the hierarchy. You start off as the programmer and then end becoming the project manager. So instead of becoming the artist, I've become an art director."
34 year-old IS project manager

"There are computer people who are in it for the short haul, just to make money quick. Then there's those who help other people more than themselves. You have the big mouths in the meetings and then the quiet computer people who make everything happen."
37 year-old computer technologist

"The mentality of big business is that they buy high-powered computer equipment. Then the company realizes that they have to train people to use it but that costs money so they don't. Instead they really only use about 20 percent of the machine's capabilities. In many cases, people have to get the latest and greatest machine, when they don't really need it. It's like having a brand new shining car on the block."
32 year-old systems analyst

"With my last job, when the computer is down, so is someone's business. So you have to run out and help them. Computer repairs are 24 hours a day, 7 days a week. In many cases, it's a mom and pop business and you want to be there."
38 year-old account executive

"Just because the client has got a lot of education, doesn't mean they know how to use computers. We get calls, like you've got to help me. My computer's not working. We ask them, have you turned it on. They say, oh yeah. We ask them are they sure? They tell us, of course, they're sure. They just don't believe that their computer is off. We ask them, are there any lights on? Do they hear any sound? They said no. Then we ask them, is the little red switch turned towards O-F-F, they say yes. We tell them, well turn the little red switch the other way. For that, we charge them $300."
40 year-old computer consultant

Take the Money and Run

For those who believe that there's money to be made in computers, it can be made. "The computer world now is like physics in the 1920's. Money can be made everywhere," says a 33 year-old venture capitalist. He became a millionaire before he turned 30.

Last year, one 21 year-old computer programmer who bought a copy of my book, *Miracles for the Entrepreneur,* was working on an Internet security software project. A quiet soft-spoken guy who ate cold pizza for lunch in a makeshift office dominated by a ghetto blaster with concrete bricks and plywood for book shelving, rationalized, "Yeah, the work is really interesting and I want to help out my friend. If it doesn't work out, I can always go back to school." He got lucky. A Silicon Valley company purchased the software he was working on for a mere U.S. $30 million. His two partners were also under 30.

> *"Find something simple that no one else has realized and keep it secret long enough to get ahead of any competition that might crop up. The Information Age is based on that largely, from what I've seen."*
> 22 year-old computer sciences student

TABLE 6-1: SHOW ME THE MONEY
CAREER PATHS/VOCATIONS RESPONDENTS RECOMMENDED FOR MAKING BIG MONEY.

VOCATION	IT-MALES	IT-FEMALES	NON-IT MALES	NON-IT FEMALES	NET PEOPLE
COMPUTERS	58 %	42 %	58 %	55 %	33 %
DO WHAT YOU LIKE	12 %	17 %	—	—	—
ENTREPRENEUR	7 %	9 %	2 %	—	4 %
ILLEGAL ACTIVITIES	6 %	—	6 %	—	13 %

Only 54 per cent of respondents dared to divulge their scoop on how to make big money. Several remarked that money would not buy you happiness or love, too. Many of the gung-ho geeks under 30, spoke of Freedom 25, or 30 or 35 goals, while individuals over 40, couldn't see an end to the rat race. The secret to creating wealthy geeks hunkered down to working anywhere in the computer world, whether you choose to work as a programmer, systems analyst, network administrator, consultant or in multi-media, sales, marketing or computer repairs. This advice was dished out by 58 per cent of IT males, 42 per cent of IT females, 63 per cent of non-IT males and 55 per cent of non-IT females. The next significant piece of advice that the IT professional had for others was to "do what you like", regardless what it was, followed by entrepreneurship, although none of the non-IT females suggested this path. About 7 per cent of IT males recommended the E-commerce and Internet as big money makers, too. Three respondents suggested on becoming SAP/ERP specialists.

Advice on making big money from the Net people warrants some close examination. Of the 33 per cent who suggested that computers was the way to go, they were in unanimous agreement that big money is to be made with anything to do with Linux, the up and coming operating system – whether it be writing applications software, sales or marketing, etc. Then 15 per cent of the Net people advised others to become a lawyer and 13 per cent were heavy on investing in the stock market. And 13 per cent of Net people and 6 per cent of IT males and non-IT males were quite explicit that illegal affairs would make a pile of money, listing everything from selling illegal weapons internationally to drugs to porn and prostitution. Network administrators should know about porn. Off the record comments indicated that Internet porn hits recorded during a working day is equivalent to the number of employees multiplied by up to five or six. One engineer conceded, "You have to do something illegal to make big money. You don't want to pay income tax." Still, another individual suggested, "Kidnap Bill Gates' dog."

> "I say you go to school and do a lot of things, so you will always have something to fall back on, in case the 'big money' never shows up."
> Student

> "I'd tell them (big money seekers) to get a life. I suppose if it's just money they want, I'd recommend day trading commodities and buying their intelligence from me."
> 55 year-old computer user

> "Be any kind of doctor…probably a psychiatrist."
> 17 year-old computer user

Besides lawyers – doctors, accountants, plastic surgeons, plumbers and dentists were perceived to have much better earnings potential than computer professionals, along with politicians, sports heroes and rock stars. A handful of men suggested money hungry souls head for the United States to take advantage of a better fiscal climate and lower tax structure. Six per cent of the Net people said that the big money would be made in technology that had not been invented yet. Last but not least, the classic and easiest way to make big money was suggested by one astute IT male – "Marry rich."

"One of the problems if you work in the information systems department of a large corporation, is that your position is never viewed seriously. You're not producing for them and it's highly unlikely that you can make your way up the corporation and become a member of the board, although this may be changing."

43 year-old techie turned lawyer, who notes that it was easier to get eight hours of work daily as a computer consultant than the two or three hours daily, as an independent practicing lawyer.

Top Ten Online Sites

1. Monster.com
2. CareerPath.com
3. CareerMosaic.com
4. Jobsearch.org
5. Headhunter.net
6. NationalJob.com
7. HotJobs.com
8. Net-Temps.com
9. Dice.com
10. CareerBuilder.com

Source: Useem, Jerry "For Sale online: You" *Fortune Magazine*, July 5, 1999 p. 67-78

L E V E L   7

DE-CODING THE GEEK MYSTIQUE

"Definition of geek – (slang) performer of grotesque or depraved acts in a carnival, etc., such as biting off the head of a live chicken.

Definition of nerd – (slang) a person regarded as contemptibly dull, unsophisticated, ineffective, etc."
New Webster's Dictionary, 1982

"I know a lot of computer geeks with nice cars, nice wardrobes, pretty wives/girlfriends and good taste in music. They are far from being Nerds…"
26 year-old lead programmer

"I don't know why there's no happy medium. They're either these skinny pimple-faced guys with coke bottle glasses and plastic pocket protectors or really fat ones, like 300 pounds."
30 year-old female IT training assistant co-ordinator

The only difference between my husband and Bill Gates is about U.S. $90 billion. That's what I tell my closest friends. The geeks have already inherited the planet. I know my younger sister and I used to shriek when we heard the term geek being used in high school. But now, the geeks have something to laugh about. Us. They call us frezzbies, newbies, zipper heads, turkeys, lusers, lamers, PEBKAC (problem exists between keyboard and chair), sawdust (because that's what our brains are made of), 404's newbies, normal, FOPS (frigging old persons) and Mom and Dad.

The majority of persons surveyed were not offended by the term computer geek, but considered it to be complimentary. Just nine per cent of respondents were offended by the term. Sometimes, confusion reigned as to which term was more endearing, geek or nerd. The majority of individuals who were offended by the term were introverted, while 41 per cent were born under the Scorpio astrological sign. Fifteen per cent of the women surveyed and 19 per cent of the men said that they were geeks.

Fast Company recently surveyed passengers on *Nerd Bird*, the daily commuter non-stop flight between Austin, Texas and San Jose, California – just two leading centers for semiconductor manufacturing and software development. They discovered 35 per cent of passengers admitted to being nerds, 37 per cent denied it. Seventy-five per cent of passengers carried a laptop, 57 per cent a pager, 52 per cent a cell phone, 12 per cent a personal digital assistant and one person a slide rule and another wore a pocket protector. Leisure time cited by one computer geek, "I work on the configuration of massively parallel computing systems." An IBM internal auditor defined the nerd, "When his electronic toys cost more than his car."

I contacted Robert Stephens, Chief Inspector for Geek Squad in Minneapolis, Minnesota, a 24-hour computer support and repair company. Geek Squad, takes pride in dressing up their "agents" in clothing from the 1950's and sends them out on service calls in "geekmobiles" like the 1953 Morris Minor, 1958 Simca Aronde or 1960 Ford Falcon.

When asked if the work "geek" in the company name is a plus or a minus, he e-mailed me back this reply, "It is a plus plus – the richest man in the world is a geek. The geek shall inherit the earth. We are not really geeks, we just play them on television. Everyone is a geek – a geek is just someone who specializes in a certain area. If you like pottery, then you are pottery geek. It's about being confident in yourself about a given subject, and enjoying it, regardless of trends."

No doubt, there were a few geeks in denial who participated in the survey. One computer geek worked 16 hours a day on the computer. He used to work 20 hours a day. That's when he was a real computer geek. Now, he says, "I'm not a geek anymore. I have a girlfriend. She can take me away from the computer for an hour or so, but then I've got to get back on."

Having a relationship with a significant other seemed to be an unwritten code as to what separated geeks from non-geeks, even though they slept in the same room with their computers on all night. Dress was another bone of contention that separated geeks from non-geeks, along with personal hygiene (or lack of). Although with the ascendance of affluence amongst computer geeks, things are changing, even if it's at a slug's pace.

One saxophone playing Silicon Valley computer gal ranted about how geeks have become more sophisticated, were beginning to wear designer clothes and were more health-conscious that fruit smoothies was the choice of drink nowadays. She offered a good explanation as to why computer geeks have been labeled poor dressers, "When the first computers came out in the 1970's, everybody wore polyester. But let's face it, we all dressed badly in the 1970's." At home with 12 PC's and never leaving home without her palm pilot to follow her to-do lists. Speaking in sound bytes, she swore by the ease to download her palm pilot to desk top, and corrected me as to what geeks in Silicon Valley were called. "We call ourselves, technoids," and pointed the finger at UNIX people as giving other computer professionals a bad rap, "Yeah, those UNIX guys are fat bald guys who wears cartoon ties."

Diet was another consideration, with Jolt being the highest strength caffeinated soft drink for programmers and pizza being the mainstay. While pizza, like Italian food, is the most popular take-out food in North America, it was not the only sustenance for computer people, whose food tastes varied according to age group and amount of disposable income.

The most comprehensive and insightful description of the geek is thought to be a re-hashed e-mail message that originated from a sighting on the Internet and provided by a 27 year-old network guy:

A geek is someone who spends time being "social" on a computer. This could mean chatting on irc or icb, playing multi-user games, posting to alt.sex.bondage.particle.physics, or even writing shareware. Some who just uses their computer for work, but doesn't spend their free time "on line" is not a geek. Most geeks are technically adept and have a great love of computers, but not all geeks are programming wizards. Some just know enough Unix to read mail and telnet out to their favorite MUD.

Geeks are generally social outcasts from mainstream America. The ranks of geekdom are swelled with gamers, ravers, science fiction fans, punks, perverts, programmers, nerds, subgenii, and trekkies. These are people who did not go to their high school proms, and many would be offended by the suggestion that they should have even wanted to. Geeks prefer to socialize with other geeks, the self proclaimed weird. Therefore, they go online to organize parties, food runs, drink runs and movie nights, and be assured that their companions would rather talk about superheros as modern mythology than the latest football scores.

Geeks are their own society – a literate, hyperinformed underground. The community accepts people from all walks of life, assuming they have access to the net and the skill to use it. Geeks are rather open-minded with regards to nonstandard lifestyles. Many geeks are queer, more practice non-monogamy, and the most common religion is neo-paganism. You can't tell if someone is a geek just by looking at them, there is no dress code. Some dress causal, some prefer silk – but few pay attention to current fashion. You are more likely to see a geek in a renaissance bodice than a dress from a glamour magazine; or a tie-dye T-shirt instead of a suit and tie.

The unwritten geek credo states that originality and strangeness are good, and that blind conformity and stupidity are unforgivable.

Take care not to confuse the terms geek and nerd. A nerd is a person with no social skills, usually obsessed with science or technology (geek is more computer specific). Nerds are known for their pocket protectors, taped glasses and plaid shirts. Many nerds are also geeks, using the Net as a safe screen to hide behind while practicing their social skills. However, they rarely come out to be seen in person at live geek events, so there is little reason to be concerned.

The term hacker tends to refer to the more programming intense set of the geek crowd. However, this term is overused in the popular media, and therefore, is no longer used much among "real geeks". Hackers also have negative connotations related to cracking, or illegally obtaining access to computer and accounts.

Geek can also be used as a verb. "To geek" is to sit online and read mail, news, chat, and otherwise waste time in front of a keyboard. This "geeking" often consumes many hours, even if the intention was to "just log in and check my mail." Some would say this time would be better spent being social in person or even just being curled up in a sunbeam...

Ten Original Definitions of a Computer Geek

"MALE, under 21, can write computer code simultaneously in 20 languages, can spout about nth level normalization until the cows come home, but has never seen the inside of a working office nor ever tried to extract meaningful information from a database. Actually the age limit probably only applies to the female of the species. Males can go on like that for years."
35 year-old Aussie female accountant

"You lock them away in a room, throw them Twinkies once a week. Leave them alone and low and behold, they emerge with new software."
53 year-old telecommunications guru

"Their offices glow green at night."
50 year-old management information systems guy

"They're in a dark room with jube jubes besides them. A programmer's cookbook would be compiled of all the stuff you could eat with one hand and dipping into something. The big computer (mainframe) computer geeks don't like other computer geeks. They could be in blue suits. It's the multi-media guys who've got orange hair and nose rings. They look like squeegee street kids. But as far as those guys with plastic pocket protectors, they're still around. These are the guys who never pull a brush through their hair. Now that they're older, there's probably less hair for them to brush."
42 year-old software marketing manager

"I don't call them geeks, I call them zeeks. They could recite 11 to 14 digit numbers on the chips and tell you what they were good for. These are the smartest people in the world, but when they tell you what to do, they give you instructions in the same manner they would instruct a computer; step by step, because that's how they're thinking. They weren't much good at communicating but they were good at what they did. We put them in research and development."
37 year-old computer technologist

"Girl who would rather spend time with her computer than me. Guy with tape between his eyeglasses, plastic pen protectors, showers once a week, yesterday's lunch in his moustache, some guy named Bernie."
41 year-old single male hardware repairs representative

"People who lack the social skills to carry on the normal conversation. A prime example is a former boss who would walk first into his office, and turn on his Apple IIe computer. He would say, 'Hi!' to his computer first and then he would walk out and say, 'Hi,' to everybody else. He regularly kept his door closed. His boss told him that the company had an open door policy. So he opened the door and put a chair in front, so nobody could enter. He was an extremely caring person, just very introverted."
32 year-old PC hardware specialist

"All geeks have Dilbert dolls covered in their cubicles. They tend to have hair where most people don't have hair. They eat a lot of day old pizza, which is the national food of geeks and tend to have skin problems. Some tend to be a bit shallow. Ones in their early 20's are still day dreaming about getting a date and looking for somebody to decode Visual Basic 4.0"
55 year-old IT executive

"Skinny short guy with flannel shirt who wears thick glasses and could go on Jeopardy and win."
27 year-old female IT account executive

"A geek is someone who needs a rolling chair to get from his main computer to his auxiliary computer."
36 year-old geek

"There's one guy in the office who's a computer geek. He knows everything technically, every nitty-gritty detail. Every time you ask him a question, he knows the answer and he thinks you should know it, too. That makes you feel stupid."
43 year-old systems analyst

Proud to be A Computer Geek

The search for the perfect geek persisted and the following individuals confided to being geeks. They embraced technology with titles like chiphead, bit head, propeller head, machine head, chief geek, data abyss terminator, Linux God, software evangelist, memories provider, bug killers, evangelists, memories providers, screwdriver jocks, computer lab monkeys and chief geeks.

"I'm a short, thin short haired brunette, pale skin, pale blue eyes. Nutty girl with wacky hobbies. Loves music (big black, shellac, punk, indie, jazz, etc.) art and plays geetar and sings in a rock n' roll band. Does computer geeky stuff and loooooooves geeks. Slightly jaded, but in a good way, open minded, talented, loving romantic, crazy… Maniac depressive… shy.

Computers peeve me because they screw with your social habits. You fall in love with some guy, but darnit, he lives 2000 miles away."
18 year-old student/musician.

"I'm communicative and helpful and I don't have any significant weaknesses. I've been on computers since I was nine years old, but repaired bicycles first. Yeah, there's not too many geeks like me, 80888 TRS 80 clone, IBM compatible, DOS, pre-DOS, cpm. I love computers that I really don't know about because I find computers natural to be with. When they do cause problems, they're not overly hard to fix. I've been assimilated with computers. That's how second nature it is for me. I feel more like a remote peripheral."
19 year-old computer student who once went trick and treating as the "Tech Improvement Man" who survived a computer explosion.

"I'm an intelligent computer nerd who's the father of two kids and am interested in computers. For my vacation, I re-installed a Linux kernel in my computer. My definition of a computer geek is somebody's who's very familiar with computer operating systems, like they know most of the Unix or system administration commands, anybody who uses the word GREP – that stands for global regular expression print…"
38 year-old software designer

"I'm a workaholic, too involved, very intense. If I see a challenge and I do it, I tell myself I can do this, even if takes 16 hours and I feel like hell afterwards. I'm very un-motivated if something is un-challenging. I'm a good listener, good at dealing with problems in a logical and emotional way, but I get way too involved with women, 90 per cent of my friends come and go because I take on too much responsibility. I've been on computers since I was 8 years old. You can't get bored with them. They're always challenging. It's kind of cool being involved with evolving technology, the potential behind technology is just exponential in your mind. Like on Star Trek, when the facts can tie the whole world together."
21 year-old Linux God

"When I was ten years old, my parents got a divorce and they gave me this computer, it was a 4K grey monster, then I got my first real computer, a TRS 80. Do you know why I like working on computers? Because people suck, because humans are assholes."
27 year-old hardware developer

"When I was five years old, I got heck for sticking things into light sockets. I was very spoiled. I told my parents that I would drop out of school unless they went out and brought me an Apple IIe computer. They brought me the computer. I think technology is very appealing. I love the Internet. It's the best thing that's happened in this world. Using the Internet is amazing. Quite coool. Used to like computer games, but the computer is becoming more or less a tool. It's not my left arm, but I definitely spend a good hour checking my e-mail messages. I'd have a fit, if I didn't check my e-mail daily."

"I'm good at public speaking. Soo good looking. Very modest. Get me a 10 gigabyte drive to put all my strengths on and I need a back up to

back my personality strengths. We don't think computers are funny. When you work with machines all day long, I pretty much laugh at myself."
26 year-old president of a very successful computer services company

"A geek at its lowest level is someone who is comfortable in front of a machine. One who can feel 'feel' their way through a problem, even if they know very little about it. Higher level of geekdom would be marked with the understanding of the system(s) they use or run, knowledge of at least one programming language, as well as a scripting language or two. And any level of geek MUST want to learn more than they know now, and (though this borders more on hacker than general geek) be willing to teach what they know to someone else who is willing to learn.

I've found that I can't really sleep anymore without the sound of at least one power supply fan running the background."
24 year-old PC software/networking consultant who lives with four computers, loves the color purple and snacks on skittles, Pringles and strawberry Twizzlers. Keeps one computer on in the master bedroom on all the time because

"Nobody wants to be a geek. We just end up being geeks."
35 year-old female website designer

L E V E L 8

GEEK GIRL POWER

"If you do something once, people will call it an accident. If you do it twice, they call it a coincidence. But do it a third time, and you've just proven a natural law!"
Dr. Grace Murray Hopper, 1906-1992

"People still do see the technology as foreign. It's something that boys do that maybe women use. But the notion that women are creating it is still a surprise."
Esther Dyson, chairman, EDventure Holdings Inc..and author of Release 2.0

Since August Ada Byron Lovelace wrote computer programs in 1842 to the time Kim Polese stomped out of Sun Microsystems in 1996 to start up Marimba, the world has been in awe at what commotion women and computers can create. Technology has always been perceived as a guy thing, with men motivated on making bigger, better and faster machines; while women questioned how technology is going to benefit the user.

The ongoing debate is not that women cannot thrive in a technology-driven world, but why they have not chosen to. Ingrained societal prejudices assume that women have difficulties with mathematics and machines. When complex technology is stripped to its essence, lies at the core, technical eloquence that is simple and logical to understand. Women have to realize, if mathematics and computers are so difficult to study in the first place, why are so many men succeeding?

Excellence in any field is derived from inner passion that spontaneously creates excitement and energy. No exception, Lovelace, the daughter of acclaimed British poet Lord Byron, adored mathematics. Her father nicknamed her the *Princess of Parallelograms*. She had many childhood interests – gymnastics, dancing, horseback riding and music – playing the piano, violin and harp. Her mother Annabella, arranged for Lovelace to study math under a tutor. When she was a teenager, she met her mentor, mathematician Mary Sommerville who later introduced the young woman to Lord William King, whom she later married and bore three children.

When Lovelace was 18 years old, she met Charles Babbage at a society party. The mathematics professor at Cambridge University invited Lovelace to work secretly for him. Babbage invented the difference engine; which was able to automatically compute and print out mathematical tables with accuracy to five significant digits. Lovelace wrote the programs for the analytical machine and a technical paper on Babbage's invention which he published and distributed, referencing the author by her initials. It was three decades later, that the initials "A.A.L." were identified. Tragically, Lovelace died at 36 years, the same age as her father.

It wasn't until a century later when renewed interest in Babbage's work, which is considered to be an important forerunner for the modern computer, that Lovelace's contributions were uncovered. To honor Lovelace, who wrote the first program to calculate Bernoulli numbers, the U.S. Department of Defense named a programming language Ada. Every year, one deserving woman in computers receives the August Ada Lovelace Award presented by the Association for Women in Computers in the United States.

After the first woman was awarded an engineering degree by an American university in 1893, Edith Clarke earned her masters of science degree in electrical engineering from MIT in 1919. Two years later, Clarke patented her graphical calculator and became the first female engineering professor at an American university.

Dr. Grace Murray Hopper, who graduated with her Ph.D. in mathematics from Yale University in 1934, came from a family with military traditions. So it was a natural for her to join the Navy in 1943. A year later, she became the third programmer to work for Harvard University's Howard Aiken, the instigator behind the Mark I – the world's first large scale all purpose paper-tape driven electromechanical calculator (also known as the IBM Automatic Sequence Control Calculator).

Upon her arrival, Aiken greeted her, "Where the hell have you been?" Hopper submersed herself to programming the machine and assembled its 500-page operations manual for the Mark computer, which measured 51 feet long by eight feet high and five feet deep.

Unknown to contemporary computer users, Hopper coined the phrase "computer bug." On September 9, 1945 at 3:45 p.m., while working on the Mark II, in a temporary open aired World War I building, Hopper discovered the cause for a computer malfunction – a large moth squashed against a panel. From that point in time, fixing a computer became known as "de-bugging." In the years to follow, Hopper made outstanding contributions to computer science both as an educator and developer, while keeping a high profile. In 1960, Hopper participated on an industry committee with the mandate to develop COBOL and was well known for developing the first compiler. Hopper thrived on change and contrary thinking. Just to prove her point, she kept a wall clock that ran counter clockwise.

Kathryn Kleiman, the Alexandria, Virginia-based attorney with Internet Matters has finished working on a documentary on the lives of the ENIAC programmers – six female mathematicians: Kay Mauchley Antonelli, Jean Bartik, Betty Holberton, Marlyn Meltzer, Frances Spence and Ruth Teitelbaum. These women were originally called "computers" by the Army during World War II to program the ENIAC which was located at the University of Pennsylvania. Their mission was to compute ballistic trajectories using the ENIAC, a massive first generation computer that required the women run around a labyrinth of 3,000 switches, cables and trays to physically route the data pulses through the machine. Unlike today's computers, these women had no help desk support, on-line help or training manuals or courses.

Once their assignment on the ENIAC was completed in 1946, these pioneer programmers went on developing tools and trained future software engineers. Antonelli designed programs for her husband's co-inventions – the ENIAC and UNIVAC computers. Bartik programmed the BINAC and designed logic and memory back up for the UNIVAC. Holberton worked for Antonelli's husband's company and designed hardware and software for the UNIVAC I. She also worked with Grace Hopper on the COBOL committee and was instrumental in the development of both FORTRAN and COBOL languages. Holberton's programming skills were such that an early colleague once said, "Betty could do more logical reasoning while she was asleep than most people do while they are awake."

In 1949, Evelyn Boyd Granville was the first African American woman to earn a Ph.D. in mathematics from Yale University. She developed computer programs that were used to analyze trajectories for the first manned U.S. space mission and for the Apollo project, when U.S. astronauts were sent to the moon.

Sadie Plant, a well-known cyberfeminist and author of numerous books about women and technology, has observed, "as computers became more intelligent, women became more liberated." The 1970's brought a surge in women's issues and equality became the rigor for the day. The year 1975 was the Year of the International Women and feminists were ready to take on the world.

Enrollments in engineering and computer science swelled in the 1970's. Support for women in engineering, technology and computers grew. In 1978, 15 women of Washington, D.C. founded the Association for Women in Computing. Since then, Dr. Anita Borg, a computer scientist at Xerox's PARC founded the Institute for Women and Technology which includes an electronic forum for women in the computing field.

"There's a perception that women working in a computer lab will be disconnected from the world. When in reality, they will be working on projects that are very, very connected to the world."
Anita Borg, 1998

Today, in Canada, there are several organizations for women technocrats, including the Association for Women in Engineering and Science; and Women in Science, Engineering and Technology. During the 1970's, women tried to emulate male counterparts, when the fashion rage was to wear three-piece pin striped suits with floppy bow ties to work. That was a strategy executed with minimal success. Nowadays, women strive to be themselves, with balance and family issues still laborious concerns.

I spoke to many women IT professionals. Some of the older women missed having other women to collaborate and brainstorm with. Still, others did not feel being a woman has held them back, even though several of them were married with children. Most of the younger women were overwhelmed by the speed at which technology changed and were conscientious about not falling behind. IT females was the group in the survey most likely to lament about the time crunch of the 1990's they battled daily with.

Several of the women ended up in the information systems departments by default, when they were hired 20 years ago in administration and clerical support. When their organizations adopted mainframe computer systems, opportunities arose for these women to be trained on the job for handling the data processing and information systems. Women employed in major corporations, and public institutions, fared well under these circumstances.

Breaking out of the corporate mold, a few women left corporate life to set up their own information technology companies with success. An outgoing personality and strong inter-personal skills were important to maintain their client base, along with high quality work and exceeding customer expectations. Having confidence in making presentations to clients was an absolute must. Some women worked with their spouses in businesses, running mom and pop computer consultancies from their homes. A former male IT executive noted that women fared especially well in technical support and enthusiastically referred me to a woman who ran a very successful high-tech company.

Today, 37 per cent of the people working in the American information technology and high-tech sector are women. Only two per cent of technology company executives are women. Carol Bartz is the CEO of Autodesk, the world's fourth largest PC software company in the world. A working mother, Bartz was instrumental in re-engineering AutoCad, Autodesk's signature product and has been a renegade for both men and women to work for progress, "Women need to jump out of their element, out of their comfort zone..."

With her uncanny resemblance to an obvious famed pop star, Kim Polese has been nicknamed by the media as the *Madonna of Silicon Valley*. Cyberfeminists preach that the web with infinite possibilities for networking and collaboration, is one technology arena, with potential to be a playing field that women could excel in. Polese might be proving a point. As brand manager for Sun Microsystems, she instigated the company's Internet strategy for Java, one of the hottest high-level languages created within the past five years.

When she left Sun in early 1996, to start up Marimba, Inc. which develops and maintains networked applications within enterprises and across the Internet, industry critics were astounded by her courage and gumption. In an interview with *Internet magazine*, Polese admitted that it's unusual for a young woman to be running a software technology company. With Silicon Valley becoming the new Hollywood in terms of mass media, Polese accepts graciously working under the public eye. She dances to keep balance in her life and distances herself from work, "I don't define myself by the high-tech industry. I've chosen this as a career because it's an incredibly exciting thing to be doing and because it matches my personality and my interests in technology."

Polese graduated with a bachelor's of science degree from the University of California in Berkeley and studied computer science at the University of Washington in Seattle.

The list of women who have succeeded in computers is far from short. Fran Allen was the first woman appointed to be an IBM fellow, then was later elected president of the IBM Academy of Technology. Esther Dyson is Chairman of EDventure Holdings, a small but diversified company focused on emerging information technology worldwide and on the emerging computer market so central and Eastern Europe. Dr. Ruth Davis founded the Pymatuning Group and also is the chair of the board of trustees of The Aerospace Corporation. Pamela Lopker is the founder and president of QAD inc., one of the world's leading producers of ERP software.

In 1978, I was one of the 600 women in Canada to have received an engineering degree, out of a profession of over 110,000 persons.

Like the United States, Canada has its share of high-tech divas. Micheline Bouchard, is the president of Motorola Canada Inc. Claudette MacKay-Lassonde is the president and C.E.O. of Enghouse Ltd, a Markham, Ontario-based company which elated investors when Enghouse received the 1998 Branham/Canaccord Software Award for Turnaround Company of the Year. Carol Stephanson was appointed President and C.E.O. of Lucent Technologies, July 1999.

In Calgary, digital cowgirls have mustered enough dust to be the talk of the town. Kim Sturgess, president of Revolve Technologies, led a group of laid-off employees to upstart a company from technology developed at their former employer Nova Corp. Christina McGill, leads Benchmark Technologies which markets and sells mainframe management software worldwide. Leslie Purkis is a partner in Technology Connections Ltd., an IT service provider. Molly Mak is president of Onward Computers Systems, a company, which provides custom-built systems, software and services. In 1998, Mak received the Canadian Women Entrepreneur of the Year Award. Nancy Knowlton, co-founded Smart Technologies, which produces an inter-active whiteboard and maintains a strategic alliance with Intel Corp. Since 1997, Smart Technologies has been named one of the top 50 best-managed Canadian companies by *Profit* magazine.

Despite the progress, the prognosis for the future of women in technology is only fair. According to Dr. Maria Klawe, science dean at the University of British Columbia, women in computing science programs make up 15 per cent or less of the enrollment across North America – half of what it was 15 or 20 years ago. Even engineering schools, which have worked hard to encourage young women, find themselves at odds with the macho male culture that the women have to integrate themselves with. In recent years, engineering school enrollments have plateauxed at 15 per cent, too.

Still, a March 1999 article in htc – *Canada's Hi-Tech Career Journal* suggests that the Internet is spurring women's interest in technology for a communication tool to stay in touch with the family and solve problems. With a desire for a balanced lifestyle as emphasized by female survey respondents, telecommuting is supposed to give women the flexibility to work from home, although studies show that people who telecommute actually work longer hours than if they worked downtown.

Women's under-participation in computers and technology is under the media glare. In September 1998, U.S. Commerce Department official Kelly Carnes was quoted on the opening day of the Women in Technology International conference, "It really says something when of the 105 winners of the prestigious National Medal of Technology, only two have been women."

The barriers have not completely corroded away. Senior female IT professionals have shared with me their feelings of isolation, lack of support and barrier to entry to the old boys club. At high-level computer user group meetings, women outnumbered by 20 to 1, cowered in the corners, tight-lipped and uneasy. While many women were able to combine career with family, one good-natured woman with several children noted that peers frowned upon her in choosing to have such a large family.

However, Carnes conceded the geeky image that society has cast upon scientists and technology folks remains to be transcended by women. "We asked a group of sixth graders to draw pictures of IT workers recently, and they drew people with pocket protectors, bald heads, glasses and high-water (pants)," Carnes said. "And nearly all of the pictures were of men."

From San Francisco, California, Kristine Hanna and Peter Crosby are producing a documentary *Girl Geeks? The Female Side of Computing* © which will examine women's roles in computing past, present and future. The following women are participating in this project – Esther Dyson, Anita Borg, Kim Polese, Judy Estrin, Chief Technical Officer, Cisco Systems; Katrina Garnett, C.E.O. CrossWorlds Software and Ann Winblad, Hummer-Winblad Venture Capital. Hanna's and Crosby's co-produced documentary is expected to be released spring 2000. The website at www.girlgeeks.com has garnered a lot of attention with on-line mentoring, says Hanna. "We receive a lot of e-mails from women who are the only women out of 100 male engineers at work. They feel very isolated and don't have a safe place to talk, but they don't know about a lot of other women out there."

Hanna, who formerly worked on special effects for George Lucas, experienced a remarkable experience working in a group, comprised primarily of women and started asking herself whether or not women were in technology elsewhere. She noted in a recent interview, "Girls can do mathematics and science, but they drop out when they are 13 years old because it's geeky, it's not cool. They don't realize that people in engineering and computers are empowering us with technology to have a life and raise a family. You can work from home. The Internet is a great equalizer. Women find that creating technology is very empowering."

Janice Glasgow is an expert in artificial intelligence and associate professor of computer science at Queen's University in Canada. She believes that things have improved for women during the past 20 years, "There is greater awareness among both men and women… Only in the last few years have I been able to find female scientists at similar career points to me. It has been very supportive to talk to them and share experiences."

She suggests that young women seek out mentors and peers for role models, get involved by serving on industry committees and help organize conventions and workshops, present technical papers, nominate other women to speak, promote and support other women.

"They like women in information systems because women pay attention to details. Now I'm not sure about women as project managers. I never found any glass ceiling. I started off as programmer, then went to being a systems analyst, over to technical support and customer support. Then I went into consulting and then I left because I got bored."
43 year-old former female techie

LEVEL 9

DIGITAL PEOPLE AND TECHNO-CULTS

Three Apple engineers and three Microsoft engineers are traveling by train to a conference At the station, the three Microsoft engineers each buy a ticket and watch as the three Apple engineers buy only a single ticket. "How are three people going to travel on only one ticket?" asks a Microsoft engineer. "Watch and you'll see," answers the Apple engineer.

They all board the train. The Microsoft engineers take their respective seats while all three Apple engineers cram into a rest room and close the door behind them. Shortly after, the train has departed, the conductor comes around collecting tickets. He knocks on the rest room door and says, "Ticket, please." The door opens just a crack and a single arm emerges with a ticket in hand. The conductor takes it and moves on. The Microsoft engineers see this and agree it is quite a clever idea.

After the conference, the Microsoft engineers decide to copy the Apple engineers (as they always do) on the return trip and save some money. When they get to the station, they buy a single ticket for the return trip. To their astonishment, the Apple engineers do not buy a ticket at all. "How are you going to travel without a ticket?" asks one perplexed Microsoft engineer. "Watch and you'll see," answers an Apple engineer.

When they board the train, the three Microsoft engineers cram into a rest room and the three Apple engineers cram into another one nearby. The train departs. Shortly afterwards, one of the Apple engineers leaves his rest room and walks over to the rest room where the Microsoft engineers are hiding. He knocks on the door and says, "Ticket, please…"
41 year-old female systems analyst

Whether on-line via the Internet on newsgroups and bulletin boards, or in musty smelling dingy church basements, computer groups congregate to share ideas and discuss technical difficulties. When help desks and on-line help are not as user-friendly or the solutions not at hand, computer people try to solve their problems themselves. You go to computer user groups to find out the latest and the greatest, the con's and pro's of the next release or upgrade, how to properly install the software, and get the scoop of who is doing what in the digital world. Granted that most of this information can be read in any computer magazine, it's just more palatable when you hear a fellow user spice up the news with an opinionated bent.

> *"There's elitism in the computer world. UNIX people think that Microsoft guys are clones and idiots and the other way, Novell and Microsoft think the UNIX guys are either dinosaurs or demi-gods. The dinosaurs understand how the programs work, but the demi-gods don't know what they're doing."*
> 43 year-old software marketing manager

Like different religious sects, computer people can get fanatic about the operating system or software program they work on. Sometimes, it's best that you don't upset the status quo and open your big mouth at one of their meetings and tell them how great the opponent's operating system is.

A snapshot of today's operating systems begins with the industrial strength operating systems for mainframe computing systems and servers. UNIX developed by AT & T in the 1960's and released in 1969, has garnered a widespread and loyal following. IBM's OS/2 was originally co-developed by both Microsoft and IBM during the early 1980's but a fall-out led OS/2 back to the arms of IBM, which began marketing OS/2 during the early 1990's. In 1993, Microsoft released Window's NT, as a means to penetrate the industrial strength operating systems, and acquired about 36 per cent of the marketshare by 1999. A derivative to UNIX, Linux was first posted on the Internet in 1991 by Linus Torvald, a Finnish university student, and has since made inroads into the server business at 17 per cent of the marketshare, in a second place with UNIX.

When it comes to the desktop and that's where personal computers are at, the most pervasive operating system at 90 per cent of the marketshare in 1999 is Microsoft's Windows which was released during the early 1990's. Prior to Windows, Microsoft also sold another operating system – MS-DOS, which was licensed to computer manufacturers by Microsoft during the early 1980's. Proponents of MS-DOS claim this disk operating system was easier to use, more reliable and required less memory.

While the Apple computers have been around since 1977, the Macintosh operating system, in its evolution especially since the release of the iMac in 1998, is being vouched as a superior operating system to Windows. However, of increasing annoyance to Microsoft is the penetration of Linux into the PC environment. Although cited as being un-friendly for luddites, Linux's reliability as an operating system is something to get crazy about. During the late 1990's, when Microsoft bashing reached epidemic proportions, Linux is a welcomed alternative. It will be just be a matter of time before its installation will be less of a headache.

"Linux is UNIX. I don't consider it to be very innovative... The profit motive will end up ruining and tarnishing the altruism people use to promote this thing."
Jim Allchim, Senior Vice-President, Microsoft quoted May 6, 1999 PC World

"Computers have this groupie image. If you are part of the group, everybody can talk a lot. But around you, these people are computer geeks."
33 year-old hardware designer

Despite the convenience of the Internet, *Silicon Cowtown* had an astonishing number of computer user groups for me to visit. Most of these groups only met monthly, yet it amazed me in the dearth of cold winter nights, how a meeting room could be packed full of members - many driving in for over an hour from out-of-town for a two-hour presentation. Contrary to popular public misconception, these meetings were not for hackers. There were no green-haired tattooed nose-ringed computer geeks in attendance. The young men and women I met were relatively sedate.

The bulk of attendees were forty-plus graying Baby Boomers who missed Computers 101 at university or college; followed by seniors and retired persons. Sometimes people came with questions about why their computer wasn't working and the technical evangelist in the group (because there always is one keener who knows it all) would reply. Often working in isolation on the computer at home, people come to have a meaningful techie conversation with somebody at their own level. Still, others come to get away from their spouses, giving them at least one night per month to play around on the home computer.

User groups targeting corporate users have quite a different flavor. I attended several Microsoft user groups in town. The meetings are often hosted by a Microsoft rep – a tall skinny guy who speaks in hyper drive and has so much nervous energy, I suspect he doesn't sleep well at night. The meetings are marketed as information and training sessions, accompanied by free refreshments and a chance to win a prize – once you have filled out an evaluation form and given Microsoft everything they need to know about you, except whether your belly button sticks in or out. I assume the free pizza and coke, or buffet lunch, is responsible for the superb attendance. Or is it that virtual golf game they give away? Twice, I heard the Microsoft rep apologize profusely for slide number 3 or 4 in the presentation, which overtly promotes beyond the realm of political correctness. He crosses one arm across his heart, lowers his voice and says, "Oh, the marketing department made me do this."

Naïve, I really thought that I would learn something meaningful at the Microsoft presentation, not a lot of gibberish going in one ear and out the next. The Microsoft rep was ranting and raving about a software package that only one out of 13 persons in the room actually used. He was upset, flailing his arms by the side like a sinking duck, "Why aren't you using our software? Christ's sakes, we give it to you FREE!!!" Just then, the temperature in the room fell about ten degrees, as the working geeks leaned back in their chairs and crossed their arms over their chests. To make matters worse, the Microsoft rep wasn't getting any feedback except blank looks from high-level programmers who were still thinking about a problem from work. The talk was pretty heavy, like most of the corporate computer user talks are, because every second word isn't really a word, but a code or acronym for something else.

Usually, at most corporate computer user meetings, people walk out politely without saying a word to anybody, after diligently filling out the e-val. Some people come to network, but that's usually amongst the people who organized the meeting. For others, it's a chance to eat one less meal in front of the computer and an excuse to get away. At one computer users' meeting, half the people who came left without saying a word to anybody. They ate their pizza, drank their Coke, then took a seat and read *PC Week*, while waiting for the guest speaker. The tension in the room was broken by the roar of laughter about jokes poking fun at high-level computer geeks. Such jokes would probably have been accepted less graciously outside the room. For many a computer geek have told me that they don't mind being called a computer geek by their peers, but find it offensive when an outsider uses the term.

I attended as many computer user groups in *Silicon Cowtown* as possible, but there were a few groups that banned outsiders (like myself) entirely altogether. Personal computer user groups definitely had better human interface than the computer professional groups. Please read on, as to how different computer users fared in terms of personality and technical savvy.

Linux Lovers

Today, Linux, is being touted as a faster and friendlier operating system than Microsoft's Windows or Macintosh. Although it's virtually impossible to estimate the numbers of persons worldwide who have downloaded Linux for their own use, a *Time* magazine columnist dared to say it was about 15 million. Linux users, are frenzied about their operating system, even though support is somewhat spartan. And why not, you can download your copy for free from www.linux.com.

On first impressions, Linux users appear a methodical and organized lot. They respond to their e-mail messages quickly and have contacts for their user support groups posted geographically.

While Apple computers have a fruit for users to relate, Larry Ewing developed a cute black and white penguin mascot that goes by the alias of Tux to brighten up the Linux website. There's even a game you can play (using Linux, of course) that Tux goes looking for some herring.

Microsoft Dissidents

The bottom line is that people use Microsoft's Windows because they have to. Just because everybody uses the system doesn't necessarily mean that it's best thing around. Its popularity has spread like peanut butter on your kitchen floor. Even if you wanted to get rid of it, you can expect an onerous task in doing so.... because Microsoft is industry standard (for now).

Bill Gates passed away and is talking to St. Peter at the Pearly Gates. St. Peter says,

"Gates, I've looked at what you've done and you haven't been particularly bad, so I'm going to give you a choice. You can choose to go to Heaven or Hell." But Gates says, "I don't know what Heaven or Hell is like." "No problem," says St. Peter. First he shows Gates what Heaven looks like, angels floating around, blue sky and bliss." Gates says to St. Peter, "That's boring, can you show me Hell?" So St. Peter shows him a glimpse of Hell - bikini babes on the beach, sex, drugs, rock n' roll. Gates says, "This looks like fun. Send me to Hell."

So St. Peter sends Gates to Hell. Instead of babes on the beach, sex, drugs, rock'n'roll, he finds it burning in Hell and that he's being whipped. After awhile, St. Peter decides to check up on Gates and finds him screaming, "Hey, what happened to the Hell you showed me." St. Peter replies, "That was only a demo."

44 year-old software programmer

There are very few, if any, computer users who worship Windows, Microsoft or Bill Gates. If Microsoft users had an alternative, they would jump ship, assuming they could afford it. The dissention and frustration that comes from working on such an operating system is bait for on-line jokes. The following epitomizes how users feel towards Microsoft –

>>If Restaurants Functioned Like Microsoft...
>>Patron: Waiter!
>>Waiter: Hi, my name is Bill, and I'll be your Support.
>>Waiter. What seems to be the problem?
>>Patron: There's a fly in my soup!
>>Waiter: Try again, maybe the fly won't be there this time.
>>Patron: No, it's still there.
>>Waiter: Maybe it's the way you're using the soup. Try eating it with a fork instead.
>>Patron: Even when I use the fork, the fly is still there.
>>Waiter: Maybe the soup is incompatible with the bowl. What kind of bowl are you using?
>>Patron: A SOUP bowl!
>>Waiter: Hmmm, that should work. Maybe it's a configuration
>>problem. How was the bowl set up?
>>Patron: You brought it to me on a saucer. What has that to do with the fly in my soup?!
>>Waiter: Can you remember everything you did before you noticed the fly in your soup?
>>Patron: I sat down and ordered the Soup of the Day!
>>Waiter: Have you considered upgrading to the latest Soup of the Day?
>>Patron: You have more than one Soup of the Day each day??
>>Waiter: Yes, the Soup of the Day is changed every hour.
>>Patron: Well, what is the Soup of the Day now?
>>Waiter: The current Soup of the Day is tomato.
>>Patron: Fine. Bring me the tomato soup, and the check. I'm running late now.
>>[waiter leaves and returns with another bowl of soup and the check]
>>Waiter: Here you are, Sir. The soup and your check.
>>Patron: This is potato soup.
>>Waiter: Yes, the tomato soup wasn't ready yet.
>>Patron: Well, I'm so hungry now, I'll eat anything.
>>[waiter leaves.]
>>Patron: Waiter! There's a gnat in my soup!
>>The check:
>>   Soup of the Day $5.00
>>   Upgrade to newer Soup of the Day . . $2.50
>>   Access to support $1.00

"I call my machine Monica because I use Windows NT and it always goes down on me."
69 year-old computer user.

Commodore Comrades

Why Commodores do not catch colds.

"I have a real computer, the Commodore 128K. It's real old. Its disk operating system (DOS) is on the disk drive. You send the command from the computer to the drive and the drive does what you tell it do. On the PC, the DOS is held in the memory of the computer. Any infected program with viruses can attach to DOS because it is in the memory. They can put the virus in the program, but it won't hurt the Commodore because when you turn it off, the virus has nowhere to stay. Commodores are not host to viruses... because there is no DOS in memory – just a 'read-only' chip on the computer. When you turn on a Commodore, it loads basic Commodore and it loads kernel ROM into RAM. As long as the power is on, the program is in RAM which is a very efficient system.

Why didn't they keep the RAM system? Because Bill Gates couldn't make any money. We Commodore people call Windows, <u>Windoze</u>."
50 year-old commodore user

They are a small but hardy group in *Silicon Cowtown*, Commodore people, that is. Their membership is rapidly dwindling, but their spirit is undeniably strong. The company that made their pet computers has changed ownership and no longer exists. Still, the big whigs at this group lug truck loads of equipment to a meeting, that you almost think you've come to a garage sale.

Commodore people are down-to-earth, techie hillbillies, who enjoy a good yarn and quality time spent with a machine that doesn't go down on them. There are no viruses on the Commodore 64K, a machine whose loyal fundamentalist following are a warm and friendly bunch, who swap momentous and trade software amongst each other. There are several electricians in the group, who are adept at re-configuring the computer, during a coffee break.

Self-righteous, you say? That Commodore users debunk Microsoft's claims of developing the click and point Windows-type user interface. Windows was developed after GEOS, the graphical environmental operating systems for the Commodore

64K, which was developed by Berkley Softworks. The Commodore 64K came out in 1982, when Macintosh also came up with its own Windows systems.

> *"I've been on computers since 1985. Computers are very logical. If the programming is done properly, they will do exactly what you tell them to. IBM programmers are into bloat. With Commodore, you only have 64K RAM to work with. Every year, new IBM software not only takes up memory, but they also take up more space. The only way to get speed, is to get hardware, software and memory up-grades. What do you think it costs to up-grade? That's every dollar I don't have to give."*
> Contented Commodore user

> *"With the Commodore Amiga, the manufacturer named the computer chips after three girlfriends - Paula, Denise and Agnes. The chips became fatter. The last version of fat Agnes was Obese Agnes and Denise became Super Denise. The Gary chip always stayed the same and we think he's gay because we knew the computer was failing when the other three girls were having pms. Commodore named their motherboards after rock songs, like B52."*
> 25 year-old network administrator

MACINTOSH MANIACS

> *"The Macintosh computer came up in the artsy world. Mac don't have users. They have bigots. You don't buy a Macintosh computer, you marry them. When you criticize somebody who uses a Mac, it's like criticizing their driving and it becomes very emotional. Mac is a very nice machine. Main thing about the Mac is that certain people absolutely adore it and become amazingly defensive.*
>
> *Real techno-weenies come from a world where OS/2 people are dead or have frontal lobotomies, like the Japanese pilots who have come out from the forest and they don't know that the war is over. People get emotional about cars and they get emotional in big corporations as whether they should use Lotus Notes or Microsoft Outlook."*
> 55 year-old IT executive

If you haven't purchased a computer yet and you go to the Mac Users group, guaranteed by the end of the meeting, everybody will have you convinced that Mac is the only way to go. Without a doubt, Mac people are a different breed of computer user, not coming from the scientific stream. They know that they are a minority on this planet and they have got to stick together to survive. Unlike other computer users, there was a tendency for them not to drink beer, but wine and indulge in visual interests like art and photography, accompanied by gardening and gourmet cooking. No blue box macaroni diners in this group, and the most sociable bunch of them all. The Mac Users group has an official social co-ordinator, which means once a year, they have a picnic in the park.

> *"I had my first encounter with computers in 1980. To load an 8K program would take half an hour. Started with Apple IIe. It was a tool. There was no mystique about it. If you run a Mac hard enough, you can push it rather hard. It's like a good pair of pliers and I like to have good tools. A computer has to be the same way. So when I buy a computer, I never buy the latest. I bought the 8600K Mac line because it was the most stable hardware around."*
> 50 year-old Mac user

> *"Microsoft wanted to diversify, so they decided that they would make condoms for computers. They did the research, but they couldn't sell it."*
> 74 year-old Mac user

While the Microsoft rep only flails arms when giving a "training session", the Apple rep waves his arms above shoulder level. He, too, speaks in sound bytes in hyper-drive and is a tall skinny fellow who barely looks like he graduated from high school. How appropriate it was for the group to meet in a church basement. The Macintosh rep was getting to his followers. People were speaking out of order, applauding and nodding in unison. By the end of the presentation, the sound level in the room had risen several decibels and people loitered around to tell me how happy they were with their machines.

Q. *"What does IBM stand for?"*
A. *"I want to be a Mac."*
Q. *"Why doesn't Microsoft get rid of Apple Computers?"*
A. *"Because it would lose its research department."*
Q. *"How many Macintosh users does it take to screw in a light bulb?"*
A. *"Just one, he holds the light bulb and the universe revolves around it."*

UNIX Undertakers

Pity those poor UNIX users, the only guys and gals who really know what computers are all about. By the way, UNIX was developed in 1969 by Ken Thompson and dennis Ritche, two programmers at AT & T Co.'s Bell Laboratories. The name UNIX was derived from UNICS, which stands for Uniplexed Information Computing System. Don't know why so many computer professionals picked on this group.

UNIX is about power and that's all I'm going write about for now.

"UNIX is much more powerful than Microsoft. Unix is 10 times more powerful, much more powerful to use, but much more difficult to learn."
45 year-old applications specialist

"Right now, I do a lot of high performance computing. Try and do it with NT. Dream on. You can finish something in a few minutes on UNIX, which takes hours on NT... Used to use OS/2 – great operating system, but no good software... Whatever operating system you need to use, they are still all stupid dumb tools. In order to make it work, the tool itself must lend itself towards what you are trying to accomplish. It's like hitting a nail into a wall. You can use a shoe (NT) or a piece of rock (OS/2) or you can use a hammer (UNIX). A 400 megahertz machine for word processing is for secretaries"
22 year-old systems engineer

OS/2

An OS/2 user had only one word to say about what everybody else was working on, "SHIT!"

Digital People Pet Peeves

Only 2 per cent of those surveyed did not have any peeves in life, not even bad drivers. Eight per cent of those surveyed were peeved by other people's behavior, which they described as being dumb, greedy or ungrateful. The majority surveyed had computer peeves, beginning with Bill Gates and Microsoft, followed by computer crashes and bad computer software. Comments were made on how computers wasted people's time, what evil things computers did to people, along with the constant struggle to keep up with the technology.

"I find computers to be a real pain in the ass."
27 year old computer user

"I hate computers. I spend more time battling them, than using them."
28 year-old Internet consultant

"I've got a lot of pet peeves. First program the computer in f--king English. Industry leads monopoly and makes it binary. Everyone is poking on Bill Gates, when they should be worshipping him."
27 year-old programmer

"I hate how computers are out-of-date when you get them. I hate it when young kids know more about computers than I do. I hate it how software vendors outsell what their software can do. The corollary is that I hate bugs and hate having to conform to one platform. I hate Microsoft."
33 year-old systems analyst

"People spend too much time on the computer and lose touch with reality. It's overkill on the computer, paralysis through analysis."
50 year-old IT executive

"Computers are schizophrenic. Like the Internet and e-mail, you gain access to information and connect with people. But computer games, it's very isolating if the kids are playing alone. I feel it's particularly important that people develop people skills. I'm concerned that they're pushing computer golf and now, computer fly fishing. Now, let's get a life. There is a game, software disk and lure in a box. Get real."
47 year-old computer consultant

LEVEL 10

Humor in Hyper-Drive,
Boolean Logic and Binary Code

Why Computer Geeks are Real Men

Computer geeks eat from vending machines.
Vending machines do not serve quiche.
Computer geeks do not eat quiche.
Real men do not eat quiche.
Therefore, computer geeks are real men.

The above is my first real computer joke that illustrates Boolean logic, says I, but the GEEK says, "Go find the bug."

When it comes to computer humor, even the geekiest of all computer geeks will tell you that they laugh. They laugh at themselves. They make jokes about computers and computer programs. They laugh about other computer users, irreverently about their customers and industry titans, who they feel have made them part of an Evil Empire. Some of their humor may require de-coding, like you almost need to be a hacker to get it.

A Partial Real Programmers Guide…

So you think you're a real programmer, do you? Check yourself against this list of qualifications to see if you are… Heresy has it that there are actually 300 lines to read.

1. Real programmers don't make comments about their code. If it was hard to write, it should be hard to read.
2. Real programmers don't write application programs, they program right down on the bare metal.

3. Real programmers don't draw flowcharts. Flowcharts are, after all, the illiterate form of documentation. Cavemen drew flow charts, look how much it did for them.
4. Real programmers don't read manuals. Reliance on a reference is a hallmark of a novice.
5. Real programmer's programs never work right the first time. But if you throw them on the machine, they can be patched into working order in only a few 30-hour de-bugging sessions.
6. Real programmers never work 9 to 5. If any real programmer is up around 9 am, that's because they were up all night.
7. Real programmers know what the user needs better than the user.
8. Real programmers don't use schedules. Schedules are for manager's toadies. Real programmers like to keep their managers in suspense.
9. Real programmers like vending machine popcorn. Coders pop it in the microwave oven. But real programmers use the heat given off by the CPU. They can tell what job is running just by listening to the rate of popping.
10. Real programmers scorn floating point arithmetic. The decimal point was invented for indecisive people who can't think big.

If you're going to keep up with the information overload, and hyper kinetic speed of learning, you need humor and your sanity from going into a malfunction mode. All that laughing helps blast your bod with a shot of substances called *endorphins*. These substances get those electric pulses zapping your brain cells and improves your ability to think and create, along with boosting your immunity and cardio-vascular system. Laughing helps freeze the frustration when computers hang up on you.

Computer professionals are more likely to pull a workplace stunt, than a computer widow is likely to avenge her live-in lover. For whatever reason, rational or not, IT males lived to tell some of the practical jokes they pulled at the office – re-placing somebody's hard drive with a smaller one or dis-connecting a corporate user's computer from the corporate LAN.

"I was in the middle of conversation with a lady who told me that her hard drive fell out. I said, 'What the heck?' She said that her hard drive fell out and now her machine was busted. She thought the floppy was her hard drive."
46 year-old systems analyst

There were classic computer jokes reported – transcriptions from Murphy's Laws, dumb blonde jokes, and more light bulb jokes than I care to mention. Humorous workplace anecdotes from unknown origins are blasted through the Internet at warp speed to other friends. Some computer professionals claim that there are really only about a hundred computer jokes in circulation.

"I like blonde jokes. Every blonde I know is intelligent, articulate and competent at almost everything they attempt. These people scare me-naturally-but they are SO far from the stereotype that I find it amusing."
26 year-old computer geek

"If it weren't for users, our jobs would be a lot easier."
34 yr-old IS consultant

"One lady brought in a box of colored diskettes to return because she had a black and white monitor. She insisted on returning the colored diskettes."
25 year-old computer sales associate

"Some lady was asked to send back a copy of the disk that she was working on. She sent a photocopy of the disk."
52 year-old IS coordinator

"There's an urban legend when an organization was undergoing a huge technical transition, moving from a simple computer environment into Windows. When the engineer was asked to use the mouse, he literally picked up the mouse and pushed it against the computer screen. The individual beside him, told him, it works better if you roll the mouse on the pad."
33 year-old senior systems engineer

It didn't matter whom I spoke to, or what part of the world they lived in, computer people seem to agree, on what made them laugh. Men particularly, were proud of their sense of humor, although only about one in five persons could remember a joke to tell.

> Q. *"How can you tell when a blonde is working on the computer?"*
> A. *"There's white-out on the screen and eraser chips in the keyboard."*
> Most popular joke for male computer users in *Silicon Cowtown*

> *"Three women are in a bar drinking, talk after a few drinks about their lovers. One says, 'Mine is a jock and a real he-man and that turns me on.' The second one says, 'My boyfriend is an artist and very sensitive.' The third woman says, 'My husband is an IBM salesman and all he tells me how great it will be when I finally get it.'"*
> 40 year-old computer user

Bill Gates is the butt of several jokes. An elaborate fictitious press release was distributed widely on the Internet.

At (COMDEX), Bill Gates reportedly compared the computer industry with the auto industry and stated that *if GM had kept up with technology like the computer industry has, we would all be driving twenty-five dollar cars that got 1000 miles to the gallon.* In response to Gates' comments, General Motors issued a press release stated by Jack Welch, CEO of GM, on July 22, 1998:

> *If GM had developed technology like Microsoft, we would all be driving cars with the following characteristics:*
> 1. For no reason whatsoever your car would crash twice a day.
> 2. Every time they repainted the lines on the road you would have to buy a new car.
> 3. Occasionally your car would die on the freeway for no reason, and you would just accept this, restart and drive on.
> 4. Occasionally, executing a maneuver such as a left turn would cause your car to shut down and refuse to restart, in which case you would have to reinstall the engine.
> 5. Only one person at a time could use the car, unless you bought "Car95" or "CarNT." But then you would have to buy more seats.
> 6. Macintosh would make a car that was powered by the sun, reliable, five times as fast, and twice as easy to drive, but would only run on five percent of the roads.

7. The oil, water temperature and alternator warning lights would be replaced by a single "general car fault" warning light.
8. New seats would force everyone to have the same size butt.
9. The airbag system would say "Are you sure?" before going off.
10. Occasionally for no reason whatsoever, you car would lock you out and refuse to let you in until you simultaneously lifted the door handle, turned the key and grab hold of the radio antenna.
11. GM would require all car buyers to also purchase a deluxe set of Rand McNally road maps (now a GM subsidiary) even though they neither need them nor want them. Attempting to delete this option would immediately cause the car's performance to diminish by 50% or more. Moreover, GM would become a target for investigation by the Justice Department.
12. Every time GM introduced a new model car, buyers would have to learn how to drive all over again because none of the controls would operate in the same manner as the old car.
13. You'd press the "start" button to shut off the engine.

"There was a product out called the computer condom which protects your software from viruses. On the side of the box, it said that the condoms could be used on hard disks only. This is a true story, I swear."
26 year-old Mac user

Q. How many computer programmers does it to take to screw in a light bulb?
A. One to do it and six to say that they could have done it.
34 yr-old computer user.

Q. How many Microsoft engineers does it take to change a light bulb?
A. None. That's a hardware problem.
41 year-old, computer user

Q. What do you get when you cross a nun and an Apple?
A. A computer that doesn't go under.
45 year-old IS manager

"In Texas, it's legal to shoot computer nerds. So there's a Texan who stops buy a pub and shoots this guy who wears glasses and pocket protector. He goes outside and drives his truck down the road. The truck turns over and a whole bunch of computer nerds come running out to pick the computers. The Texan shoots them and gets arrested. He says to the Sheriff, Hey what's going on? It's legal to shoot computer nerds down here. The Sheriff says, It's okay to shoot them, but not bait them."
47 year-old computer trainer

"Car breaks down and in it is a mechanical engineer, electrical engineer and computer programmer. The mechanical engineer says, No problem, let's get out and take this car apart and see what's wrong. No, says the electrical engineer, May be it's the ringing. We should check out the ringing. And the computer engineer says, Not a problem. Just put the key in ignition and start the car again."
25 year-old computer representative

"A guide at Pearly Gates sees what looks like Bill Gates in Heaven. The guide says, I didn't know that Bill Gates was dead. Somebody replied, That's not Bill. It's just God. He likes to think he's Bill Gates."
56 year-old IS guru

"Artificial intelligence is not a substitute for stupidity. I'm not a complete idiot, just some parts are still missing."
23 year-old programmer

"Microsoft's new 'softer' approach,
File Not Found – Would you like me to fake it?"
40 year-old computer network geek

Technology has gone too far. The president of a company decided for the year 2000 and beyond, all desktop computers would be replaced by Etch-A-Sketch for several reasons – including no probability of dealing with computer bugs, no technical glitches keeping work from being done and no more time wasted reading and writing e-mails.

To assist users to make the transformation from being a computer user to being an Etch-A-Sketch user, an Etch-A-Sketch

Technical Support group was set up. Here were some of the frequently asked questions:

Q. My Etch-A-Sketch has all of these funny little lines all over the screen.
A. Pick it up and shake it.

Q. How do I turn my Etch-A-Sketch off?
A. Pick it up and shake it.

Q. How do I create a New Document Window?
A. Pick it up and shake it.

Q. How do I set the background and foreground to the same color?
A. Pick it up and shake it.

Q. What is the proper procedure for rebooting my Etch-A-Sketch?
A. Pick it up and shake it.

Q. How do I save my Etch-A-Sketch document?
A. Don't shake it.

Last, but not least, the following e-mail was sent to me by a Mac user. Now I know what it is consultants do!

>>ANDERSON CONSULTING FINDINGS
>>LAST WEEK I TOOK SOME FRIENDS OUT TO A RESTAURANT, AND NOTICED THAT THE WAITER WHO TOOK OUR ORDER CARRIED A SPOON IN HIS SHIRT POCKET. IT SEEMED A LITTLE STRANGE, BUT I IGNORED IT. HOWEVER, WHEN THE BUSBOY BROUGHT OUT WATER AND UTENSILS, I NOTICED HE ALSO HAD A SPOON IN HIS SHIRT POCKET.
>>I THEN LOOKED AROUND THE ROOM AND SAW THAT ALL THE WAITPERSONS HAD A SPOON IN THEIR POCKET. WHEN THE WAITER CAME BACK TO CHECK ON OUR ORDER I ASKED:
>>"WHY THE SPOON?"
>>"WELL," HE EXPLAINED, "THE RESTAURANT'S OWNERS HIRED ANDERSON CONSULTING, EXPERTS IN EFFICIENCY, IN ORDER TO REVAMP ALL OUR PROCESSES.
>>AFTER SEVERAL MONTHS OF STATISTICAL ANALYSIS, THEY CONCLUDED THAT CUSTOMERS DROP THEIR SPOONS 73.84 PERCENT MORE OFTEN THAN ANY OTHER UTENSIL. THIS REPRESENTS A DROP FREQUENCY OF APPROXIMATELY 3 SPOONS PER TABLE PER HOUR. IF OUR PERSONNEL IS PREPARED TO DEAL WITH THAT CONTINGENCY, WE CAN REDUCE THE NUMBER OF TRIPS BACK TO THE KITCHEN AND

save 1.5 man-hours per shift."

>>As we finished talking, a metallic sound was heard from behind me. Quickly, the waiter replaced the dropped spoon with the one in his pocket and said: "I'll get another spoon next time I go to the kitchen instead of making an extra trip to get it right now."

>>I was rather impressed; the waiter continued taking our order and while my guests ordered, I continued to look around. I then noticed that there was a very thin string hanging out of the waiter's fly. Looking around, I noticed that all the waiters had the same string hanging from their flys..thingy.

>>My curiosity got the better of me and before he walked off, I asked the waiter: "Excuse me, but can you tell me why you have that string right there?"

>>"Oh, certainly!" he answered, lowering his voice. "Not everyone is as observant as you. That consulting firm I mentioned, also found out that we can save time in the restroom."

>>"How so?"

>>"See," he continued, "by tying this string to the tip of... you know what... we can pull it out over the urinal without touching it and that way eliminate the need to wash the hands, shortening the time spent in the restroom by 76.39 percent"

>>"Okay, that makes sense, but... if the string helps you get it out, how do you put it back in?"

>>"Well," he whispered, lowering his voice even further, "I don't know about the others, but I use the spoon."

L E V E L   1 1

Nerds in Love

"If Bill Gates can get laid, so can I."
31 year-old computer guy

"Money is kind of like sex and it's best to get it by not going for it. Use the indirect approach. Either case you can go direct for it, although I've not been good personally at this. Men have a problem in they are too direct about going to have sex. Women may have the problem in being too direct in going after romance."
38 year-old single computer technician

"Computers break down according to how important the job is and how many people are waiting for it. Relationships break down, according to how hooked (connected) you are to the other and much you have been waiting for someone like them to come along - inevitably, they're the ones that don't want you."
36 year-old female computer user

Romancing the Byte

He was only 28 years old. But in *Silicon Cowtown*, with all his peers paired off, Romeo was wallowing in self-pity that the right gal hadn't come along yet. Things were much worse 20 years ago, when black velvet nude paintings sold well on street corners. Let's face it, *Silicon Cowtown*, like any Silicon civilization is a guy town, even though there are 2,000 more ladies living here than men.

"The geek boy finds a talking frog. The frog says, 'Kiss me! I'm a beautiful princess trapped in a frog's body and can only be freed with a kiss! If you kiss me, I'll marry you and give you all the riches in the world!' The boy looks at the frog, smiles and puts it back in his pocket. The frog says, 'Why won't you kiss me? I'll love you and do anything you want!' The boy smiles at the frog and says, I'm a computer geek. I don't have time for girls but a talking frog is pretty damn cool.'
24 year-old female techie

Over half of the IT males that were gainfully employed had still not tied the knot, at the average of 34.8 years. About 40 per cent of them had steady girlfriends, but the other 60 per cent were shooting arrows in the dark or licking wounds from previous relationships. There were a few divorced men who preferred not to speak of their ex-wives. Now some of these dateless 20'ish guys honestly admitted they were on the look out for great looking babes, who could make them laugh. By the time, they reached 30 years, they whined about the lack of intelligent women to talk with.

"I just want somebody I can talk to."
16 year old computer guy

Now, all these single guys and gals tell me that they want to get married and raise a family. But you start to wonder when someone is 40 years and single, if he or she is still going to bother. No doubt that some of these people were a little picky. Some men in particular, provided eloquent descriptions of their ideal woman including hair and eye color, height and body type. What the heck, they've probably figured out her bra size, too.

"Compatibility, common values, interests."
44 year-old never married computer guy

"I'm looking for a woman who can put up with me. I've got crazy hours. They've just got to understand they're not the only person in my life. I can't be there for them all the time and I can't stand a woman who lets herself go (looks)."
21 year old self-prescribed computer geek

"Somebody who understands me."
39 year old mathematical genius who likes dancing

Okay, I admit I interviewed some stereotypical computer geeks, with shoulder length hair that hadn't had a comb pass through it since the turn of the century – the kind you don't really want to get to close to, in case, you contract lice. There were a few with lily-white pasty complexions, who should get more radiation than what they received from the computer monitor. But there were also some men, who were sensitive and caring with all those attributes of the New Age. There were cute fashionable guys with tight butts that could have stepped off the set of *Melrose Place*, emanating charm and confidence, but were caught up with lusting bytes after hours.

> *"Humor. If a girl is real good-looking but anal, forget it. But if a girl's funny then she's can be attractive."*
> 29 year old computer guy, good-looking fit, average height, dark, outgoing into funk music and might end up in Miami one day

When it comes to romance, the shy guys have it the worst. Possibly, it's just a figment of their imagination. About 94 per cent of these digital cowboys who were looking said they were introverted. But when they do fall in love, it's the stuff that could last forever. I spoke to a very bashful guy who is married with two kids. Elated about his marital status, he giggled nervously on the phone, "The fact I met my wife is a minor miracle in itself."

Computer Geek, tall skinny blonde, 36, looking for super-model for play and adventure.

Internet Freak – Serious single male, 38, with brown hair and a mustache, who enjoys fishing, camping, surfing the internet, reading and writing, would like to meet a humorous, understanding, patient single female.

Single guy. Owns home, smokes, drinks once in a while. Tall and works out with weights regularly. Problem: main interest in life is his PC. Relationships with non-PC types haven't worked. Seeking single female, 29-35, in reasonably good shape, who is happy spending time helping develop multimedia software. If you know the difference between a *.WAV and a *.BMP or *.TIF, we need to meet because we will get along just fine.

Personal adds in local newspaper

When you consider the odds in *Silicon Cowtown* for mating with someone from work, the picture isn't pretty. Remember only about one in seven students who graduates in engineering or computers is female. Information technology departments are mainly male institutions. The single guys gripe but she's already married or living with someone. Many couples often meet at the office, but those kind of romances can get dicey at times. Once is enough, for most to realize what a *faux pas* that can be, because human gossip travels faster than most office LAN's. Sometimes, maternal or paternal staff act as matchmaker, but if the average age at work is 30 years or even younger, this option is just a lost cause.

> *"I don't think anyone could put up with me. We're so distant. We don't see things in a romantic way. Computer people are too hard bitten for romance that they don't feel it's a worthy effort."*
> 40 year old computer guy, single but going steady

It was in disbelief that many young able-bodied men confided in me, their forsaken love woes. Some were brave enough to ask me to set them up. Once their single male friends had found girlfriends, they were immediately ex-communicated from further social contact. So rather than make an effort to join a club to meet someone, they hid at home, playing on the computer. Social gatherings, a few men have told me, make them very uncomfortable. Geek love is not something that people talk about either. While there were over 250,000 web sites on the topic of *The Geek Shall Inherit the Earth*, there were only 737 mentioning the words geek love.

> *"I've been on the computer since I was eight years old. That's right, for the next 26 years, I spent all my time in front of computer. Then I looked around me and realized that I didn't have a life, no wife, no family, like other people I knew. Then I went to this dance and met a gal. So now I have a girlfriend. I now have a life."*
> 34 year-old hardware developer

Women who date computer geeks like them because they know where they are, they get cool electronic gadgets for presents, on-line help is quick, and you can have some interesting conversations about what's happening in the Universe. Intellectual capacity, claimed one woman, was the way to a computer geek's heart. She suggested that if you're looking at the stars on a date, just rattle off all the constellations. The trivia should impress him enough.

> *"I have a good sense of humor, romantic and punctual (chicks really dig the whole punctual thing). Also, women don't run away in terror at the sight of me. Most of the time..."*
> 25 year-old computer guy

Men need women more than women need men is obvious. About 10 per cent of the men, upon defining success, emphasized the need for harmonious relationships in their lives, especially family and wives. The women couldn't care less about significant others or being married. They wanted to make money, have time for themselves and be balanced. One single lonesome digital cowboy, summed up his sentiments about success in life, "Having a wife."

SLEEPLESS IN SILICON COWTOWN

> *"I'm young and dangerous:"*
> 20 year-old computer entrepreneur

> *"I'm looking to meet people who are honest and have a weakness for women in Birkenstock sandals"*
> 33 year-old modest, Allan Ad man of the 1990's, sensitive and understanding.

> *"I am old one day, young the next, messy but can be a clean freak. I can be a bitch and I can be your lover."*
> 24 year-old systems consultant

> *"I'm looking for an independent, feminine, charismatic, ambitious, romantic, spontaneous girlfriend who can sweep me off my feet, loves to share and is open to life's many offerings. I'm 27 years old, 5 ft. seven, about 185 lb., who loves to laugh, go out, watch movies, go for walks, go to amusement parks, cuddle and be romantic. I have an intuitive mind... I enjoy dancing and being social. I'm a young kid at heart and seek someone who is a young kid at heart, too, but is also mature and stable... I'm funny, loyal, wise, good communicator, good listener, talker, teacher and love to learn. But I'm self-conscious, and nervous when it comes to impressing a woman with the intent of dating... perhaps, at times, I worry about a lot of simple things too much."*
> 27 year-old hardware developer

"I'm flamboyant, mutilated in some gardening accident and not seeking a romantic interlude all the time. When they see me, they think of Nintendo. I ask these women, 'What do you want to with your life?' It's exciting. Then I meet others who like to end hunger on earth and find that they're hypocrites. I am an extreme stickler. Is it by random that your protoplasm in this universe has given you life? You should be happy... I'm looking for integrity - the morality of something else. When I meet a woman, I ask myself, do I want her to have my children. Women nowadays are expected that everything is handed to them on a plate and then when they don't get it, they cry."
27 year-old shy hardware developer

A SOAG IS BORN

After nine months of assembly, John and Jane Doe are pleased to announce that their new model, Java Doe, became fully operational on January 1, 2000 at 12:00 noon. This lap-top is 21.22 inches long, weighing 7 lbs., 12 oz. Basic features include blue eyes, auburn hair and HUE (Human Urine Extender). Batteries were not included.

Also included are two monitors, John and Jane and one speaker with no volume control. Java has virtually no memory but is pre-programmed to accommodate future upgrades. Compatibility with Lisa Mac Doe, a 1986 model, is currently being tested. Java arrived with no operating manual. System support is provided by Java and Martha Doe, of Santa Cruz, California and Mac and Lisa Smith of Boston, Massachusetts.

LEVEL 12

Forever On-Line

"The fact is that Etch-a-Sketch was the personal computer for my parents' generation. One day, all Etch-a-Sketch's will be hooked up to the Internet."
22 year-old computer user

"It's just ignorance. If they only knew what a wealth of information is available at their fingertips! You can find info about anything and everything you may be interested in. I think senior citizens would benefit immensely from surfing the Net. Another reason is the fear of new technology (I know people who won't even use the automated teller at the bank! Or CD player!) And also the media's horror stories about child pornography. People hear the bad things and assume that is ALL bad, when in fact, the bad stuff is only a tiny fraction (and easily avoided segment) of the wonderful information available on-line!"
38 year-old store clerk

"The Internet is for the exchange of information. Talk about commercialism. The Internet is the epitome of mob mentality."
26 year-old software programmer

When Paul Baron of RAND Corporation in 1964, announced to the public his vision for a totally centralized network, I wonder if he thought things would get so big. During the early 1960's, the American Department of Defense's Advanced Research Project developed a small network that shared information amongst computers of researchers. It would be decades later, before this network would become known as "The Net" or "The Web," radically revolutionizing the way companies conduct business and people communicate. In 1981, the term Internet was coined.

Today, about 50 per cent of Canadians have at least one family member hooked up to the Internet and growing. In January 1996, there were over 40 million Internet users world-wide, a number anticipated to grow to more than 1 billion by early 2000. The possibilities for the Internet seem infinite. We have only just begun.

It's not unusual for families create their own personal websites of themselves and their pets. It's not unusual to hear about some friend who went after a sexual tryst on the Internet that soured another relationship. It's not unusual to find out that a lot of people on the Internet use phony names.

> *"I have a 23 year-old friend who maintains two web sites that run banners paid for by advertisers. He gets compensated by the number of hits his web sites receive daily. His first web site was risqué and full of naked women but he got diddley squat. Then he decided to put himself up on one of the web sites as a naked woman. All of a sudden, he got a lot of interest. I guess he must be feeding somebody's fantasy."*
> 50 year-old Internet consultant

The Internet is also setting the stage for another revolution. E-commerce has become the latest buzz. The Internet has become a level playing field for anyone who participates, whether they're a one-person operation, a multi-billion business or multi-level marketer. Some companies use the Web to solicit customer feedback; others accept that it's just another dimension of doing business. Like cocaine to a drug addict, the Internet to multi-level marketers has become an obsession.

World-wide E-commerce last year was estimated to be U.S. $70 billion and growing. It's a still far cry from total world-wide retail trade estimated to be U.S. $2.5 trillion or the money that's made from mail order and catalogue sales. But E-commerce is growing business to business and business to consumer. Eddie Bauer and Lands' End are the two retailing giants with on-line spiraling sales. And companies like Starbucks use their website to survey customers, test out new concepts and identify where they should be opening up their next location.

Terminal Illness

You don't need a license to drive the information highway. You don't even need an e-mail account or a computer at home. Better than driving, you don't even need to take out insurance. Nothing is sacred anymore in cyberspace. There is no censorship, industry watchdogs lurking or enforceable government controls.

Whatever you lust, somebody has it for you. In cyberspace, you can find willing buyers and sellers – whether it be human eggs or sperms, guns or bombs.

There are over 500 million web pages indexed by leading search engines; of which 3.5 per cent hunker down to pornography – raw, pure and unadulterated. No questions asked. Just a credit card number will do fine, thank you. It's the kiddie porn, which is most disturbing. No child is safe, not even a baby. The Internet is a pedophile's fantasy too good to be true.

Are you lonely? Do you want to meet people who are interested in what you are interested in? Are you looking for a bridge partner? There are newsgroups, on-line dating services, bulletin boards and listservs to sign up. One respondent filled his appetite for pornography off the newsgroups. He claimed that using newsgroups were the most affordable and virus-resistant way of viewing pornography. No ID required either.

In cyberspace, everybody is connected. Websites are a free for all. It's true that nobody is physically watching you on the Internet as you key in a message to send you to wish Uncle Harry a happy birthday. But put it this way, there is an even darker side that you need to protect yourself from.

> *"I have met someone who thought that if you used the Internet there was someone watching you through the screen…"*
> 23 year-old computer geek

Conspiracy websites have traced links back to the CIA and FBI. Hackers ran amok in cyberspace. It's play time for them, and if by chance they imbed one of their viruses in a file that's been sent to you, watch out.

Computer viruses are pathogenic to computers. About 300 new viruses appear monthly.

The GEEK innocently opened up an e-mail attachment from a friend living in Indonesia. Literally speaking, the attachment was a joke. But what happened to the GEEK wasn't so funny. Within the attachment just waiting to rip through his computer's innards, was the HAPPY-99 virus. Worst still, HAPPY-99, which originated from Israel was a WORM – one of the most incurable. WORMS disguise themselves as messages from a friend or acquaintance. Once they are opened, they contain malicious programs that can wipe out documents, spreadsheets and graphics. Once they get inside an organization, WORMS replicate themselves at the speed of electrons.

Within one week, the latest WORM (June 1999), Worm.Explore.Zip infected 12 countries and infiltrated computers at technology leaders – Compaq Computer, Motorola, AT & T, Boeing and General Electric. Worm.Explore.Zip's forte was deleting data on computers.

The GEEK tried several virus scanners to rid his computer of the pest and received threatening calls from our Internet Service Provider, who had detected the virus on the lam. Finally, HAPPY-99 was destroyed. Lucky, for me, I never read e-mail messages from the GEEK or open up file attachments (ever).

In April 1999, two dreaded viruses had already cannibalized computers world-wide. The Melissa virus masquerading as an innocent e-mail message attacked corporate networks and Chernobyl virus arrived as an executable file that made sure computers failed to start.

Viruses can also be found attached to files downloaded from the Internet, too. For further information on viruses, check out these websites – AVP Virus Encyclopedia at www.avp.ch/e/avp-news.htm, Norton Anti-Virus at www.symantec.com/avcen ter/index.html, McAfee Anti-Virus at www.mcafee.com and Virus Expert Doug Muth at www.claws-and-pqs.com/virus/index.html.

COMPUTER VIRUSES:

Ellen Degeneres virus - Your IBM suddenly claims it's a MAC.
Monica Lewinsky virus - Sucks all the memory out of your computer.
Titanic virus - Makes your whole computer go down.
Prozac virus - Screws up your RAM, but your processor doesn't care.
Lorena Bobbit virus - Turns your hard disk into a 3.5 inch floppy.
Martha Stewart virus - Takes all your files, sorts them by category and folds them into cute doilies to be displayed on your desktop.

AT & T virus - Every 3 minutes it tells you what great service you are getting

MCI virus - Every 3 minutes it reminds you that you're paying too much for the AT & T virus

You've Got E-mail

> *"I've been resistant against technology. But one day in Cancun, I went into one of those internet cafes and later checked back and found that I had 13 e-mails waiting for me. I stopped because I couldn't stand the thought of having 13 persons waiting for me while I was attending to patients."*
> Lenna Mazur, therapist and author of *The Naked Therapist*

I wasn't the first person to run out and get an e-mail address. I handed out husband's e-mail address to people I knew. What if I never got any e-mail? Now that would be a really disappointment. These are the 1990's, right? Everybody gets e-mail. Checking your e-mail is like brushing your teeth. I have had some people send me an e-mail message and disturbed that I hadn't responded within an hour or so, to receive a cranky call, "What do ya mean? You didn't get my e-mail yet??" I suppose the speed at which you respond depends on what hyper speed the sender is running on. My guideline is within 24 hours, but others might feel that's not fast enough.

Nowadays, you go to a business networking function and depending on who you met, some people will shake hands and say to you, "Hey, drop me an e-mail sometime, won't you?" Of course, I prefer to phone people, but now it's to the point where e-mail is better when you're dealing with busy people. They can't be bothered to return phone calls, but react with urgency when it comes to e-mail. A realtor friend who typically drove his clients around the city showing off houses was really frustrated by a high-tech guy who was ready to buy a house on-line. He insisted that all their communication be on-line, including photos of the houses. Who knows? Some day soon, we will all be going to on-line meetings, introducing ourselves by our e-mail addresses, nicknames or "handles".

Eventually, my husband was perturbed by the excessive amount of e-mail that I was receiving, stuff like jokes and business-related matter. Like a mad hyena, he would pounce on me for not responding immediately, because of his latent urgency to delete everything that wasn't important. Finally, I got my own e-mail address. Initially, I would check it two or three times daily, but after the novelty wore off, once before going to bed at night, seems suffice.

In the world of electronic correspondence, I have probably broken most of the rules that e-mail etiquette experts are preaching. Most of it is common sense. It's suggested that you use correctly spelled words, appropriate grammar, including capitalization of words and proper sentence structure. Be familiar with whom your audience is. My close friends send me jokes via e-mail and I don't mind. Unsolicited or junk e-mail is considered to be SPAM and like the cholesterol-laden stuff from cans, it can plug up somebody's inbox.

Type in a subject header, a summary of your e-mail message. It helps the recipient prioritize his or her message. Keep your e-mail short and sweet. Break up your paragraphs in small chunks, so the recipient can readily respond to each question or statement separately. Business messages needs to be clear and concise, but if you have further information to send, use a file attachment. To emphasize text, which is really important, do not use capital letters because it comes across being rather offensive.

Instead if you need to emphasize an important piece of text, use the underscore or asterisks, before and after the word. Newbies or new e-mail subscribers may not be familiar with all the e-mail buzz like smileys or emoticons which are ASCII glyph to convey an emotional state in e-mail and are viewed by rotating your head by 90 degrees. User is winking ;-). User is kissing :-*. User is crying :,). User is tongue-tied :-&. A rose is depicted by @}->---. Many hyper drive e-mail communicators would go nuts without acronyms that are in essence code for full length phrases, such as BTW for "By the way", IMHO - "In my humble opinion", FYI - "For your information", TIA - "Thanks in advance", TTYS - "Talk to you soon" or TTYL - "Talk to you later."

Business users often end their e-mail message with a signature file. According to Ted Holmes, founder of The Canadian E-mail Business Network, signature files should be thought of your electronic business card. He suggests that your "Sig file" be kept to a maximum length of 6 to 8 lines with a character width of 58 characters or shorter. Anything much larger than what he suggests comes across as being too self-serving.

Before you send your e-mail message, re-read it and check that it's going to somebody at an e-mail address. If you have friends or business associates who share an e-mail address, be sure to put "Attention: so and so," in the subject header. That little detail makes it easier for them to receive your message.

If you have a home computer without Internet access, you can still log on to the Internet at public libraries and cyber cafes around the world. Still, others can locate computers at 24 hour per day photocopy shops that often lease out computer time. One photocopy shop clerk conceded that the web cruisers showed up after midnight. They often would argue afterwards that they were only on for two hours, when four or more hours had passed. Cyber cafes attract an eclectic bunch, including globe-trotting travelers with band width anxiety, and the young and restless crowd, under 35 years, who come to oggle at other patrons and sip a cup of java.

The American daycare worker who spent 20 hours on-line didn't keep a computer at home, but he lived within walking distance of three public libraries, where he could cruise the Web for free. The Netherlands was a different story. Dutch libraries charged U.S. $2.50 per minute for Internet access, enough to convince him to give up his cyber life until he returned home from his vacation. He kept a web-based hot mail account. Unlike the typical server-based e-mail account, a hot mail account gave him the flexibility to log-on to the Internet anywhere in the world from a library or cyber cafe. By keying in a password, he could access his hot mail messages without a home computer.

The Listserv – A Brave New World

For several months, I signed up to a listserv, which are typically set up for information sharing and problem solving. There are listservs dedicated for special hobbies and interests, like cars, genealogy or pets. You give the monitor your e-mail address and then you're hooked up to receive all the listserv messages on a daily basis. The flaming got so bad that eventually the listserv got shut down. Flaming is when people go after somebody because of what they said. When I first started on this listserv, people would get angry because I would press the wrong key or send a message that should have been sent privately instead publicly. I also noticed that people had low tolerance thresholds for obvious typo errors.

For the first few months, I thought the listserv was great. I made some good contacts and procured good feedback, during the development phase of this book. If you had a problem, you could post a question to the whole listserv group In a day or two, somebody would have responded with a suggestion or two. I made a point of responding to everybody's problems and found that I was spending at least two hours daily on the listserv.

Not all was rosy about my listserv experiences. I met a book publicist, who also ran a bed and breakfast in a city I was making an upcoming book tour to. Oops, did this person forget to tell me? That the bed and breakfast was located smack in the middle of the city's red light district. No media splashes were procured as proposed. As far as I know, this person is still on the Internet looking for more work.

On this listserv, an upset mother warned others about a man she met. Let's call him "Jim". He came on-line and introduced himself. Then "Jim" told everybody that he had been kicked out of his apartment and needed a place to stay for a few months. It so happened that there was a single mother who had spare room available. So "Jim" moved in with her and then moved out. After his departure, her four year-old daughter told her that "Jim" had molested her. Instead of support from the listserv members, she got nothing but riff raff and was kicked off. They accused her of being a rabble-rouser, while the accused remained on-line.

Most of the people I interviewed who participated on listservs did so to gather information. Many had no intent of actually meeting listserv mates face to face. And some listservs are spin offs from trade and technical organizations, which hold meetings and seminars on a regular basis.

LEVEL 13

CRUISING CYBERSPACE
FOR LOVE, FRIENDSHIP AND SEX

"The Internet gives you the opportunity to be what you want. It is not lying. The Internet is an ego boost on part of yourself that you would never see. You can have connection with people you don't normally have in real life. It's a different type of connection. On the computer, even if you're completely honest, you can highlight things in your personality, even if people are telling you lies, they are telling you what they want to be and it is their perception."
17 year-old female teenager

I signed on icq, a chat group to participate. I expected fireworks, action and color. There were only five persons signed up that uneventful Saturday afternoon. Four persons had identified themselves by raunchy handles, which were a little hot for me to handle so early in the day.

The fifth person I electronically chatted with, mentioned that he was physically-challenged. The flow of communication was jolted by long moments of silence, too long, for my impatient personality. I felt like I was playing some sort of long drawn strategy game. My opponent was trying to figure how much information he could divulge at once. Understandably, worst case scenario, I could be a con-artist, multi-level marketer or any other societal bottom feeder trying to be-friend somebody for personal gain.

So, this was it? Keying in words, communicating on-line is what chat is all about. If so, I felt awkward. After 45 minutes, I signed off. For the reasons I didn't like chat, are the same reasons why other persons prefer chatting on-line to meeting people in real life or on the phone. Teens chat to kill time. Men and women cruise looking for Mr. Right or Ms. Right. Some people see cyberspace as another frontier, a place by chance to connect with another human being - because no one, likes to feel alone in this world.

"Don't give out your real name or tell them where you live. When I'm bored or there's nothing interesting on television, I go chat on-line. You can talk to kids from out of town that you wouldn't normally consider. You can meet more people. There are teen chat groups where you can talk about everything or if you're interested in certain sports or your favorite television show, like Dawson Creek. It's kind of cool. You could pretend that you're really older than you are and everybody believes you. You could make yourself sound so good and you're totally different than that. All of my friends go on Yahoo. You can talk to more than one person at once. You can set up mini-windows and mini-screens. You can send private messages. You can create a big screen between you and a whole bunch of people. You can make smiley faces and you can change the color of your words and that adds to it. There's at least 15 to 20 persons going into a chat room and there are different categories depending on the topic. I just chat. I've never met anyone on the chat groups, unless they are my friends and we know each other beforehand."
13 year-old female chat group user

"There's more women on chat groups than men. You go to chat groups that's defined by your age or your interest. There are tons of divorced women and unhappily married women on-line. They go on-line because it's practical. They've got kids at home. They can't go out or maybe they live in a real small town and they're a single mom. They've got to look elsewhere or maybe they've got a career where all they're doing is working and they don't have time to go out and meet somebody. I went to a chat re-union with 20 members. There was a girl from Australia, a fellow from San Francisco and others who came from Saskatoon, Edmonton, Calgary, Kamloops and all over. It was quite an experience when you meet these people and all you know them by is their handle. One of the women in the group was going over to England to marry this guy.

You can't tell what people look like on the Internet. A lot of people ask me for my picture and how I look. I tell them that I'm fat and ugly and if they don't want to talk to me, I say forget it. If they're only interested in my looks, then they're just trying to come on to me, you can tell."
41 year-old chat groupie

"I found a date and got a job on-line. I've been on the Internet for three years and would tell others that there are too many wackos out there. I know when somebody's bullshitting me and when they're not. If it seems too good to be true then it is. You can't see these people.

You find that a lot of newbies to the chat groups expect the people to be nice. Expect 99 per cent of the population to be assholes. People tend to get involved. You just got to understand that it's chat. Don't get involved. You've got to dissociate yourself from virtual reality. It's just a computer screen. Granted that somebody's telling you dick. People get all flustered. You've got to keep your sanity or you're going to go insane."
21 year-old computer programmer

"I don't see any harm in looking for dates on-line. At least, you'd get a good grasp of my personality. I've seen people on-line who argued all the time. I met a couple and they failed expectations miserably. They lied about their looks. I'm just so happy to be alive, so what if Bill Gates buys me for 15 million years. I prefer people to be happier with themselves. This mental aspect that you need to accept people, confuses me. People are looking for band-aid solutions. If people did a psychoanalysis on me, they would probably put me in jail.

Why is that every girl who names herself lurid and sexy is over 300 pounds and why every masculine guy alias so skinny and tall?... I've cut myself back on chat groups. Something happened that was quite offensive. This 40 year-old guy, a pedophile was sending quite lurid messages to a 14 year-old kid. Kids are tomorrow's leaders. This guy challenged me in public, but he didn't show up. One chick on-line accused me that I raped her and then they (chat monitor) suspended me. This lady was totally lying. This lady was mad because I turned down a date with her."
27 year-old hardware developer

"The best thing that happened to me was that I met wife on chat group. We happened to be members. You can tell who has just logged on. We started talking. We played a game, what do you think I look like? We started yakking and we formed some emotional bond. We found that we had a lot of things in common, like similar taste in music. It was a wonderful chance to know a person, committing your thoughts to paper.

You can't go for the package of person and soul, but if you just see the body type, (like in regular dating), you just can't see the person well. Like when you read in a magazine about a strawberry blonde, you think of somebody that's really attractive. We tend to think of the best when it comes to attributes physically. When my wife and I met for the first time after chatting on-line for a few weeks, we were disappointed, but we got over that pretty quickly."
41 year-old E-commerce specialist

"I always used icq as a communications tool for technical problems to connect with technical and business people. Never got into the dark side. About two months ago, I thought that I would show my wife how to use the computer. She met her lover on icq and left. So then I decided to see what goes on in the chat rooms and talked to literally dozens of women who could become instant cyber candidates. The chat rooms gives them an anonymous means to express their fantasies and frustrations. There's never a medium like this on the plant. You get this random chat where you can be totally anonymous. You can have real-life inter-action. People think that it's totally anonymous, but PING in software is like sonar on the submarine and you can virtually track anybody. They think they're anonymous but they're really not.

In four months, eight women have sent me their photos. Two of them were solicited and one of them has become my friend, whereas the rest are just people on the Net."
45 year-old project manager.

"I signed up to a on-line dating service. I got two inquiries, but I didn't say much more than my age and that I was breathing. I have heard some horror stories. One acquaintance started a long-distance chat line relationship on AOL which ended when she got a collect call from a penal institution in Florida.

I never give out my real e-mail address. I always give out my hotmail address first, until I get to know them better. There are too many con artists out there. I'll tell you, I'm finding the computer so-called dating scene somewhat more foreboding than I originally thought. But maybe I should expect more fruitcake than usual, now that it's heading into December.

You do come across some nice people. A widow of eight months answered one of my ads. I'm not sure what she expected to learn on the net, but e-mails are not a real substitute for face-to-face meetings or even telephone discussions... I have seen some interesting ads out of Calgary. Have you ever come across a woman named Melissa, 45, brunette and self-employed? I haven't answered the ad, but her picture is intriguing."
51 year-old single male

"One guy dressed up as a woman. He needed support on-line. He met my friend (21 year-old single male) in a hotel room. Another time, my friend met a 45 year-old married mother of three in British Columbia. They met in Whistler for a weekend rendezvous. He broke it off because he didn't want to be a father. Then there was this was this 21 year-old chubby virgin he met on-line. She told him how slutty she was. Expecting to encounter a sexy babe, he met this young woman who lived at home with her parents. She paid for his plane ticket out, but he was so disgusted by her, that he immediately left."
26 year-old computer user

"I go on the Internet for the hell of it. I meet friends and made some friendships. Some of them are really god awful. Some of the guys are really ugly. Please stay at home. Is that a mole on your face or is that your nose? You are still taking a risk when you go on-line. You do get to meet a lot of people, where basically, you get to know their personality then you get to see them the next week. The gay community is a one night kind of stand. Gay relationships that last three months are like two years re-incarnated with the same mate. It's a lot easier over the Internet. It's pretty cool."
25 year-old computer user

"I end up communicating with a lot people by e-mail because it is easier for each to express ourselves, before we say talk. With e-mail, you can spill your guts and deal with it. Granted, this whole e-mail thing about the Internet is going to lead to anti-social behaviors. I met a woman from Iowa on-line. We met in real life and we didn't get along at all. We didn't know what to say, but we would talk for hours on the Internet or on the phone. But in real life, we don't know what to say to each other.

With e-mail, you can get back at people at your convenience. With places like hotmail, there are an incredible number of people who are having affairs. Married women have an e-mail account at home but they get a hotmail address, which their husband doesn't know about to communicate with their lover. Four women have admitted me about doing this.

People are more comfortable with the keyboard. On the phone, you can detect emotion by the tone of the voice, but the keyboard is emotionless. It's is harder to see how the other person is feeling. Basically, it's easier to bullshit. You have no idea what I look like. You wouldn't know if I'm beating my wife in the background or what. My god, if you met them in real life, they're completely off the wall or neurotic. I wouldn't call any of these people I've met on the Internet who are friends. There's many cases of 40 to 50 year old men who portray themselves as being somebody much younger and different and they befriend a child and molest them... I'd stay away from chat groups. I don't have time to waste. It's okay to e-mail back and forth, but chat rooms. What's the point? It's something to do, and granted as a professional, you can exchange ideas... but what's the point?"
32 year-old divorced software programmer

"You've got to be crazy to be on chat groups. I should know because for eight months, I would come home and run up to the computer and spend all my time on chat groups. Then one day, this guy starts calling me up, 'Hey, I know who you are. I know where you live. And I'm coming to get you.' It's spooky being stalked and eventually, I had this guy got arrested.

I was on this chat group once and there was this guy who was a real creep who hit up on the women on-line. I complained to the chat monitor but they would not do anything unless I had proof. So I

created this personal of this newly wed gal from Texas to trap this guy from Arkansas. I logged her on as "Marion" being an unhappily married person and let him go at her for 30 minutes. His stuff was so slimy that I posted the whole conversation on the chat group and finally he got kicked out. There are some rules about decency on chat groups."
42 year-old hardware specialist

"I like the anonymity that leads people to believe they're somebody else and watch how they inter-act with others. There was a man on the chat forum and right from the start, implied that he was a woman himself and opened up areas that were taboo. You see how people act thinking they are anonymous. You can get people who have hit it off and then there are stories where people have been stalked. All the social queues and social facades are gone and you're left with communicating with the truncated English language.

Generally, if there's a chat forum, there are few women who admit that they're women. There's a reluctance to admit that you're being a woman. There's always the fear that they could be uncovered.

It's interesting to note that men think they can have their own way eventually with women. They're superficial enough to think it will happen and men are gullible with what women will say and are equally thwarted just as quickly."
26 year-old male network administrator

"Whenever you express your opinion on-line, you can expect harassment. You also get kooks who talk about committing suicide and monitors who think that if you swear too much, they will stop your access."
41 year-old chat room user

"Men always think they're invincible. It's a teenage mentality. You're immortal as a teen. On the Internet, it's a big fantasy. Look at their mindset. They make themselves thinking that they're single. They're cruising for chicks and looking for sex. That's an adolescent mentality. They say it's safe because they don't see each other or touch each other. It's not because they form a particular emotional bond with a woman on the Internet which is stronger than their bond with the wife and one of them will say, 'let's together. It's that sneaking around that adds to the excitement."
37 year-old computer widow

"He was a seemingly happily married man with a gorgeous stay-at-home wife and two young beautiful children, about four and six years old. She suspected that something was going on and hired private investigators that worked between Canada and the United States. He told his wife that he had to attend a convention in Atlanta. He flew from San Francisco to Atlanta, checked into the hotel for the convention and then walked out to catch a flight up to Toronto. There, in Toronto, he met his cyber lover, a very homely looking middle-aged woman and they spent the weekend together. Then he flew back to Atlanta to officially check out of the hotel and caught his return flight back to San Francisco. When he arrived back home, his wife served him with divorce papers. Why? He seemed to have everything going for himself."
Source: private investigator

"A cousin of mine got into one of these chat rooms from Seattle. He met this Singaporean girl and two weeks later, she sent him her photo. She's actually quite good-looking. After five months of on-line chatting, she borrowed money from my cousin and his dad and she flew up to Seattle. They've been living together now for 18 months and she wants to immigrate to the United States. She's a teacher and he's an engineer."
28 year-old computer analyst

"I wouldn't go surfing on the Internet for dates. That's dumb. It's not normal I guess. It's like you know the people on the Internet got to be geeks."
16 year-old website designer

"If you're on the chat groups, you need to change your judgment of people. You can't take people at face about anything. People say things to get a reaction. You have to judge someone by gut feel and gut response. You still can't judge by body language. There's no audio and no visual."
40 year-old computer training instructor

"I'd say 80 percent is good and 20 per cent is bad about on-line dating. I went to a wedding in Chicago. We were all on the same chat group. I knew the bride for three years and the groom for one year. He was a Chicago cop and she was a Missouri school bus driver. They are real

happy. *The con's about on-line dating is the distance and I've met some psychological sick women.*

I think this is funny. The guy looks like a slob and she looks like a slob. They're both sitting in front of the computer chatting to each other on-line. He says he's a Chip N' Dale dancer and she says that she's a beauty queen."
34 year-old web designer

WHAT A PSYCHOLOGIST WHO RUNS AN ON-LINE DATING SERVICE HAS TO SAY

Today (May 24, 1999) search using Altavista noted that there were more than 32 million web pages in English pertaining to on-line dating. I interviewed Dr. James Sempsey, a Philadelphia, Pennsylvania-based psychologist and president of an on-line dating and consulting service at www.couple-link.com, which has 40,000 members world-wide.

Q: "What advice would you give to people before they consider on-line dating?"
SEMPSEY: "I would advise people that on-line dating is much more efficient than attempting to meet a compatible partner in the face to face world. Face to face meetings are greatly subject to change and geographic proximity. So on-line dating services are a great way to meet people. However, they should exercise caution since there is no telling what sorts of people one may encounter on-line (people may lie or at least exaggerate). Thus, one should attempt to acquire as much information about someone that they have met on-line as one can before agreeing to a face to face meeting. Also, any first face to face encounters should definitely be conducted in a very public place (for safety reasons) and "private" meetings should not take place until well after one has gained level of confidence in the caliber of the person they have met. In other words, they should exercise some common sense.

As far as on-line dating per se, one should be as honest as reasonably possible (do not exaggerate or brag), and keep in mind that others may be doing so (or at least they may not have a realistic perspective on themselves).

Keep in mind that people tend to behave differently on-line than they might in face to face encounters, thus one should try to "read between the lines" in text based conversations. What they write is not always what you get. They may also appear more outgoing in –email or chat room correspondence, so don't be surprised to find that person is actually a bit shy when meeting face to face.

Do no offer any personal information that might enable you to be "tracked down" until well after you have a gained a degree of confidence in the relationship.

Do not focus too much on any single individual when searching. On-line dating is sort of a numbers game and there is no harm in writing to 20 or more people in order to find that special someone.

Do not judge too harshly based on photos. Many people do not photograph well or know how to select a good representation of themselves (plus the fidelity of these photos is sometimes dreadful). However, the TYPE of photo one chooses to upload can be quite revealing. Consider a picture of a man with his children, which implies he is family oriented and expects that his children will be accepted along with him. But a man in a tuxedo standing next to a rented stretch limousine may imply that they believe such things to be of greater importance than honesty or self disclosure (i.e. don't look so much at ME but what I promise to provide)."

Q. "What should people expect of on-line dating?"
SEMSEY: "Be realistic. If you've got a few extra pounds, then perhaps you shouldn't dismiss others have the same. On-line correspondence is an opportunity to get to know the PERSON before judging their appearance (typically the other way around in face to face first encounters).

Do no be disappointed if someone you are interested in doesn't write back. Many people are only "fooling around" on-line or may be engaged in other relationships by the time you write (or may be too shy to reply. Such behavior should not be viewed as rejection (indeed, a non-response says more about the person to whom you writing than about yourself)."

Q. "Who ends up being happy with their on-line relationships?"
SEMPSEY: "Difficult to say from a statistical perspective. But qualitatively, those who have realistic and honest expectations concerning relationships."

WHAT SURVEY RESPONDENTS HAD TO SAY

"I tried an on-line dating company from Israel. They asked you 120 multiple choice questionnaire and it was run a psychologist. I send my application in the evening and received 10 matches. You could pick the countries, so I picked Canada, United States and France. I received one from Canada and nine from the United States. One of them sent me an e-mail, but she later married another American guy. There was a real attractive women from Oregon, at least, we had similar interests, but I never heard back from her. One of the problems with dating on-line, even though it didn't cost me any money, is that you have no feelings. You know somebody is out there looking but you don't know what they look like. It's too abstract. Lots of people lie when they fill in the questionnaire to sweeten the pot, but the picture is pretty important, that makes her a bestseller."
50 year-old divorced computer user

"I have dated on-line, and it's been mostly a positive experience. Friendship is important in a relationship. Be with somebody that makes you feel good about yourself. Without a doubt, I can handle dumb people. I dated attractive girls who are dumb. But I can't handle girls who are out to control me."
49 year-old Mac user.

L E V E L   1 4

COMPUTER WIDOWS SPEAK GEEK-FREE

"My father is a computeraholic. Five years ago, my parents separated for a month. It's a lot better now. A lot of people think that technology is where it's at, but people is where it is at."
29 year-old ex-computer widow

I'm amused. The GEEK barges into my office totally paranoid about the amount of SPAM he has been receiving. You think that Revenue Canada just told them that his income tax return was under investigation. Sex SPAM has been chasing him. He demands that I open up my e-mail box. NOW. I click on my e-mail box, to proudly reveal my lack of such illicit inquiries. I probed the GEEK further as to why the hoopla. He confesses that he was seduced by some of those sex sites. "You know, the first few minutes are always free," he replied coyly. Of course, that's just enough time for some server to really dig their claws into his e-mail address, which they did. No wonder, hot babes, vixen ladies, and kooky chicks were more then willing to pounce on him. Exciting… The GEEK was being spammed a gazillion times a day and feeling harassed. Am I supposed to take pity on him? "So how long has this been going on," I winked at him. Sheepishly, he replied, "A few times." "What do ya mean just a few times?" I demanded. "Oh, about two months," he admitted. I'm thinking to myself, so this is why you're so tired at night, and I'm trying hard not to laugh too hard because he's so paranoid about this SPAM stuff. "It's not like you gave them your credit card or anything like that, did you?" He assured me that did not happen. I shrug my shoulders, and carry on with my life. It's not like the kids have seen anything they shouldn't yet.

But for some other computer widow who called me up out of the blue one day, her encounter with on-line pornography wasn't such a non-threatening experience. Her eight-year-old son stumbled across her husband's shortcut to this porn site. She was devastated. The family computer room was stashed away in the basement, but accessible by their young children, all under the age of 8 years. She had no idea about her husband's secret cyber life and how long it had been going on. He wouldn't tell. For all she knew, he could be spending three hours daily on Internet porn sites for the last 12 years of their marriage. At the crossroads of a marriage on the rocks, she explained to me that with the exception of meals, mowing the lawn and tucking the children in bed at night, her husband spent every waking moment in front of the computer.

Resentment for time committed in front of the computer, neglect of the significant other, lack of participation in household chores and disinterest in the children's school projects, are par with the course for computer widows and widowers. Computer lovers reported learning to compromise, after marriage, like not eating dinners in front of their joy boxes and even logging off, to spend time with the family on Friday nights. The majority of computer widows I interviewed didn't know what their significant others were doing on the computer. Some assumed they were working, programming new software, playing computer games and cruising the Internet. Dr. Kimberly Young, a clinical psychologist at the University of Pittsburgh, has thoroughly researched and documented the issue of Internet addiction in her book, *Caught in the Net*, published by John Wiley & Sons 1998.

One computer widow I interviewed lamented, "I didn't know that I was marrying a computer geek. I got married in the 1960's. You couldn't take a computer home back then."

Still, many of us knew. One 49 year-old computer widower told me, "I knew I was marrying a woman with a computer. I didn't know it was going this way. I know the computer does something for her. She's on it 20 to 30 hours a week. But the computer does nothing for our relationship." While this couple both worked full-time, he does all the laundry, cooking and cleaning, "She does things once in a while and when she does, she expects me to bring in the brass band and thank her with fireworks."

His wife is into computer games and the Internet. He has a conspiracy theory for some of her antics. "I get home from the office before she does. She plays on the computer from 4:30 to 6:00 p.m. because the traffic is too busy to drive home. So by the time she comes home, I've made her a nice warm supper."

An independent computer widower with lots of his own hobbies and interest, he says he's entertained by his wife's marathon computer sessions that begin on Friday nights and don't end until Sunday night. Whether it's a gaming or programming binge, the computer user is rendered useless for all activities except eating and sleeping. After three and a half years of marriage, this couple's relationship is working. He's proud of his wife's education and career accomplishments and they do take vacations together, "She does her thing and I do my thing."

Let's face the facts. Over 90 per cent of couples marry opposite personalities. I'm the social butterfly. He's the tardy turtle with his head tucked in the shell. I'm impatient. He is patient. I'm not romantic. He's good at buying flowers for no special reason. I just pray my checks don't bounce every month. He monitors every penny earned and spent, on the computer daily complete with bar graphs, and total financial analysis that calculates his return on investments. Some people think that it's good to marry an opposite personality. We've seen too many couples of similar personalities split up and they tell us that they were competing in their marriage. We don't compete. We just fight. But we do agree on a few things. We don't take laptop computers to bed at night and we tolerate our irreconcilable differences.

Good relationships take time and lot of work. Probably, far more work than most of us imagined when we took our marriage vows. I interviewed several couples with computers at home, on why their marriages worked. Time and time again, you will read about how important good communication is. And it's not just the women who have commented on this, it's the men, too. One husband credited sticky notes for communication within their marriage as their prime means because they both have their own businesses and not much time for each other.

> *"My husband (a computer programmer) used to spend close to 30 extra hours a week on the computer. We didn't live in the same city during our engagement period. Still, when he came to visit me, you could tell that his mind was on something else. You see computer guys get focused on something and they can't think of anything else. So that was a big shock when we got married to find out that he worked an extra 30 hours a week on the computer.*
>
> *I wasn't going to fight him, so I thought that I would join him and went back to university to study computer sciences to become a computer programmer. But that was a disaster for our marriage. We fought more because he was so much more advanced than I was. He would explain something to me and he would be frustrated as why I didn't get it and that made me feel stupid. I finished second year computer science and quit. He quit being a computer programmer and we got rid of all the computer stuff at home.*
>
> *We both became financial planners. We used to be introverted, but now we're more extroverted. We've learned that in a marriage, you have work towards a common goal. You need to work towards a common goal, where you each use your own complimentary strengths. Before in our marriage, we had two separate goals and I was working hard to be more like him."*
> 29 year-old former computer widow who now has a marriage

> *"When we got married, I was only 18 years old and he was 23 years old. Everybody said that we wouldn't make it. We always talk things out. We share everything, our hopes, our dreams and whatever is on our mind."*
> 35 year-old computer widow, on being married 17 years

"When we got married, I was 32 years old and he was 34 years. We were stubbornly independent and equally strong-willed. We have to put our strong wills aside to make better choices. We've had to learn to compromise.

My husband has all the making of a computer nerd. He has a compulsion for knowledge. He has no time for junk television. His sense of security comes from knowledge. When he's feeling tense, he isolates himself from people and becomes a walking encyclopedia and uses his compulsion as a cross-reference in life.

Life is changing and society is changing so much. You have to figure out the system for the kind of relationship you want. Society is changing around each other and figuring out a way to adapt to this change. That's the same thing with computers, which are here to stay.

I am aware of how computers have helped my husband. He used to be more introverted, but his knowledge about computers has given him more confidence. I used to be threatened by computers and pissed off at them. From the beginning, I would over-react and we'd be open and honest how I felt about computers. I went through a time, when I really hated computers. But my husband was very encouraging. He was concerned that I would be technically left behind. Basically, he realized that he needed to let go and not shove technology down my throat. Now, on my own initiative, I have the desire to know and access computers."
40-plus computer widow.

"One positive thing about my husband working on the computer late at night was that when the children woke up, at least he was up. He was up more often than I was, but then he would lose his train of thought and all hell would break loose. Men are like that, you know. They're one-minded.

You could talk to my husband while he's on the computer and he wouldn't hear a frigging thing that I was saying. Men's minds just don't have the same capabilities of ours (women's). They cannot sort tasks and do several things at once. I know that's a fact. I read about this is some journal at the doctor's office."
36 year-old computer widow and mother of two children, ages 9 and 6 years

"If I have a computer problem, I expect him to fix it right now. If he doesn't do it, I'm very hard on him.

It doesn't bother me that my husband is looking at porn on the Internet. What's the difference between that and my father's generation that had a stash of girlie magazines? Why can't I look at good looking guys on the Internet, too?

I do my own thing. If I didn't have a computer, I'd go nuts. If he didn't have a computer, he would drive me up the wall. He knows his limits... I think most women wouldn't tolerate our situation. It takes a certain type of woman who will tolerate a man who's on the computer all weekend.

These talk shows blame the Internet as the problem in relationships. The Internet is not the problem. The relationship was the problem before the Internet."
34 year-old computer widow, who's been married 12 years

It would be incomplete if I did not write about the abandoned computer lovers, when relationships soured. Few men were brave enough to share what went wrong. One young computer lover who had been divorced for two years resigns himself to drown his sorrows, playing computer games he doesn't like and spending excessive time on machines he hates. He is only 28 years old and quite good-looking by DOAG's standards, so I boldly asked him if he would consider marrying again. Remorseful, he clipped off eye contact, wrung his hands and cracked his voice, "Who would want me?"

One 40 year-old computer professional didn't know why but he spent 40 extra hours weekly after 5 p.m. idolizing the computer. Now divorced, he has become computer celibate. And for one under-30 ex-computer consultant, the departure of his wife traumatized him so much, that he left the IT profession entirely.

"If people want to stay in love forever, they've got to learn to fall in love, again and again and again."
7 year-old SOAG

LEVEL 15

CROSSING THE DIGITAL DIVIDE
OVERCOMING COMPUTER PHOBIA

"The revenge is over... I just feel sorry for anyone who isn't living with computers, who isn't moving with this technology."
Albert Lai, 20, quoted in *The Globe and Mail*, May 27, 1999, one of the three amigos who sold their web site mydesktop.com for an undisclosed seven digit price.

It was at technical school in the early 1970's, that I progressed from pencil and paper to Monroe calculators. We had the privilege of working with the antiquated models that were clumsy and cumbersome but durable devices. No carpal tunnel syndrome here. You took the lever and cranked it clockwise or counterclockwise, depending on whether you needed to multiply or divide, to complete the proper computation. As the crank was forced one way or the other, a bell would ding to let you know that you've gone far enough. Who says you can't burn calories while calculating?

In those days, when plastic pocket protectors were the ultimate symbol of geekdom, I was quite a slide ruler aficionado. Slide rulers were quite capable of three decimal point accuracy and I possessed three – the full-length plastic slide ruler in a gray case, a full-length wooden one in a red case and a six-inch slide rule in a blue plastic protector for guesstimations. My favorite was the bamboo slide rule, for its redeeming frictionless quality, as sliding plastic stuck on occasion.

During the 1970's, when people spoke of computers, visions of monolithic machines came to mind. Just like the first computer I became up front and personal with – an IBM mainframe system at the University of British Columbia, in 1978. I never saw it, but I heard its beastie noises. As a fourth year engineering student enrolled in FORTRAN IV programming, the climax of the course was to write code for a program that would produce an over-sized kangaroo calendar. It seemed to be a course in futility. You fed information into this mainframe computer, via code on keypunch cards. With quality time with this computer a premium, you were rationed a few coupons that would have to last the whole term. If you had the keypunch cards in the wrong order, forgot your password, or had a typo error, inevitably, your program bombed and you had to start all over again. Didn't somebody say that if you feed garbage in, you get garbage out?

In 1979, the GEEK had already purchased his first Tandy Radio Shack Color Computer 8K, which used the television for its monitor. By 1980, he up-graded it. He consumed three Tandy Radio Shack Color Computers (consoles only), before purchasing a self-contained personal computer with its own monitor.

Computers became up front and personal for me. While working for Fluor Daniel during the early 1980's as a scheduling engineer, our department was allotted one Apple computer. People fought over its use. Not a chance that my grubby fingers could play with it.

Then I worked on a Commodore 64K computer, for an oilfield service company. I wrote BASIC programs to plot the data and compute the third order differential equations for reservoir production analysis. This first workplace experience was less frustrating than the university one, "I couldn't believe how easy it was to program in BASIC, compared to FORTRAN!"

As for computers and me, I was on a roll. My next job was working for an oil company in project planning and development. Some ex-NASA Californian guy (friend of departmental head hauncho) came to work for us and threatened to leave because there was not one computer at his desk. Shortly thereafter, our group had access to two computers – the Apple and the Lisa, a $13,000 special. The 20 - minute audio-tape was all the formal training I needed.

Back at home, I lived with an IBM PC-clone kind of guy and a Macintosh system was totally out of the question. We were still a one PC household, so I began my freelance writing career on an electronic typewriter. In 1987, the GEEK brought himself another computer and I inherited the Tandy 8086 MS-DOS computer, which I used as a glorified word processor, with a program called "deskmate". No mouse at hand, I memorized the keyboard commands that started with "c\:".

In 1994, the GEEK purchased a Compaq 486K computer with Windows 3.0. He is reluctant to purchase a computer with an Intel Pentium, after Andy Grove apologized to 2 million owners and agreed to replace the defective floating-point chips for a cost of $475 million. That year, I purchased a Sharp palmtop computer for $500. It's an over-priced battery sensitive word processor and electronic organizer in one and garners much attention during my Japan trip that year. A Japanese palmtop computer would have to be at least twice the size of an English-based version because the Japanese language comprised of Kanji characters requires so much more memory.

Tokyo's *Akihabara*, an electronic and computer discount district comprised of over 600 vendors, is Disneyland for any engineer – with every possible gadget you could think of, in every imaginable size and color. I wish I had more cash because credit cards aren't well received in Japan. I brought the GEEK a credit-card sized radio, after bargaining the price down about 30 per cent.

In 1998, the GEEK purchased his umpteenth computer, this one is for me - Acer Pentium II computer 200 megahertz speed with a 1.6 gigabyte hard drive, loaded with Windows 97. No sooner had the computer been un-packed, it's become obsolete. As of June 1999, personal computers can come with Pentium 400 MHtz microprocessor, 32x's CD-Rom drive, and 19 gigabyte hard drive capacity.

> *"Humans fear what they don't understand. All it takes is one well meaning geek to throw a little computer jargon at a normal person and BOOM - a computer phobe is created."*
> 21 year-old computer user

So you are on the verge of crossing the digital divide, that great abyss that separates you from the 21st Century and the 1960's. It's that imaginary barrier that you've come to terms with. Most computer users think you're normal and that you probably got a life. There's nothing to fear but fear itself.

"I've been on computer for five years now and I went through five phases. The first phase was what on earth is this thing? Second phase, now look here this computer can actually do something. Third phase is now how can I get it to do something for me? Phase IV: How can I make it do things faster? And Phase V, how can I get to do things to fill my demands and now I don't want any more crap, I want the meat, nothing else."
21 year-old systems engineer

Becoming a computer geek has no prerequisites, just courage and attitude. Age has nothing to do with a computer phobic mindset. When asked what she thought of computer-illiterate people, one 81 year-old woman hissed into the telephone, "Stupid!"

"I'm really ticked on how they display computers in movies. How people bang on the computers to make them work. That's downright horrible. If they showed a real computer, at the most a computer will ever do is smoke. It will not flash to spark. There's not enough electricity to flash."
21 year-old Linux God

Now that I've empowered myself by smashing the computer on this book's front cover to smithereens, I have learned that you control the machine. How come kids have already figured this out? SOAG or DOAG sit at the computer, goof off, push the mouse around, pull down the icons and play. If they screw up, they just laugh and say to themselves, "Cool."

To be a little paranoid around computers is perfectly understandable (but not necessarily, healthy). My computer programmer friend of 20 years speaks of computer anxiety. He confides that when he sits in front of the computer, he tenses up. After an hour, his eyes gets blurry, so he has to leave the monitor for a break. On the job, he's never sure that the computer is going to do what he wants it to do.

It took me awhile to get used to the personal computer, but I persevered. That's why I enrolled myself in all-you-can-stuff-your-brains computer training program that lasted a year. Eventually, I figured things should sink in through osmosis and they did. After the third computer course, I realized software programs had some sort of logic to them.

There was a time when the computer held me hostage. You know when the computer screen freezes on you, leaving you with that blank kiss of death. You push a key and nothing happens, unless you press "alt, ctrl, del" simultaneously. In dire straits, I've learned to calmly turn off the computer and re-boot it and pray that I saved everything. Nowadays, a Microsoft word message reminds me daily that "Your files are corrupted. Do you want to…" The computer will not allow me to shut down the machine, until I clean up my act literally. I've spoken to many computer consultants. The solution is to just re-install the software. For now, I just say "yes" to whatever the computer wants and eventually, the irritating messages stop and I'm able to exit Windows. The GEEK was flabbergasted about how I treat the computer upon exit, but I tell him, my system works (for now, that is).

Respondents offered a lot of reasons for resistance and theories for computer anxiety.

> *"I think people have computer phobia because a lack of understanding. There's a lot of propaganda surrounding the computer. You look at computer games with bits and bytes, there's the psychological advantage to the computer. It just sits there and for you, there's this frustration factor."*
> 27 year-old hardware developer

> *"People think that the computer controls them. When I teach computer classes, I tell my students to remember that you have the upper hand. You can un-plug it. But it cannot UN-plug you."*
> 25 year-old network administrator.

> *"People with computer phobia are right brain and not left brain. The artistic type of people are right brain, but computers require a particular line of reasoning which is left brain thinking."*
> 50 year-old statistical software developer

"It's a visual thing about computers. Some people are intimidated when they walk into a big library. They don't know how things are organized. Computers are the same way. Once you know the system, computers can be adapted to quite quickly. It's the lack of visual sense, so you have to use the metaphor of file cabinets and folders for a visual reference."
38 year-old computer training co-ordinator

"There is the belief that computers are powerful and infallible. If you make a mistake, it's your fault. When you start using the computer, you're afraid of pushing the wrong key. This appliance hasn't evolved. We still have to use a keyboard, which forces you to conform. If you are a little uncertain about your ability, it's a major conflict."
33 year-old senior systems consultant

It is the consensus of most computer professionals that computers are still in their infancy. They have not evolved into intuitive enough tools yet.

"Technology doesn't work as well as it should. You do something and the system crashes."
29 year-old programmer

"Computers drive me up the wall, sometimes. They're so complex and they're so poorly designed that they become like magic boxes – nobody knows how they work anymore. There is not much logic anymore. I get frustrated at the amount of complexity they've become. Computers are not designed well. They are not friendly. They should be as easy to use as a toaster."
32 year-old hardware specialist

In March 1998, Markham, Ontario-based research firm AC Nielson conducted a survey of 6,740 persons across Canada. They asked people why they purchased a personal computer. Twenty-eight per cent of users brought the PC for educational purposes, 17 per cent to start up a home-based business and 10 per cent for entertainment. Seventy-four per cent of users, once they brought a computer, couldn't be bothered with the up-grades.

The PC account executives that I interviewed claim that as many of one-half of the PC's purchased are not used at all, but are sitting around collecting dust. A 55 year-old retired computer retailer says, "I ask them why they are buying a computer. They tell me they want one just like their neighbor's. But I ask them what are they planning to do with the computer?"

> *"Computers used to be number crunchers, but the reason to own a computer today is because it's a communications device. I have seen people go spend $2,000 on a computer, which gives them no pleasure. They are better off spending that money on a holiday. The interface between computers and users are not totally intuitive. It should be seamless. It should be like a $1,000 suit that should follow you around and you shouldn't have to think how to interact with it."*
> 47 year-old hardware consultant

Seniors, I've noted are very thorough about purchasing a computer. They are more apt to buy one that's several years old for a few hundred dollars out of the classified ads, instead of a brand new one. They flock to home computer user groups to analyze what a local reseller will have to say about up-grades and they've got all the time in the world to learn the computer at their leisure. They know all about how much RAM or memory their computer should have, how fast the modem should be, how many gigabytes on the hard drive and what microprocessor speed to get.

With more people using computers and at an accelerated rate of participation, it's easier to find someone to help teach you about computers. This person could be your significant other, an eight year-old kid or a teenager who is acclimatized to a computer like a peripheral. There is one big advantage to living with techies. Your help desk is only a shout away.

A woman called the Canon help desk with a problem with her printer. The techie asked if she was "running it under Windows." The woman responded, "No, my desk is next to the door. But that's a good point. The man sitting in the cubicle next to me is under a window and his is working fine."

You will find that computers are fun and easy to use, once you have psyched yourself up. The best way to learn about them is to play with them first. Teaching yourself is one of the most rewarding ways to learn. You do have to understand that the computer is far from ideal. The techies' biggest beef about computers is the lack of good software around. If you read the following, you will understand why.

Murphy's Computer Laws

1. No matter how many resources you have, it is never enough.
2. Any cool program always requires more memory than you have.
3. When you finally buy enough memory, you will not have enough disk space.
4. Disks are always full. It is futile to try to get more disk space. Data expands to fill any void.
5. If a program actually fits in memory and has enough disk space, it is guaranteed to crash.
6. If such a program has not crashed yet, it is waiting for a critical moment before it crashes.
7. No matter how good of a deal you get on computer components, the price will always drop immediately after purchase.
8. All components are obsolete.
9. The speed which components become obsolete is directly proportional to the price of the component.
10. (Hofstatler's Law) Things always take twice as long as you anticipate.
11. Software bugs are impossible to detect by anybody except the end user.

For a more complete set of Murphy's Laws, check out www.bugcomputer.com/cpuidle/murphy.htm.

Murphy's Laws were derived from Edward A. Murphy, an American aerospace engineer who worked in the military. He said in 1949, "If there are two or more ways to do something, and one of those ways can result in a catastrophe, then someone will do it."

THE LEGO EFFECT
RAISING YOUR COMPUTER QUOTIENT

*"Chaos is the most creative environment.
Teach kids how to survive in chaos, by being creative."*
Frank Ogden, a.k.a. Dr. Tomorrow

When SOAG was a baby, he'd crawl around the house and pull electric plugs out of the receptacles. DOAG never did this. I looked down at SOAG, gasping that he hadn't electrocuted himself yet. When SOAG was nearly two years old, we caught him playing with one of the GEEK's computer. In fact, he shoved a screw driver into the floppy disk drive and destroyed it – all in a few minutes. When SOAG was four years old, my credit card went astray and I called the VISA people in a panic. SOAG strongly denied any wrongdoing. Then I noticed how screechy my floppy drive sounded, so I peered into the disk drive. Low and behold, using a straightened out paper clip, I pried out my credit card. Still, the floppy disk drive sounded cranky. I probed further and pried out a quarter, a nickel and two pennies. It seems that SOAG was wondering why you could not get money from your computer (well, at least, not yet.)

SOAG's behavior is typical for many individuals who will grow up thriving in computers and technology. Ada Lovelace was known to take apart alarm clocks for fun. Simply put, SOAG is driven to find out how things ticked. To-date, he has dissected three walkman tape recorders, his Disney watch, felt tip marker pens and other miscellaneous electronic devices including a dead virtual pet and calculator. Working with mechanical items isn't enough.

SOAG combs through the kitchen and bathroom, looking for materials to play scientist with. He has mixed hand lotion with white glue, baking soda with olive oil and tried to grow crystals. He is adamant about his secret experiments that he uses first aid adhesive tape to bind the jars his cocktails are in. But when mold grows over, I walk in and flush everything down the toilet. In his spare time, he studies the AMA Repair Guide, especially the isometric drawings of the car engine.

Other parents have told me how their sons were incredibly fast and good at taking apart so-called child-proof toys. Said one mother, "By the time we had pulled the Fisher-Price toy off the shelf and taken him to the check-out in the buggy, he had taken the toy out of the box and pulled it apart."

> "There was no point in buying him toys… I was fed up with him wrecking these toys. So when he was three years old, I brought in an old car engine and put it in his bedroom. I gave him a screw driver and told him that he could take it apart and put it back together. I don't know if it was a safe thing to do, but it kept him busy. After he was finished with the engine, I brought in an old carburetor."
> 55 year-old computer guy and father of 30 year-old computer analyst

> "My father repaired electrical appliances. I grew up in a household where I could take apart vacuum cleaners and not get reprimanded."
> 34 year-old hardware developer

So if you always wondered how today's techies became so good at computers, when there were no computers back then, it's because they had the opportunity to learn about things by taking them apart and putting them back together. Putting a child on a computer at an early age is not always the solution. The 34 year-old hardware designer who spent most of his time on a computer since he was 8 years old, frets that he missed 26 years of life.

There are acrimonious debates on whether today's parents should shove their children in front of a computer monitor, as early as possible. "People ask me if they should buy a computer for their children. I say, 'yes', but I tell them, please don't use the computer as a babysitter," says a 37 year-old technologist. Still, a 47 year-old account representative wonders if people should buy a computer at all for children, "Everybody thinks that you should put kids on computers at an early age. But what's the point. By the time the kid is in high school, technology will have changed and he will have to re-learn new technology."

Software manufacturers are rolling out programs for babies and toddlers, targeting parents who want to have smart children. Usually, these products appeal to IT professionals who have children. One IT professional didn't like the idea of pushing her daughter into computer training at 3 years of age, but did so for fear her child would be left behind.

All the major children toy manufacturers, like Fisher-Price and Sesame Street, have "lapware" available for children under 3 years of age and as early as 9 months. The software often features singing animated animals, videos, counting and simple reading exercises.

One IT professional proudly told me that his four month-old daughter already was a using a computer. That was hard for me to imagine, considering she's still contending with passing gas and other bodily functions. But her father re-assured me how computer literate she had become. At four months old, perched on daddy's left knee in front of the monitor, she was able to press "any key" to continue and she was able to put her CD in the disk drive.

"Go to art school to embrace the other side of your brain. It's easy to pick up technical stuff but you need creativity for computers."
31 year-old IS vice-president

"They put computers in front of kids at school nowadays, which is taking up valuable time, which could be used otherwise. They don't need to teach the kids about computers until they are in high school. Kids need to learn to socialize and get along with each other. Why not teach kids to type. All they're learning now is how to push a mouse."
42 year-old software marketing manager

What's the rush? According to the Software Human Resources Council, children with an aptitude for computers and technology are identified by the time they are eight years old. By this age, they would like to see young girls and boys sold on a career in high-tech. Educators push for computers in day cares, kindergarten and first grade.

But Dr. Otto Weininger, a childhood play expert at the University of Toronto, isn't so sure that software for toddlers and babies is such a good thing. The speed at which a computer can respond is more instantaneous than human response. Children who get used to computers at an early age, expect instant gratification and many computer users cited impatience as one of their personality weaknesses. The end result Weininger anticipates will be aggressive children.

> *"I learn through my heart. My heart is much bigger than my body. Adults learn through their heads and that's a really slow way to learn."*
> 7 year-old SOAG

What does a child know? Probably a lot more than you think. You can pick up a few pointers from a computer kid to raise your computer quotient. I asked DOAG why adults might be fearful of computers. She calmly replied, "Adults worry so much when they are on the computer, about all the things that can go wrong. Children couldn't care less." Being child-like is essential claimed several computer professionals to keep yourself motivated and curious in front of the computer. Play and having fun on the computer is very important to increasing your computer quotient.

Perhaps, educators and parents should note that 47 per cent of female respondents and 44 per cent of male respondents reported playing a musical instrument. This figure was much higher for Net people. Sixty-three per cent of the Net people played one musical instrument; 43 per cent of Net people played more than one musical instrument. Of the techies within the Net people who responded, 87 per cent played at least one musical instrument. A handful of persons interviewed played in bands or were concert pianists. The correlation between working with computers and solving mathematical mysteries and playing a musical instrument is uncanny. The world's first programmer, Ada Lovelace, was both an accomplished mathematician and musician.

An article written by Sandra Blakeslee published in *The Globe and Mail*, May 25, 1999 entitled "Intuition, language keys to helping brain solve math equations" may be on the right track in suggesting that we use more than one part of brain to do math and solve problems. The piano was most popularly played by the 27 per cent of the women, while the guitar was most popularly played by 16 per cent of the men. About six per cent of IT males played more than one musical instrument, several reporting up to six instruments. After the guitar, piano and drums were most popularly played by IT males. For IT females, the order was piano, saxophone and violin. Other instruments that were mentioned included the trumpet, clarinet, flute, banjo, keyboard, accordion, harmonica and trombone.

LEVEL 17

GAMES PEOPLE PLAY

"Computer games satisfies some primal need to destroy. It's rationalized because you're saving earth from aliens. I was addicted to DOOM, absolutely had to play it constantly. Can't remember whether DOOM II had 30 or 32 levels, just had to work it into my personal life. I was laying in bed pretending to be a sleep. My wife fell asleep and I slipped out of bed and went into the second bedroom. I turned on the computer and turned the sound down. I had lost myself into the game. Now I was one with the computer and culminating with reaching another level. I noticed the light turned on. I caught the silhouette of my wife in the hall. She wasn't friendly because she hadn't said anything. Then she spoke, 'At least you could have the balls to turn up the speakers,' and left the room and went back to bed. In effect, I was cheating on her. The time I spent on the computer is like cheating. She would have to have my time. That one-liner really put me in place. After that I was more open about it with my wife. We had been in our second year of marriage."
33 year-old senior systems analyst

For years, I witnessed the GEEK playing games on the computer. The GEEK says he's not on the computer as much as he's used to. But often before going to bed, I notice that he equates meditation with 20 minutes of solitaire, something which I could not understand because I don't have the patience to play card games, never have and never will. In the GEEK's upbringing, his parents often played board and card games every evening for an hour or so. So, it's not too surprising that the GEEK has been programmed to play computer games for sport.

Many computer lovers claimed that computer games strengthened their mental dexterity, helped them relax or be the ultimate escape into another dimension. But I sometimes wonder, when I see my husband on edge. His blood pressure is curdling, eyes fixated to the screen with a salivating jaw and clenched fingers on the keyboard pushing down as fast and as hard as humanly possible. The air in the room is silenced, except for the keyboard clicks and noise from the power supply fan. You tell him that dinner is ready and he screams at you to leave him alone. He's so worked up that you wonder, maybe you should call 911, because if he doesn't make it to the next level, he might have a cardiac arrest.

During the earlier years of our relationship, I noted how the computer games he played were essentially little Pac men scurrying through a maze gobbling up everything in sight. They progressed to mythical themes, where in this world of make-believe, the GEEK rescued damsels in distress and slayed dragons. Was he addicted? Temporarily insane? Probably. The GEEK had a pattern, a fetish for Radio Shack on Saturday afternoons, where he could be amongst males at his own level (usually teens and pre-teens). He would check out weekly what new games, new gizmos, and new upgrades would be available. On impulse, he would blow what I made as a freelance writer on an average length assignment on a computer game, with the flash of his credit card. I would be horrified, sigh and then act dumb.

For this book, it was essential that I check out at least one computer game. It's called *Hunter* and it reeks of sweat, survival and manhood. It's the kind of game that guys are infatuated with. Like many computer games, you click on the icon and you enter a different time, different space and different place in history. There are good guys and bad guys. In this game, you're the one who's being hunted. A Darth Vader voice rendition speaks to you in digital bytes and you feel heavy footsteps pounding through cyberspace, made as eerie and spooky as possible. Your mission, should you accept is move yourself through this three-dimensional maze comprised of dungeons, traps, surprises, fire, monsters and locked chambers, that gets increasingly trickier as you progress up each level. Lights flash and disintegrate like fireworks. You direct yourself with vertical and horizontal arrow keys. You get points for killing off creepy-looking aliens and for the speed at which you can make it through. You get choice, whether to go right or left, decisions that many gamers call strategy. And for this game, you play alone.

I tried out *Hunter* for the first time. I was too slow and too frustrated and didn't last longer than 30 seconds. The GEEK kicked me off the computer he played. But then a year later, I inherited the GEEK's computer and he installed *Hunter* on it for the benefit of SOAG, who described the game simply put, "Cool!" After a few times, he got bored. After witnessing the GEEK and SOAG on *Hunter*, I decidedly to give it another try in secrecy, with the doors to my home office closed.

This time, when I played *Hunter*, I made it to level 3. I jumped and soared through the narrow passageways, leaped across barriers, escaped the fire of death. I was immobilized. It was like I had stepped into the seat of the roller coaster at an amusement park. Adrenaline purged my systems and my hands were paralyzed by the intense activity. I could feel my shoulders lean forward, my breathing become shallow and my body tighten up. Then the game stopped to inform me that I reached level 3. Maybe two minutes of my life had passed. Now I could understand, but quite frankly, I wouldn't call this relaxing. Not at all. And I proceeded to finish folding the laundry.

> *"I like playing games like Dungeons and Dragons because I use my mind and I'm not beating the crap out of people. I'm learning to figure out stuff."*
> 16 year-old computer user

Gender and age were two factors as to who plays computer games, which were introduced to the world during the early 1960's. The youngest group had the highest computer game playing rate. Eighty per cent of Net people play computer games. Of those Net people who play, 68 per cent play standalone games vs. 32 per cent for inter-active games. Fifty-two percent of males surveyed played standalone computer games, the higher percentage were for non-IT males at 62 per cent vs. 46 per cent for IT males. By the same token, only 30 per cent of IT fenales played standalone computer games versus 47 per cent of non-IT females. There was a significant spread as to which gender played interactive computer games, about 27 per cent of men and 8 per cent of women played interactive games. Again, non-IT males led the way with 30 per cent playing inter-active computer games versus 25 per cent of IT males. About 9 per cent of female computer users played inter-active computer games versus 8 per cent of IT females.

The discrepancy in game participation between males and females is incentive for game makers to lure women with more appealing product. After all, computer games mean big money. In 1998, the sales of video and computer games leaped 35 per cent to 181 million units in the United States, almost two games for every household with total industry revenue of U.S.$5.5 billion, of which U.S.$1.8 billion worth of games used on personal computers.

"With computer games, you have four different scenarios. Different aliens have taken over Los Angeles and they're hanging out in a grocery store. They've taken over, kidnapped the canine population to make burgers, so you've got to save them. Or on a moon base, the aliens have taken over the moon. I actually find playing computer games very relaxing.

Another has mining colonies in the solar systems and you get to build various robots in these planets. But Myst is the most amazing game, you are the only person on this island and you have to get off the island and you end up in the strangest places. I'm not addicted to computer games. I only play about 30 minutes at a time. The chips challenge you and the 3-D graphics are just beautiful."
32 year-old hardware developer

Controversy reigns over the use of computer games known as the "first person shooter" games, which actually account for about six per cent of the games sold, and appeal strongly to men. Quake and Doom have been cited as the best types of games in this category. There are 74 monsters in Quake 13. As users build up immunity to the amount of violence and gore, game makers work on creating more realistic but gruelsome illusions, with more 3D mayhem and some with sex and violence concealed in the same package.

In November 1997, Angie Beal launched www.GameGirlz.com, as a place for female gamers to congregate. On the type of computer games women like to play, Beal says, "Female gamers don't all like the same kind of game… Overall, though I think you can find that many female gamers all seem to appreciate the same types of elements in a game. For instance, most women gamers will tell you that they like to have the option to play a strong female character, not a bikini clad goddess who exists in the game for novelty or titillation. Another issue is thought provoking challenges. Very few women play hardcore 3D shooters. The largest female consumer base exists in games, which provide both action and puzzles. One of the wonders of game technology, multi-player on-line gaming is also breaking more women into the gaming curve. The ability to communicate in a more "social" online gaming server is another element."

> *"They put viruses in computer games, so then they would have to find a cure. Then they would sell you the cure later. It's a fact. That's how computer game manufacturers work. Money has to be their incentive.*
>
> *Once I was downloading software from an Internet site. It was a real big program. The download took 30 minutes with 33.6 Baud modem. Since it was such a big file, the computer asked me to re-start the computer. Then I press yes and re-booted. Then the computer crashed. My God, I thought my baby was dead."*
> 30 year-old computer user
>
> *"On-line MUDding (multi-user dungeons) are role playing games and they are usually quite a bit different from chat. You have descriptions of people and games, rooms have themes and you play a character within a theme. There are differences between MUSH (multi-user shared hallucination), MUD, MUX, and MOO. This inter-active virtual role playing at best is a regular conversation between characters. You can get very absorbed by it to the point that you can say what your character would do without thinking. Most people know that it's text-based, so it's hard to lose touch with reality. There are no images. Some people get upset if some people sees someone get killed.*

You can MUD 24 hours a day and most places will have anywhere from 10 to 50 people playing. Peak hours are in the evening. Part of it is the escape is getting into a different character, in a world where you'd have to wait in line or go to the bathroom. Part of it is talking to other people...casual chat with other people. People will boast that they can manage to go into this situation and survive. My character managed to politic her way into being a duchess and there's a feeling of accomplishment that you've been given the role. There is staff on MUD sites. Usually one person who owns the actual computer and several people take care of the server and re-boot the MUSH. The only way to make money is to provide the server. I've been MUDding for five years and been on staff on three or four places. One of the MUD groups has a yearly meeting and potluck dinner. I can only spend 21 hours a week MUDding, but I used to spend 40 hours."
21 year-old female student

L E V E L   1 8

STAR-GAZING
FOR WEB CRUISERS, LUDDITES AND SUPER GEEKS

No way. You wouldn't spend a penny to have your tarot cards read or your fortune told by some hairy fairy psychic. You got to be kidding. That's for flakes like that kooky kid sister of yours or Aunt Edna. Unless you're buying your groceries on-line (which I doubt you can do yet), you've probably picked up *The Enquirer* or *Star* to lap up the latest sleaze and smut. But there's a higher probability, without a doubt, that you've read your horoscope at lease once in the local daily newspaper, even passing up the column of the matriarchal know-it-all Anne Landers.

Unbelievable? That 99 per cent of respondents filled in the blank about their astrological sign. Responses were fairly evenly distributed from around the Zodiac. Why? Do you believe that celestial bodies play a pivotal role in our lives? Is it possible that our destinies are pre-determined by the alignment of the sun, the moon, the planets and the stars at birth? With ancient origins as far back as the Assyrian and Chaldean empires, which flourished around 6th Century B.C., astrologers combine astronomy and mathematics to chart celestial influences based on your time of birth and geographic location. But free will can change your future, as you risk it.

It was not black and white that all those high-strung computer programmers were Virgos or that all flamboyant Leos had their own high-tech companies. There were some tendencies for persons born under certain astrological signs to relate to technology in a certain way. Would you suggest that the findings are merely coincidental?

ARIES THE RAM — MARCH 21 TO APRIL 20TH

Speed. The Aries leads life in the fast lane and computers helps keep life that way.

I should know because I am one. Confident, forgiving, fun-loving and optimistic, we just ram our way through life. We are risk-taking hustling go-getters with an itch in our unmentionable body parts... the reason why many of the Aries I interviewed were happiest being self-employed or head of the company. It's not money that the Aries craves for, as much as recognition, and having the freedom of not being told what to do. We just like to do things our way.

I used to be conceited, but after therapy, I'm one of the nicest persons you could meet. That's a fib because diplomacy is not one of our stronger virtues, or patience, for that matter. When it comes to computers, the Aries sees the computer just as a tool. It helps get the job done faster, maybe not better. Many Aries interviewed claimed they had a love-hate relationship with the computer. When it doesn't work, I'm apt to chuck the damned thing out and get another one.

There were a lot of Aries surveyed who naturally held positions with a lot of freedom and independence - in sales and marketing, were entrepreneurs and IT consultants. You won't find many Aries on chat groups, because we don't like to sit still, but you will, if we need to get information to help get our work done. It was the majority of computer professionals under this astrological sign, who felt strongly that schools should teach children art and music, instead of computers at an early age, to develop their creativity.

TAURUS THE BULL — APRIL 21 TO MAY 21

The Taurus is a stoic and staid creature. The GEEK is a Taurus. Some people call the Taurus stubborn, others will say that he's patient. But they have zero tolerance for screw ups. And when there are computers involved, the shoddy software that's out there is surely to tick them off. "Memory hog," the Taurus belches my way about Microsoft's Windows.

If you work for one, they demand perfection and competence in your work and can be aggressive when they want. They like their material comforts and their computers, too. For the record, one proud Taurus commented on how he could not understand people who could not make one pair of jeans last at least a year. Now, let's talk underwear. The Taurus in my life can hold onto his briefs until the threads give way and render them useless.

Money makes the Taurus tick. It makes them feel secure. Working in high-tech is a likely proposition. It was the Taurus who was glad that he could triple or quadruple his salary in a year, or drive an extra hour to dine at that cheap Vietnamese restaurant at the other side of town. The computer is the perfect tool for the Taurus to have. If there's time, these bulls will fill in spreadsheets to monitor every penny they own, and then groan at the end of the day, when the stock portfolios have fallen a notch.

Sometimes, it takes a lot to arouse the Taurus. Watch out, there's a steam roller in your path. More than one male Taurus considered being too emotional or too excitable their personality weaknesses, the aftermath of which upsets their daily routine.

GEMINI THE TWINS — MAY 22 TO JUNE 21

Boredom and routine are two things the Gemini likes to avoid. That's why computers and Geminis can be matches made in Heaven. Multi-talented and multi-faceted, often charming and witty, Geminis can talk fast, think fast and move fast, being some of the world's greatest promoters. Computer sales and marketing might just be the IT position to keep them happy, giving them leeway to call some of the shots when they can. But so can working as a website designer that enables them to express themselves freely and creatively from one client to the next.

Playful and young at heart, Geminis like to have fun, too. That's where computers come in. Just another toy to play and have fun with. Several individuals born under this zodiac repeatedly told me that learning about computers was intuitive, "Computers are so easy to use. All I had to do is sit down and play around to figure things out."

The dual personality nature of Geminis enables them to manage two things at once, while the rest of us, fumble around. Chat groups attract Geminis where they can create themselves a whole new on-line persona, which nobody will know about. While computers takes off in one direction and telecommunications in another, trust a Gemini to link both technologies together and keep him or herself up to speed.

While most people just want to be happy in their life, the Gemini wants balance, too. One Gemini who worked on computers all day made a point of sharing the fact that his fiancée wanted to install a personal computer at home. His response, "No way!"

Cancer the Crab — June 22 to July 23

Many individuals born under this sign, male or female, remarked how sensitivity was one of their personality weaknesses. Their computer skills may be impeccable, but for some reason they feel shy about their abilities. It's the people, not computers that attracts them to technology. Training is one area in which they can excel in readily and enjoy. Some Cancerians are content to sit in front of a computer monitor for hours, creating new hardware and software. But they talk about relationships, like the loved ones in their lives, as if they've been together for the 100th incarnation. Spare time is best spent with people.

Perhaps badly burned by a personal relationship, only then will the Cancerian retreat into his shell and seek solace in front of a monitor. Even if they use the computer for research, the end all will be the relationships with others that they seek.

The Cancerian is a saver or hoarder, if you must say. The computer lover, who confided in keeping every single one of his 40 computers purchased over the past 25 years, was a Cancerian. The home is a sanctuary for the Cancer, with or without children, a place to retreat and relax.

A small home business appeals strongly to Cancer, keeping watch dog over the home front and distant from the calamity of the corporate rat race that they dislike so much. With a bit of encouragement, the Cancerian's creative side can really outshine others, too.

Leo the Lion — July 24 to August 22

Technology doesn't scare this astrological sign very much. These cats just have too much ego to be intimidated by a dumb box. Risk-takers, the Leo doesn't mind entering unknown territory and blaze the path for others to follow. It's a natural for the Leo to take over a company or build one up. He or she doesn't mind leading the group and they pretty much get passionately involved with computers.

Brash and brutally-honest, the Leo makes no bones that a career in computers means money and power. A few born under this sign were most reluctant in sharing their opinions on how big money was to be made with comments, like, "If I knew, I wouldn't tell you."

With the exception of a few Taurus respondents and Y2K consultants, the Leo was the sign that most likely declined to give to charities. Said one, "There's only one charity and that's me." Perhaps, the Leo was just more honest than the other signs.

Several individuals who shared a passion for MUDDing and chat groups turned out to be Leo. "When you're MUDDing," said one 21-year-old, "You get respect and you have power in the role that you play." Not surprising to note that she just didn't MUD, but often worked as a monitor for a MUD group.

For some silly reason, individuals born under this astrological sign were the most diligent in filling in the survey for the book or were willing to be interviewed.

Virgo the Virgin — August 23 to September 23

The right way. That's the only way for the Virgo. Don't kid yourself. These are the people who can find the flea on the elephant when nobody else will notice. A survey completed by a Virgo is a joy to review because often every question is answered precisely and concisely. At times, care is taken to even add comments by the questions. They will put their minds over-time to get the problem solved which inevitably leaves them mentally exhausted. When the Virgo doesn't promptly answer a question, he will ask you why first. Don't feel challenged by the Virgo's cross-examination, they're just out to get the facts.

When it comes to computers, the Virgo will tell you that problem solving is what turns them on. They work well in a supporting role within an organization. It's not their style to be up front and center.

When it comes to finding a mate, the Virgo (both male and female) can be in a quandary. If they can't find someone who can live up to their expectations, they'd rather go through life solo. But if they do find someone to love, they can make great partners, even if they need to compromise along the way.

Libra the Scales — September 24 to October 23

SOAG is a Libra, a bright cherub child oozing with charm. Most of the time, he can be the sweetest and best-behaved kid you've ever seen, going on 40 years, instead of 8. The next moment, he's every parent's worst nightmare, throwing a tantrum from his room, smashing glasses against the door, peeing on the floor and gouging holes in the wall. With computers, one moment, he wants to be programming as soon as he can read and write properly and grow up to be a computer geek 'cos computers are cool'. The next moment, he wants nothing to do with computers because they don't do what he wants them to do.

With the affairs of the heart, he's madly in love with Cindy S. and saving all those rings from the dentist's office to give to her when she's ready to marry him. The next moment, he rationalizes that maybe she won't marry him, so there's always Susannah or Ashley or even, Chantal from grade 1 to go out with. He wants kids, enough to fill a van with; but some days, he says that he just wants to live alone in a big house by himself for some peace and quiet. Are we talking about a Libra or what? Could this be the same person?

If you can understand the Libra's personality that can swing from one extreme to the next, then you can understand why so many extroverted Libras chat on-line. They have a ton of friends around them and enough dates to keep them busy every Saturday night, but still, at the end of the day, they insist on logging on to see what they've been missing. They can be lazy when inclined to, but if a Libra has made up his or her mind to develop this software package and succeed, watch out because nothing can stop him or her.

SCORPIO THE SCORPION — OCTOBER 24 TO NOVEMBER 22

Outwardly laid-back, with intense eyes and a paralyzing gaze, the Scorpio can speak in a very slow and soothing manner. The Leo may be passionate, but the intensity of the Scorpio exceeds the Fahrenheit scale. When a Scorpio gets involved with computers, we're not talking about lip service treatment of technology. "It's not enough for me to know there's a computer sitting on my desk. I want to know how those electrons move through the circuits, how they make an image on the computer monitor," says one Scorpio. Learning about one more operating system is always on the back of his mind.

When it comes to starting a computer game, the Scorpio will want to master it to the nth degree. That means reaching the highest level and possibly at one stretch.

Many a Scorpio said that they like to withdraw from the rest of the world, whether that be at home or in front of a computer monitor. When it came to this survey, there were a handful of suspicious Scorpios who refused to answer all the questions, as privacy is something many revered. Scorpios don't like doing a job half-assed, so a computer obsession could shut out those who are closest to them.

If there's a mystery to follow, the Scorpio will be attracted to it. Many Scorpios told me how they spent countless hours in chat groups, with no intentions of revealing their true selves on cyberspace. They come to lurk and to study why people behave the way they do.

Scorpios have high ideals on what life is about, and the way computers should work. This was the astrological sign reported in this survey to be most likely to be married with children, and very willing to work hard to accomplish what they're striving for. Bill Gates, born on October 28, 1955, comes under this sign.

Saggitarius the Archer — November 23 to December 21

Sagittarians are often adventuresome, gregarious and hard to pin down. If you ever go out for lunch with a Sagittarius and they've run into somebody they know by first name, please excuse them for a moment. They're apt to holler half way across the room and tease the other guy why he hasn't asked them out for lunch yet. Better still, they'll get up and walk across the room. Sagittarians don't like to sit still. They're always in constant commotion. If you're doing business with one, be prepared to hit the greens with one or walk swiftly besides them. If you do need to get a hold of one, try their cell phone first.

There's something child-like about Sagittarius, who keeps young by experimenting with new things, going new places or trying out new machines. Ask them about what they do for a living, a likely response may be, "Come on, take a guess!" They thrive on change and challenge, two needs that the computer will give them, along with freedom, assuming they own a laptop. Seriously, the computer may be a tool for them to get their job done, but there's much glee to be gained from playing on the computer, too. So when one computer system isn't working out, there's always another one to try.

Settling down is sometimes problematic, as one Sagittarius told me, "If I think about something too long, I never get it done." If somebody was having fun with the survey, it was the Sagittarian who quite often gave some off the wall answers. Two very famous Saggitarians in computers were Ada Byron Lovelace, born December 12, 1815 and Dr. Grace Murray Hopper, born December 9, 1906.

Capricorn the Goat — December 22 to January 20

Ever try to rush a Capricorn? Forget it. These sure-footed goats move at a pace of their own. They know what they want. They are not slow, nor stubborn. They just know the meaning of the word perseverance.

They're practical people who can be ambitious, too. Computers are a practical tool to have around, and possibly the means with which Capricorns can get what they want – to get to the top of that mountain. They're not snobby people, just selective. If the executive suite within a company is what they're looking for, they're not willing to quit and find another job, they'll sit and wait. Eventually, that long-awaited promotion will fall into their laps. If sacrificing evenings and weekends for completing a computer course will make them more money than they are earning, they'll gladly do it.

When asked about success, the ideal Capricorn's formula would be doing nothing and getting paid for it. Management doesn't seem to be bad, now does it? Just watch him or her go.

AQUARIUS THE WATER BEARER — JANUARY 21 TO FEBRUARY 19

She has these awesome large brown eyes with a far off look to them, as if she could be in a trance. The DOAG is no different than others born under Aquarius. She talks about her friends, as if they are demi-gods and acceptance amongst her peers, though not the end and be all is first and foremost on her mind. She appears calm, cool and collected, in the midst of a crowd, but underneath, her mind is a cesspool of information, de-coding and processing it all. Then she speaks, as if she is blessed with some supernatural powers with statements that sends you on a tangent. "Computers are fine", she says, as she manipulates the keyboard and mouse, as if it's putty in her hands. But the real action in for this tomorrow child's, is going to be working with children because adults are just frightfully stupid to be around. DOAG may be no different than other Aquarius men and women I interviewed. They just love children.

They say that the Aquarian mind is always one step ahead of everybody else's. That their vision of life is so far ahead that it would take years to catch up to them. A Californian Mac evangelist I received a survey from was an Aquarian to the "T", citing the spiritual connectivity of the computer and the Internet as why she liked computers, how she could keep in touch with her friends, adored the color purple and New Age music. Her view of computers was a philosophical one, while other respondents were not as deep.

But, by far, perhaps, her enlightened viewpoint about the Macintosh computer says it all. Computers tomorrow will be easier and more intuitive to use, and Aquarians already know that the Internet is where they want to be.

Pisces the Fish — February 20 to March 20

"Think like a fish," says my Pisces friend, "We don't want to stir up a lot of conflict. Sometimes we say 'yes' to your face, but then don't do anything about it." If there's troubled waters, the Pisces is apt to swim away.

Pisces are creative, intuitive, sensitive and sometimes, a bit wishy-washy. While some see computer programming as a science, the Pisces sees it as an art form. When the Aries or Taurus programmer is enraged at what the computer isn't doing for them, they don't get hot under the collar. Instead, the Pisces just sits back, contemplates and then tries another strategy.

While the roaring Leo, ambitious Capricorn, or enthusiastic Aries wants to be head of the corporation, the Pisces may try but experience only a varying degree of success. Steven Jobs, founder of Apple Computer was born on February 24, 1955. The Pisces are great at helping others. It was one Piscean programmer through his expertise helped create four *Silicon Cowtown* millionaires.

Several Pisces worked alone, away from office distractions and on their own terms. When it came to extra-curricular activities, water sports or travel to tropical climates with beaches and sand were definitely on their agenda.

LEVEL 19

REVENGE, INDICTMENT AND BLACK WIDOWS

In the mid-1970's, personal computers invaded the home, with names like the Commodore VIC - 20, the Radio Shack TRS-Model 16, the Altair 8080, and the Timex Sinclair, another console computer toy, like the Radio Shack color computers. Apple computers went up for sale in 1977. Barbara Henderson of Santa Marla, California wrote an article entitled *"Computer Widow"*, published January 1977 in the now defunct *Kilobaud* magazine, pleading other Central Californian wives to band together and plot rabid acts of avenge. By 1980, over one million computers were in use in the United States. The computer geek had landed. And the rest is history.

> *"I've left my wife for a computer. At least, that's what she thinks. I'm in the den every day and most weekends clacking away, tinkering, moving files, downloading new Internet trash to clog up my ever-shrinking hard disk, while she sits in the living room, all alone, with no one to talk to, no one to share her day with. At least, that's what she thinks, and says, repeatedly. And, by jingo, she's right. My poor dear wife is a COMPUTER WIDOW...*
>
> *I can't help it. I'm hooked. I can't leave it alone. There's always more to discover, more to learn. It's true. I'm a COMPUTER JUNKIE. I do it for her, for us, for my students who I need to teach Introduction to Computer Hardware and Software...*
>
> *I have a hardware manual next to my bed for easy reading that is as thick as the Old and New Testament combined, and twice as cryptic.*

Beside it is the Whole Internet Guide, a book on creating Web Pages with HTML, a stack of software manuals, Bill Gate's new book on the future, and two new computer magazines...

My wife wants to talk but we don't understand each other. I tell her that I zipped files for seven hours to free up 20 megs on the hard disk... and she doesn't ask how, what or where. She tells me about the latest findings in estrogen therapy... I'm wondering if I should clear the cache in Netscape. This causes me to miss the vital part of her story that results in her rolling over in bed and turning out the lights.

Sunday night, during the East Coast storm of the century, she nagged at me to call my mother. I intended to, just as soon as I installed the 32-bit version of Paint Shop Pro and reviewed my 2,430 pieces of clip art. When I had finished at 1:00 a.m., it was too early to call, so I went back to sleep.

Monday morning, my wife woke up at 4:30 a.m. to call my mother. They spoke for an hour and she kept all the lights on, as I pretended to snooze. Her conversation ended with our rift surfacing like Moby Dick smashing the Pequod when she said to my mother, "Why don't you fly out and visit? Then I'll have someone to talk to." With that, she hung up the phone - didn't even hand it to me to say Hello. I knew then that I was in the doghouse. I wonder if I can run an Ethernet cable out there?"

A true confession from one indicted for computer addiction was posted on the Internet at http//:cris.com/~stangel/1-11-96.html, but nowhere to be found was his e-mail address.

"One woman was so teed off at her husband for spending time on those newsgroups. She wanted to install an Internet filter without her husband knowing it. We told her that she needed a marriage counselor, not an Internet filter. Anyways, we mailed the Internet filter to her neighbor's house and her neighbor installed it for her. Later, this husband called the Internet service provider up and complained that they screwed up his connection."
29 year-old software programmer

For those who feel humiliated, and dumped for a computer, Japanese computer widows and widowers have an option. Retribution specialists, who see themselves as doing a community service for keeping the murder rate down, are available for hire. Charging anywhere from $500 to $100,000; and calling themselves *shiokinin*, such modern-day *samurai* work in secrecy only identified on their business card by a name and cell phone number. Working within the confines of the law, most requests are turned down because they are too unsavory to conduct to get back at an ex-lover, ex-spouse, ex-boss or ex-business partner.

> *"Well, I tried sexy underclothes. He asked me to follow him into the bedroom because he wanted to show me something. I thought I had won. It turned out he wanted to show me something and he wanted me to watch. It gives a whole new meaning to the word voyeur.*
>
> *For my birthday, he promised we'd have a date. He bought me RAM and we spend the evening installing it and seeing if it would fix the computer freezes. Do they make RAM to install in husbands?"*
> Computer widow, 20 years married, but still looking for Mr. Right

Few computer widows and widowers I interviewed did anything to even the score with their spouses. Although here's a few ideas, computer widows and widowers have thought of – spill pop on the keyboard, put a magnet in the disk drive, give it a virus, let a child loose on the computer and quit paying the electric bills. We thought the last time the GEEK was out of town, that we would sell off his office computers and re-place them with Etch-A-Sketch. But considering how his office computers naturally crashed during his last business trip, we thought that he had suffered enough.

One geek girl was reportedly embarrassed by one of her husband's shenanigans. He had installed on her computer a continuous banner crossing the monitor that read, "I want you. I need your hot bod now. You're so sexy, Laura." She discovered the banner while she was accessing some information for a client who was looking over her shoulders.

In the early days, the GEEK only had one computer at home and worked it out with industrial strength vigor. Eventually, his under-rated joy box would pass out and require time at the local computer repair shop. Usually, the ordeal would take two weeks. The computer repair people would call when it was fixed, but I never was able to bring myself to tell the GEEK, exactly when the computer was fixed. When the GEEK hasn't been working on the computer for two weeks, he's almost ready to re-join the human race; after four weeks of computer withdrawal, he's almost normal. But after two incidents, when it took the GEEK three to four weeks to get his computer back from the repair shop, he suspected some wrong doings. Immediately, he rectified the situation by purchasing another computer.

The GEEK is lucky to live in *Silicon Cowtown*, where the air here is dry. I understand in Hawaii and Florida, ants in keyboards are no laughing matter. Avengers could seek to smear honey on the bottom of a keyboard to create or aggravate the situation. Because once you have ants in your keyboard, you've got a pretty itchy problem. You better not be laughing because somebody on that listserv I used to be on, was frantic for a solution to this problem. And if you do get ants in your keyboard, as I recall, your options are to freeze the keyboard and kill off the bugs, suck them off with a vacuum or put up a sweet placebo nearby to encourage them to shift their living quarters.

> *"I go to bed without him. I wake him up without him. Then I take the car in the morning without telling him. That pisses him off. But sometimes, he doesn't even notice it, so it only ticks him off."*
> 37 year-old computer widow

> *"When we first got the computer, my husband was such a bad boy. He got on it. He typed the word 'sex' for a search on the Internet. The computer crashed. It's 2 o'clock in the morning. My husband wakes me up and is totally scared. We only had the computer for six hours."*
> 40-ish computer widow

"After he's called down for dinner, for every minute she has to wait, his wife charges him a dollar a minute."
40 year-old computer user on another couple's computer usage management strategy

Angie's Complaint Corner – *When the Computer Takes Over*, is an article that first appeared on a website and is being re-printed in part with permission by author Angie Rothery, an British–based computer widow. Her suggestions may be invaluable for prospective computer widows and widowers.

Never complain when your husband/boy friend spends hours on end at the computer.

1. Not even when you have to give at least an hour's notice to do the shopping.
2. Not even when you are tearing your hair out because the kids are running riot, the phone is ringing, somebody is knocking the door and you are trying to make the dinner.
3. Not even when you are decorating and four hands would be better than two.
4. Not even when you are washing the car and he gets dirty.

After a while, you get to recognize your husband more by the back of his head than the front. You can get quite used to having a conversation with the back of someone's head. You could also practice this when they are out working by getting a large football and painting it in the color of hubby's hair. Just like the real thing, if you put it on his favorite chair.

You only know that he is still alive by the confirmation that the coffee you made an hour ago has been consumed and grunt would suggest another is required.

Don't get too alarmed or excited when he moves, he is only going to get up to go to the toilet.

Don't get over excited when he crawls into bed beside you at 3 o'clock in the morning. He's got to get up for work in five hours and he's cold…

A great way to get 10 minutes conversation from him is to polish his beloved desk (while he is at work) and put all his important papers away. It will be the first thing he'll notice on arrival at home and will spend at least ten minutes moaning about it. Then you can sit back and watch him find it all and put it back into the place again.

Always be wary when he wants to extend his desk space by six inches. Turn your back for an hour while decorating and you will find the computer area spreading half way across the lounge area.

Be prepared to spend at least 90 minutes in B&Q while he picks out a set of drawers in which to store his endless stream of computer bits and pieces. Would he do that while you were choosing wallpaper?

Just count to ten and scream silently when he moans about the electricity bill. I often wonder if he takes into consideration the 14 plugs under the computer desk.

Notice that he will never moan about the BT phone bill, even a causal glance at the itemized list will show the Demon ISP number listed 9 times out of 10. God help the teenagers (mainly Samantha) if they pick up an extension phone to make a call while he is "surfing".

Always remember that if you ask him anything, the answer will more often than not arrive half an hour later when you are least expecting it and you have forgotten the question.

If you are bored in any spare time that you get, you could always try reading one of his many computer weeklies that he eagerly collects. Make sure that the news agents don't mess up one week or he will moan constantly until the missing number 14 book turns up.

Don't be fooled into thinking that he's got all he wants. When after a trip to Curry's and scores of boxes later, he unpacks the computer and set it up, you think that is it. Wrong, months later and he is still adding to it, i.e. another modem (separate this time), not one printer but two, scanner, joystick, desk lamp and even a fan for when things get too hot. A good investment is to buy him a paper shredder, the waste paper from notes and scrap printouts are great for the kid's rabbits…

By Angie Rothery

In May 1999, I lived out the ultimate computer geek's fantasy of smashing a computer for this book's front cover. A highly controlled environment was set up for the deed. The computer monitor and keyboard were rescued from the dumpster of a computer repair center. We were warned about the cathode ray tube of the computer monitor, which contains pressurized inert gases with potential to implode upon impact. In attempt to open up the computer monitor for inspection, the GEEK and Gerry sprung a leak in the tube and the gases hissed out.

I donned protective eyewear and rubber gloves and whacked the computer with a hammer to no avail. "How hard do I have hit this darned thing?" I wailed. Gerry who could not stand my feeble efforts shoved me aside and grabbed the sledgehammer, "You've got it hit hard, like this!" He smacked it once and nothing happened. Then he lunged at it with all his might. This time, the upper right hand corner of the monitor collapsed. Then I took another swipe at the monitor with the hammer. The glass in the upper left section cracked around the hammer's circular impact. Somewhat taken back, I whacked the monitor again and more glass shattered.

On further examination, we realized that we had killed a black and white monitor. Gerry carefully brushed his finger on the inside of the glass monitor to pick up a yellow powder, phosphorus He explained how only a single cathode ray came from the back of the computer would make its way across the screen to create the image that you view. In the event that a color monitor is involved, three rays would zap across the screen - one for yellow, one for red and one for blue. When mixed together in the right proportions, you can view any color of the rainbow. It took us over two hours to set up, bash and shoot the pictures for the back cover.

Afterwards, the first thing a friend asked me was, "Did you feel good when you smacked your computer?" Still, wired up, I replied, "Yeah, it feels good. It actually feels really good."

LEVEL 20

HOMO GEEK
THE NEXT GENERATION

"Why are houses only painted one or two colors? Why can't they be painted like rainbows? I'd like to walk into a house that looks like a comic book and you can change the comic on your house, whenever you want. I'd like to eat a bowl of jello and have it laugh at me, too. I don't want to walk. I want to get up and fly.

I want the robot to do all the housework for me, clean my room, pick up my clothes and mow the lawn. When I make big money, I'm going to have 200 robots work for me. They will walk over to the computer and the computer will tell the robots what to make. Robots can do anything. They can make sewing machines, other robots, cookies, just anything. I'm going to have robot kids because they're going to work for me."
7 year-old SOAG

"There will be clones around and they'll be killed for their organs. It will be kind of sad, that you wonder why they were born in the first place. So there's a person around who thinks he or she is kind of great, they'll just clone themselves and carry on. I'm not so sure things are going to be so great.

My fantasy would be in a room, where the walls and ceiling are filled with water and the ceiling is filled with water. When you look up from a soft bed, you could see all these fish swimming around you. Then when you want to feed your fish, you'd climb a ladder to the roof and feed them, or maybe even jump into the water and swim with them....

There will be more single mothers in the future and parents who really don't care about their kids. There will be all these lost children. Teaching will be a harder and harder thing to do, but what you got to do, is make teaching a game, so people don't even know that they are learning at all. I'm going to care for some of these lost children as a teacher, and care for them as much as I can. But I'm going to have kids of my own and their father better be real."
11 year-old DOAG

Homo Geek[1]— the homogenized geek, comprised of a little bit of everything.

Frank Ogden, is the Vancouver, B.C.-based pop futurist, who I met in 1987. Back then, he preached that information was power and the future was in the hands of the technical aristocrat. Educational credentials are to mean nothing and that, employers would hire individuals on the basis of their potential. He anticipated women to set up small businesses in droves, and entrepreneurs create a new economy by operating virtual corporations.

As I reviewed what the 426 survey respondents told me, I realized that the future Ogden described a decade earlier has arrived. The virtual corporations are thriving. People work from their homes or wherever they want to be, communicating via e-mail and the Internet, meeting face to face once or twice a year, at a trade show or convention. Countless computer programmers and IT professionals told me how what they learn about technology is self-taught by doing. Academic credentials were procured to appease employers. With rapid change, our lives and workplace are chaotic, a fertile breeding ground for creativity. Tomorrow's communication calls for sending holographic images with birthday cakes and for aromatherapy scents with virtual greeting cards.

In 1998, Dolly the first female cloned sheep and Cumulina the first cloned mouse, joined an elite club of designer animals, cloned from cells related to the reproduction. But in June 1999, the world heard of Fibro the mouse, cloned at the University of Hawaii from the skin cells of a male mouse's tail. Although not published in a scientific journal yet, it is believed that the Japanese have cloned a heifer from a calf's ear. Fibro's odds of survival was one out of 274 attempts, and now it's likely that human clones are just a matter of time.

So to end this book, which is an ongoing saga, I interviewed Ogden for what he sees ahead.

Q. "If we review the headlines in 1999, we read about the burgeoning growth of biotechnology and bio-engineering. We see that the coding of computer programs is shifting to the re-coding of DNA. Frank, is it obvious to you that the next Millenium is about biotechnology and bio-engineering?"

OGDEN: "Biotechnology is certainly an explosive field and certainly controversial. You haven't seen anything until you see someone with green hair and their hair is made of broccoli. That's right, broccoli grows as hair and you can eat it. Your body can create your own food. It's already happened where you transfer a plant gene into an animal gene or vice versa. In Alberta, there are thousands of acres of land growing rapeseed which contains the anti-freeze gene of the Atlantic flounder. In places with too short of a growing season, now you can grow this rapeseed plant which is resistant to the cold and land which wasn't being used for agriculture can now be used. Gene transfer is very common now. You can buy a tobacco plant that glows before it's being lit. They (scientists) have even transferred the gene from the glow in the firefly to the tobacco plant. That's moving from an animal into the plant. In the future, you may have a brother-in-law that's part giraffe. There's no limit, he could be one per cent giraffe and 99 per cent human or he could be 99 per cent giraffe and 1 per cent human."

Q. "How will the next generation be affected by these implications of bio-technology?"

OGDEN: "Biological coding, is just another program, it's like going from text to images. No different. They will be teaching DNA 101 to eighth school graders. You will see the rise of the bio-hackers, young kids playing in the basement with $50 worth of supplies, creating new life forms. Parents are always worried what their kids are doing on the streets at midnight, but at least you will know where these kids are... creating new life forms."

Q. "In what direction is the education system moving towards?"
OGDEN: "We are moving from a teaching environment to a learning environment. You don't need teachers. You need knowledge navigators... And all those kids diagnosed with attention deficit disorder and put on drugs. Well, in a few decades from now, you're going to see teachers and school boards being sued because there was nothing wrong with these kids because they are just bright. It will be like the sex abuse crimes from 20 and 30 years ago that you hear about in the papers. Well, this is what you will be reading about in the future because our school systems are failing."

Q. "What do you see booming in the near future?"
OGDEN: "You're going to see granny hackers. They may be widowed, but they've got the time and money to play around on the computer. Cybersex is going to be booming. A 71 year-old woman tried on the cyberglove and she liked it!"

Q. "What role will computers play in our lives?"
OGDEN: "Computers will be a lot like the electric motor. Most people have 15 to 20 motors in the house, but they won't even know that they are there. The same with computers. There will be computers that will turn on the water in your bath for you when you want and at the temperature it's been set for."

Q. "Scientists are already installing chips in their bodies. Where is this research going to lead us?"
OGDEN: "They will put chips in the brains of persons who have lost their limbs or suffer from any other disability. The brain gets used to the chip and then an artificial limb is installed and the person moves it without even thinking about it. They can put chips with a lens, one-half the width of a pin that can see color and transmit via radio. They can have that chip hooked up to your optical nerve and put in the kid when it's born, or even before it's born, when it's in the womb. Everything that that kid hears, sees, learns and does is recorded in that memory chip which is extracted when that kid dies. Then the memory chip is installed in the kid's clone and gives the clone the history of a lifetime. The clone will be smarter than the humans, because it will have two life times of memory."

Q. *"Do you think we'll see human clones?"*
OGDEN: "We're going to see human clones and it doesn't matter what the Royal Commission on New Reproductive Technologies has to say. Because somewhere else in the world, somebody's going to do it and there's nothing to stop them. Some country will want superior smarter people, probably homophrodites, devise a male and female in one. The homophrodites can't help but be smarter, because they have male and female in one. They can't help but be smarter, because both viewpoints and feelings built in, and they will be cloned. You have 3 million people of these superior people after 30 years on this planet, guess who's going to be in charge?"

Q. *"What will be life be like for us in the future?"*
OGDEN: "I think it's going to be benevolent times for those people who know. For the people who resist change, they're going to have a hard time. They're blocking out change."

Q. *"Do you see the United States the hub for all this progress?"*
OGDEN: "No, maybe Singapore, the United States is too large. Twenty-five years ago, the average Singaporean used to make one-fifth of the American wage per capita, now they make about 15 to 20 per cent more than the average Canadian. They are very well paid and you don't need vast acreages to develop this technology."

Q. *"What kind of lifestyle do you see for the future?"*
OGDEN: "There's going to be more varied lifestyle. There's going to be bigger economic differences between those who have and those who don't. We're approaching the end of the age of credentialism. Credentials don't mean anything. The Industrial Age extended our lifespan. I wouldn't rule immortality out yet, but I don't see it in the immediate future. We will be going through another transformation, some will be good and some will be bad. The average police force as we know them is at a disadvantage because they don't know what's going on."

> *"I strive for geekdom. I want the computer to be the extension of my brain. I know that's the next evolution. Homo geek."*
> 40 year-old computer consultant

Q. "Do you see man thinking with his computers?"
OGDEN: "Yes, the next thing is mind link. We have gone from wire to fiber optics and wireless communications. Beyond that, we will be able to link minds. Intuition will come with it. It's already happening."

Q. "Any advice for middle-aged persons wanting to live in the future?"
OGDEN: "Yes, go spend time with an eight year-old kid. Just because they are little people who don't have the press agent to let the world know what the world is going to be like, these are the new titans."

Q. "One last question, what will happen to today's computer programmers?"
OGDEN: "They will have to re-train."

> *"I started programming computers when I was 13 years old with those IBM old punch cards. The sense of mania wears off after a decade or so. I don't program for fun anymore. When I was a kid, I used to program, let's say do prime numbers. The goals increased. That attitude changed after university. Programming pushes you too hard. It's been turned into work. The thing that keeps me in front of the computer frankly is communicating with other people on the Internet."*
> 40 year-old engineer

Seventy-one year-old Japanese engineer Dr. Yoshiro Nakamats, holds over 3,000 patents and invented the computer floppy several decades ago. His attention is now directed on sex drives, not disk drives. His latest libido producer, is spray to fire up the groins of both men and women, stimulating the body to immediately release the sex hormone DHEA. Nakamats, who has gleefully tested the love potion on himself, hopes to rival Viagra in terms of sales.

> *"You see my two sons, those Net heads. How are they going to mate? Who will they send their sperm samples to on the Internet? Are they going to asking prospective mates if she has a great bod?"*
> 49 year-old computer widow

Epilogue

He says, "Who says I like computers? They are just easier to handle than my wife."

In July 1998, my husband went to work for six weeks in Indonesia. Immediately upon his arrival, his laptop computer made an unexpected gravitational descent and was dysfunctional for its tropical duration. The hope to learn C++ during the evenings proved futile. Instead of pounding the keys of a computer keyboard during his off-hours, he had to socialize with other expatriates, window shop, play tennis, swim, and sip his one cup of evening coffee very slowly. During his first week, he e-mailed me a note that he had finished buying gifts for family and friends and was bored after work.

Further e-mail discussions centered on the lifestyle of his room mate, a software programmer. It began with the rejection he felt when he prepared for "John", his infamous Greek salad – splashed with an olive oil and balsamic vinaigrette. "John" balked at such sophistication and resorted to Kraft dinner, hamburgers, and salads comprised of lettuce, artificial bacon bits and Kraft dressing. The GEEK or soon to be ex-GEEK was bewildered as why "John" was not interested in savoring some of the local cuisine, like nasi goreng and sate. Like Jane Goodall studying her chimpanzees, the GEEK noted how "John" entertained himself during the evenings, manipulating two laptops with limited human interface. The GEEK was turned off and shut out. He dared not ask the "John", if he could borrow one of the laptops.

When he arrived home in *Silicon Cowtown*, the GEEK volunteered to cut back on his recreational computer usage. In fact, he vowed to quit permanently.

I thought to myself, "Let's see how long this lasts." After all, I had seen him return from overseas assignments before and quickly return to his after hour computer thrills, when jet lag subsided. In disbelief, I observed how he actually did not touch a computer keyboard at home for two weeks. He returned to the keyboard during the evenings, but lacking the vigor he previously had been accustomed to.

Meanwhile at his downtown office, he discovered that his networked computers crashed, leading to more frustration than ever. It meant more trips to service repair centers over the next four weeks. Even to this day, the computers have never fully recovered from the system's crash and the scanner is still impotent.

For a three-month period, the GEEK went from viewing the computer monitor to the boob tube. After spending years and countless hours programming and learning Visual Basic, C, then C++ and HTML, he was bored with computers. They didn't do what he wanted them to do. He ranted that computer programming wasn't satisfying his urge to be creative.

Then we observed a new man emerge. Pay back. It began with the purchase of a trendy leather jacket at an after Boxing Day sale. Then his interest shifted from computer stores to hardware stores, drooling over table saws, routers, industrial vacuum cleaners, and other mechanical parts. Instead of sleeping in on Saturday mornings, he now rises early to view his favorite home improvement show. His visits to Revy and Totem have subsided from daily visits to weekly ones. In the three months that he's gone into woodworking, he's retro-fitted three desks, built two bookcases, two armoires, and a computer table (for *moi*).

While the GEEK has kept his word on divorcing himself from the computer, I confide on slipping over to the Dark Side. During the time I worked on this book, I actually woke up one morning with tingling sensation in my right hand, a feeling that freaked me out enough to get checked out by the family doctor. The diagnosis was *carpal tunnel syndrome*.

Finally, I figured out the problem. Since I had moved my computer from a table in the rumpus room to a closet in a spare basement room, the keyboard was at a level straining my wrist. I then placed the computer keyboard on an ironing board (pre-Geek's carpentry days). Within a week, the *carpal tunnel syndrome* disappeared.

Although our seven year-old son has expressed a strong interest in computers, his time is being better spent learning how to read and write first. Our 11 year-old daughter announced that she plans to take computer courses in junior high, although her preferred career vocation will be teaching.

Listening to everybody's comments about their computer experiences encouraged me to lose the intimidation I realized the computer was having on me. I soon taught myself to use some features from Microsoft Word without consulting a manual. I even showed the GEEK a trick I learned, (which made me very proud). It seems that our household roles have changed. I'm geekier than I once thought. As for the ex-GEEK, he's "normal" again and is mildly receptive to signing up for ballroom dance classes this fall.

Working on *Revenge of the Computer Widow* was a very intriguing project. I hope that you will benefit from the insights presented. There are no conclusions. Technology is just changing too rapidly. Should you have further experiences to share, please e-mail me at platypus@cadvision.com. I will be publishing this new information in subsequent editions of this book. Thank you for your interest.

INDEX

Abacus, 11

Anxiety, computer, 149–156

Association for Women in Engineering and Science, 91

Bartz, Carol, 52

Babbage, Charles, 11, 88

Baina, Papua New Guinea, 9, 10, 13, 14

Beal, Vangie, 167

Benchmark Technologies, 93

Berners-Lee, Tim, 211

Brown, Dave, 68, 69

Borg, Anita, 91

Bouchard, Micheline, 93

Calgary, The City of, a place to live, 14–19

Campbell, Bruce, 47, 48

Career, Information Technology, 63–76
    Computer programmers, 63–76
    Growth of IT jobs between 1989–1998, 2, 64
    How computer people work, 72–73
    Mid-life career switching, 67–69
    On-line job hunting, 64, 76
    Overview of the IT profession, 63–65
    Salary expectations, 69, 219, 218
    Work ethic of young techies, 65–66

Carnes, Kelly, 94

Chat groups, 131–138
    Experiences, 131–138
    Why people like chat groups, 131–132

Chocolate Preference over computers and sex, 33

Clarke, Edith, 88

COBOL, a programming language, 90, 205, 223

Computer chip, 10

Computer security, 44, 125–127

Computers and Survey Respondents, 23–62
  Computers per household, 41
  Eating in front of computers, 38
  Keyboard commands vs. mouse, 37
  Location at home, 41
  Preference over sex and chocolate, 33
  Preference over socialization, 36
  Shopping for computers, 39, 40
  Sleeping with computers, 42
  Taking laptops to bed, 43
  Time spent on computers after 5 p.m., 35
Computer Games, 163–168
  DOOM, 163
  Experiences of computer users, 163–168
  MUDding, 167, 168
  Reasons to play, 164
Computer Groups, 97–108
  Commodore comrades, 104, 105
  Linux, 98, 101, 102
  Mac, 105–107
  Microsoft, 102
  OS/2, 107
  UNIX, 107
Computer history, 11–13, 203–210

Computer intelligence, 157–161
  Children and computers, 158–160
  Developing computer skills, 157–161
  Impact of music, 161
Computer humor, 109–116
  Cars and computers, 112, 113
  Jokes, 97, 102, 103, 105–116
  Murphy's Computer Laws, 156
  Programmer's guide, 105–110
Computer phobia, 149–156
  Coping mechanisms, 151–154
Computer usage and astrology, 169–178
Computer viruses, 125, 127
Computer widow(er)s, 179–185
  Advice for Computer widow(er)s, 183–184
  Coping mechanisms, 180–184
  Experiences, 179–185
  Revenge, 182–184
Cyber Affairs, 131–141
Disneyland, 20
Dyson, Esther, 87, 93
E-mail etiquette, 127–129
Emoticons, 128
Employment, 2, 18, 19, 30
ENIAC computer, 11, 89, 90, 206
  Jobs of information technology professionals, 30
Engineers, definition, 22

INDEX

ERP, Enterprise Resource Planning, 68, 212, 225

Ethernet technology, 13, 208, 225

Etch-A-Sketch, 114, 115, 122

Fisher, Anne, 67

Flaming, 130

FORTRAN, a programming language, 12, 150, 206, 225

Future of Technology beyond the Millenium, 187–192

Garnett, Katrina, 5, 95

Geek, definition, 77–85
    Flophouses as a place to live, 20, 21

Geek Squad, 78, 79

Glasgow, Janice, 95

Granville, Evelyn Boyd, 90

Greenizan, Kim, 44

Hanna, Kristine, 95

Hopper, Grace, 86, 89

Hot mail, 129

Intel Corp., 12

Internet, 123, 124
    Filters, 180
    History, 123, 124
    Impact on relationships, 123–148
    Usage, 124

Java, a computer language, 12, 211

Jobs, Steve, 178, 209

Klawe, Maria, 94

Kleiman, Kathryn, 89

Listservs, 129, 130

Local Area Network, 13

Lovelace, Ada Augusta, 88

Mainframe computer, 12, 13

Marimba, Inc., 92

Mackay-Lassonde, Claudette, 93

Metcalfe, Robert, 208, 225

Modem, 228

Nerd, definition, 77

Ogden, Frank, 56, 187–192

Olson, Kenneth, 13

On-line relationships, 131–141
    Advice for dating, 139–141
    Cautionary measures, 131–141
    Dating experiences, 131–141

Onward Computers, 93

Operating system, 11

Pedophile, 125

Pentium, 10, 212

Personal computers, 13

Personnel Systems, 69, 217

Peters, Harvey, 68, 71

Plant, Sadie, 90

Polese, Kim, 92

Pornography
    In the workplace, 75
    On the Internet, 143, 144, 148

Profile of survey respondents, 21–62
   Age and marital status, 25
   Automobile ownership, 48, 49
   Choice to take computers on holidays, 36, 37
   Commuting to work, 48
   Frequency of pierced body parts, 56
   Frequency of tattoos, 56
   Home ownership, 48
   Personal shopping habits, 55
   Personality descriptions, 27–29
   Pet ownership, 59
   Preference for coffee, 50
   Preference for color, 54
   Preference for music, 58
   Preference for snack foods, 53
   Preference for soft drinks, 49, 50
   Preference for take-out foods, 52
   Recreational activities, 60
   Spending lottery money, 40
   Vegetariansm, 51
Radio Shack, 1, 150
Revolve Technologies, 92
Romance and computer users, 117–122
Dating computer geeks, 120, 121
Rothery, Angie, 183–184
Sex, 33–35
   Preference of sex over computers and chocolate, 33, 34
   Thoughts of sex while working on a computer, 33, 34

Shiokinin, 181
Slide Rule, 11, 149
Smed International, 18
Smart Technologies, 67, 93
Software Human Resources Council, 160
Spam – unsolicited e-mail, 143, 144
Statistics Canada Labor Force Up-Date, 2
Stephens, Robert, 78, 79
Women and Computers, 87–96
Young, Kimberly S., 144

BIBLIOGRAPHY

Berger, Jennifer "Geeks in the Hood" HUES on-line www.hues.net/docs/911article/html

Black, Shannon "Smart Babies – Software for toddlers may inhibit development, experts warn" *Calgary Herald*, August 27, 1998

Blakeslee, Sandra "Intuition, language keys to helping brain solve math equations:" *The Globe and Mail*, May 25, 1999

Boulton, Scott "Beware the Mid-life Career Change" letter to the editor *Workplace Today*, May 1999 p. 5

Brethour, Patrick "Internet tops education as reason to buy PC: survey" *The Globe and Mail*, March 16, 1998, p. B9

"Happy chocolate lovers live longer" *Calgary Herald*, Dec. 18, 1998, p. A17

Canadian Council of Grocery Distributors and Food Marketing Institute *"1997 State of the Industry Report – a CCGD/FMI comparative study of the food industry in Canada and the United States"* 1997

Carter, Chelsea "So you want to be a world leader? Consider running Web sites instead." *The Globe and Mail*, March 18, 1999

Chase, Lorne "bits and bytes – Melissa may be history, but lots of other viruses infect cyberspace" *htc- Canada's HiTech Career Journal*, May 1999 p. 3

Coldman, Corey "Headquarters head for open spaces" *The Globe and Mail*, November 2, 1998 Report on Business, p. B1 & B3

Cougar, J.D and McFadden, F.R. *"First course in data processing with BASIC"* John Wiley & Sons 1981

De Lisser, Eleena & Morse, Dan "More men work at home than women: U.S. studies" *The Globe and Mail*, May 19, 1999

Dempster, Lisa "No child is safe, not even a baby" Special Report on Child Pornography *Calgary Herald*, January 31, 1999 p. A4

Dorr, Doug *"Ten Symptoms of Power problems – And How to Solve Them"* published by Best Power Technology Inc.

Dubowski, Stefan "Linux opens windows of opportunity" *The Globe and Mail*, May 27, 1999

Evans, Mark "Net 'playpen' rattles Web spinner" *The Globe and Mail*,

p. T1-2, May 20, 1999

Evans, Mark "High-tech sector expected to add 30,000 jobs in two years" *The Globe and Mail*, Feb. 10, 1999 p. B8

Exner, Raquel "Beware of e-mail faux pas" *Calgary Herald*, February 27, 1999 p. K1

Ferguson, Ted "Revenge of the Pink Lady" *The Globe and Mail*, January 9, 1999 p. D4

Fisher, Anne "Readers Weigh in on Virtual Work and School" *Fortune* June 21, 1999 p. 200

Fisher, Mike "Get wired and travel the world" *Calgary Herald*, January 23, 1999 P. H1

Goodman, Linda *"Sun Signs"* Bantam Books 1968

Hamilton, Tyler "Tech shortage hurts firms" *The Globe and Mail*, January 19, 1999

Hofstadter, Douglas "Of machines and men, what next?" *The Globe and Mail*, May 29, 1999 p. D5

Holmes, Ted "Using email as a business tool" *Business Dynamics*, October 1998 p. 16-17

Imperato, Gina "Flight of the Nerd" *Fast Company* issue 6 p. 42

Laurence, Charles "Manners make the Difference" first appeared in *The Telegraph*, Silicon Valley, California, re-printed The *Calgary Herald*, July 5, 1998

Lazarus, Eve "Getting Girls into the game" *The Globe and Mail*, December 10, 1998

LeBlanc, Alfred "Pair swims against brain-drain tide" *The Globe and Mail* Enterprise section May 18, 1999

Lee, Jenny "A clean machine runs better" *The Calgary Herald*, January 14, 1998

Little, Bruce "Job bonanza for those who know what works inside the magic box" *The Globe and Mail*, May 31, 1999 p. A2

McNaughton, Derek "Child Pornography" Special Report *Calgary Herald*, Jan. 31, 1999 P. A4

Menzies, Peter "Calgary rising" *The Globe and Mail*, January 16, 1999 p. D10

Meyerson, Bruce "FBI probes source of computer bug" *Calgary Herald*, June 12, 1999 p. E9

Nolen, Stephanie "Mating Bytes" *The Globe and Mail*, February 11, 1999 P. A17

Nolen, Stephanie "The ascendence of the nerds: How 3 Web whizzes found wealth" *The Globe and Mail*, May 27, 1999 p. A1 & A6

Quinn, Michelle "3Com ads ignite controversy" *Calgary Herald*, April 19, 1999 p. E7

Research Digest, *The Globe and Mail*, May 27, 1999 p. D5

Riga, Andy "Game-makers say they're not to blame for violence" *Calgary Herald*, May 20, 1999 VS10

Roston, Margo and Prentice, Michael "$1M outfit sets Ottawa on its ear" *Calgary Herald*, April 8, 1999 p. A17

Roy, Piali "Fear of a black galaxy" *The Globe and Mail* Arts & Leisure May 19, 1999, P.C1

Server, Andrew "Revenge of the Preppies" *Fortune*, June 21, 1999 p. 112

Shaw, Andy "Subtle shifts indicate promise for women working in IT" *htc – Canada's Hi-Tech Career Journal* March 1999

Statistics Canada Census 1996

Stephens, Margaret and Treays, Rebecca *"Computer for Beginners"* Scholastic Inc.

Stueck, Wendy "Computer-crazy teen juggles business, studies" *The Globe and Mail*, April 19, 1999 p. B10

"Scientists clone first male mammal" *The Globe and Mail*, June 1, 1999, p. A9

Townsend, Peggy "Geek Life" *Santa Cruz Sentinel*, Dec. 29, 1996

Tuck, Simon "Techies who clink together, think together" *The Globe and Mail*, December 3, 1998, p. C11

Uhlig, Robert "Bill Gates becomes $100-billion man" *Calgary Herald*, April 8, 1999 P. C6

Vamos, Peter "PC wars erupt into free-for-all" *The Globe and Mail*, May 6, 1999 p. T1

Verhovek, Sam Howe "Ground-hugging jet-setter takes plane view toward living" *The Globe and Mail*, Jan. 9, 1999

Watson, David "Wizards turn mere mortals into programmers" *The Globe and Mail*, Feb. 4, 1999 P. D8

"It Grads Willing to Move to U.S., Survey Shows" *Workplace Today*, May 1999, p. 8

"Where will Canada Find Knowledge Workers" *Workplace Today*, March 1999, p. 24-25

Young, Kimberly *"Caught in the Net"* John Wiley & Sons, 1998

WEB SITES WORTH SEEING –

www.advancingwomen.com/networks/phtml

www.ai.mit.edu/people/ellens/Gender/ieee/netsrq.com/~dbois/computer.html

www.aimsedu.org/Math_History/Samples/ADA/ada.htm

www.awc.~hq.org/lovelace/1997.htm

www.chatham.edu/inftech/grace.htm

www.Cybergirl.com

Http://doc.ecn.purdue.edu/Escape/special/women/histore/wiehistm.htm/dock.edupurdue

www.geekfest.net/other/geekdefhtml

www.geek.org/

www.infotec.org/history A time line of Computer, Business and Association History

www.jupiter.guestworld.tripod.lycos.com/wgb/wgbview.dbm

www.norfolk.navy.mi//chips/grace_hopper/file2a.htm

www.pbs.org/internet/timeline

www.ruku.com/polese.html

www.salon.magazine.com/Sept97/21st/tech2970911.htm

APPENDIX I

Computer History 101 Time-Line

Prior to
1800 BC Dust and pebble versions of the abacus were being used by the Greeks, Chinese and Romans.

1800 BC The Babylonians were deriving empirical mathematical formulae.

1300 AD The Chinese recorded the use of the abacus in the Yuan Dynasty.

1457 The Gutenberg printing press was invented.

1622 Mathematicians discovered the logarithmic principles, which enabled slide rules to multiply and divide by addition and subtraction. William Oughtred in England invented the slide rule. The first prototypes were circular shaped before the classical linear models were devised, and became the common calculating instrument of the 17th Century.

1623 Germany's Wilhelm Schickard produced the first adding machine.

1642 France's Blaise Pascal invented the world's first numerical calculating machine. These mechanical calculators with guts of steel used rotating gears, drums and keys that moved proportionately to the numbers being manipulated.

1833 England's Charles Babbage designed an analytical machine that followed instructions from keypunched cards, and in hindsight is recognized to be the world's first computer.

1870's	Frank Baldwin and later Willgodt Oldhner developed calculating machines, utilizing moveable pinwheels. Baldwin's designs became the basis of design for Monroe calculators, which were used widely amongst accountants and scientists, until electronic calculators came of age.
1876	Alexander Graham Bell invented the telephone.
1886	The popular soft drink, Coca-Cola, was concocted and was served at restaurants.
1906	Kellogg's began producing crispy cornflakes.
1918	World War I ended.
1924	International Business Machines (IBM) changed its name from Computing- Tabulating-Recording Company.
1925	Massachusetts Institute of Technology produced the analog calculator.
1927	The cathode ray tube is invented. It provides the guts for computer monitors.
1936	Black and white television sets go up for sale.
1937	German engineer Konrad Zuse developed the first digital calculator in 1937, and later the programmable calculator in 1941.
1941	The world heard from the first electronic talking machine, the Voder. And Hewlett-Packard Co. was founded in America to make electronic equipment.
1943	The British designed a code-breaking computer, the Colossus.
1944	The Electronic Numerical Integrator Analyzer and Computer (ENIAC), a first-generation computer was built at the University of Pennsylvania.
1945	World War II ends.
1947	Bell Telephone Laboratories developed the transistor-liberating vacuum tubes from computers, for its circuit elements.
1951	In 1951, the UNIVAC or Universal Automatic Computer is released. Then IBM introduced a

commercial mainframe computer, the IBM 701 EDPM.

1953 Color television sets go on sale.

1954 IBM's John Backus created FORTRAN, the first successful "high level" language of its era. At the same time, Commodore is founded as a typewriter repair service company.

1956 Is this déjà vu? But in 1956, IBM settled a government antitrust suit, and began selling computers, in addition to leasing them out.

1957 Ken Olson founded Digital Equipment Corporation (DEC). Honeywell partnered with Raytheon and shipped out the Datamatic 1000.

1958 The first electronic computers were built in Japan by NEC and the laser was invented.

1959 Jack St. Claire Kilby at Texas Instruments invented the first semi-conductor computer chip – integrating transistors, resistors and capacitors.

1960 Common Business Oriented Language (COBOL) became official, while ALGOL, the first international algebraic language (developed in 1958) went into remission. COBOL is first used on the UNIVAC II and RCA 501, while Control Data Corporation delivered its first scientific computers, the CDC 1604. Removable magnetic disks for secondary data storage appeared, reducing dependence on magnetic tape.

1962 The Internet was conceived and the computer flirted with entertainment. Computer games become popular. Ken Iverson from Harvard University and IBM introduced A Programming Language (APL). And Ross Perot, fired up Electronic Data Systems (EDS) in Dallas, Texas.

1963 With the influx of computers on the marketplace, A Standard Code for Information Exchange (ASCII) is the first standard developed amongst the different brands of computers. Computer-aided design (CAD) emerged, along with the light pen, developed by Ivan Sutherland. Charles Tandy also purchased Radio Shack Corporation.

1964 Beginners All-purpose Symbolic Instruction Language (BASIC) was created by Tom Kurtz and John Kemeny. Rand Corporation released a graphic tablet, the precursor for the computer mouse. IBM coined the phrase "word processing", and introduced the world's first large scale, real-time, on-line reservation system for American Airlines and announced the IBM 360, which would generate over $100 billion in revenues over the next two decades.

The next generation of computers emerged with integrated circuits replacing individual transistors. Thousands of transistors could be fabricated on the surface of a silicon chip, on a size less than a quarter of an Aspirin. The first chips housed only a thousand components.

Computers became smaller, faster and more reliable. With the shift towards magnetic disks for data storage, users utilizing interactive operating systems could gain access to their data files.

1965 DEC's PDP-8 becomes the first true mini-computer.

1967 Swiss Niklaus Wirth developed PASCAL, another high-level programming language, while the first computer magazines were published.

1968 Gordon Moore and Robert Noyce co-founded Integrated Electronics (Intel) Corp., to release a year later the 1 KB RAM chip.

1969 Dennis Ritchie and Kenneth Thompson from Bell Labs developed the UNIX operating system, while Edson de Castro started Data General Corp. with the introduction of Nova, the first 16-bit minicomputer.

1970 Gilbert Hyatt filed the patent for the microprocessor, a single chip which integrated the circuits for a computer, after which Intel began manufacturing the 4004 microprocessor.

IBM introduced the 370/135 and 370/195 mainframe computers and floppy disks emerged. Then Intel developed the 8008 chip for Computer Terminal Corp. with 8-bit bus, 108 KHz, 3500 transistors and 16K bytes address space. Nolan Bushnells started Atari and shipped out PONG – the world's first commercial video game.

1969 Bill Gates and Paul Allen were de-bugging software for Computer Center Corporation, in exchange for free computer time. Xerox also opened the Palo Alto Research Center (PARC), in the heart of what becomes known as Silicon Valley. IBM shipped out its first System 370, a fourth generation computer that utilized Very Large Scale Integration (VLSI) technology with circuit densities approaching 100,000 components per chip and access time approaching one nanosecond. UNIX operating system became of age.

Xerox introduced its CF 16A. Two of Gates' contemporaries, Steve Wozniak and Bill Fernandez salvaged computer parts to build their first computer.

1972 The 5.25 inch floppy disk with a capacity for 360 k (bytes), arrived and C Programming language was introduced. Gates and Allen formed the Traf-O-Data Company, which developed an 8008-based system for recording highway traffic flow. From (PARC), Xerox unveiled the Alto workstation.

1973 Robert Metcalfe outlined in his Harvard University thesis, the basis for Ethernet technology, which enabled computers to communicate with each other within an organization. When networked together, the computers were part of a Local Area Network (LAN). As telecommunication companies built faster and larger networks, computers would then be able to communicate with each other in different cities, on a Wide Area Network (WAN). The acceleration in modem speeds, bandwidth capacity, advanced fiber optics and satellite technologies, pushed computers into the communication age of the 1990's.

1974 Intel introduced the 8080, an 8-bit microprocessor that will be used in several personal computers – 8-bit bus, 2 MHz processing speed, 6000 transistors and 64K bytes address space.

1975 The first computer store opened in Santa Monica, California and the first personal computer users group was formed. For $9000, you could buy the IBM 5100 educational computer that supported BASIC programs, 16KB Ram, tape storage, five inch screen and weighed a bulimic 55 pounds. MITS introduced the Altair personal computer, designed by Ed Roberts and Bill Yates. The kit cost $397 for a 256- byte computer. Bill Gates and Paul Allen co-founded Microsoft.

1977 Apple Computer was co-founded by Steve Jobs and Steve Wozniak. The Apple IIe were being sold. Oracle Corp. was founded.

1978 There was an explosion of personal computers. Commodore and Tandy jumped on the bandwagon, too, selling personal computers. Barbara Henderson of Santa Marla, California wrote an article entitled *Computer Widow*, published January 1977 in the now defunct Kilobaud magazine, pleading other Central Californian wives to band together and plot rabid acts of avenge. The first COMDEX trade show was held.

The 1970's saw the proliferation of workstations and software for applications like accounting, spreadsheets and word processing, database management, and networked operating systems. Computers moved from the realm of solving fancy scientific equations to solving everyday workplace woes. Much of the application software was being prepared for personal computers. VISICALC, a spreadsheet application concept emerged in 1978. Intel released the 8086 chip, which now had a 16-bit bus, 29,000 transistors and 1M bytes address space

1979 The Source and CompuServe Information Services went on-line.

1980 Over one million computers were in use in the United States. The disk-based operating system (DOS) is created by Tim Patterson. The computer geek has landed.

1981 The personal computer market was filled with the Commodore VIC – 20, the Radio Shack TRS-Model 16, the Altair 8080, the Timex Sinclair (another console computer toy, like the Radio Shack color monitors). James Clark founded Silicon Graphics and

Microsoft began work with Graphical User Interface (GUI) and IBM jumped to sell personal computers. The Osborne Computer Co. marketed the first self-contained computer (precursor for laptops), but goes under in two years.

"640,000 bytes of memory ought to be enough for anybody." Bill Gates, 1981

1982 Intel released the 80286 chip (16-bit bus, 134,000 transistors, 16M bytes address space for $360). Sun Microsystems is founded. Microsoft licensed operating system MS-DOS to microcomputer manufacturers. And three ex-Texas Instruments managers founded Compaq Computer, which produced portable computers that looked like electric sewing machines hacked into two parts.

1983 Mitch Kapor released LOTUS 1-2-3, which replaced VisiCalc as the spreadsheet software of choice for personal computers. At & T Labs developed C++ programming language. NEC announced the SX-1 and SX-2 supercomputers. There are now estimated to be over ten million computers in use in the United States. Apple has sold a million Apple II's. IBM and Micro-Soft began developing a new operating system known as 0S/2, which is widely used by financial institutions.

1984 Over two million Apple II's had been sold to-date. Steve Jobs delivered the Macintosh computer, with mouse and icon. The Tandy 1000 personal computer became the number 1 selling IBM-PC compatible computer in its first year.

1987 IBM shipped a million units of its PS/2 computers. Cray Research released the Cray 2S. ETA Systems launched the ETA-10 family of supercomputers. Sun Microsystems unveiled its first workstation based on a RISC microprocessor. Apple introduced Macintosh II. IBM introduced Systems Applications Architecture (SAA). Aldus released Pagemaker and desktop publishing was born. Texas Instruments introduced the first artificial intelligence microprocessor chip and Apple spun off a software application company named Claris.

1988 to 1991 The activity amongst computer software and hardware companies seemed pumped by steroids. DEC introduced the VAXstation 8000. Cray Research introduced the $20M supercomputer. IBM released a new mainframe computer operating system called MVS/ESA, announced its mid-range computers called AS/400 and ES/3090 S series mainframe computers. Motorola launched the 88000, a RISC microprocessor. Apollo, Ardent and Stellar revealed the first graphics supercomputers. NeXT, Inc. unveiled its workstations that utilized optical compact disks for storage. By now, the wimpy floppy 5.25 inch disks were being replaced by 3 inch hard diskettes that could hold 10 megabytes. The Compact Disk (CD) could hold 640 megabytes. Intel announced the 80486 chip, which combined the 386 and 387 math co-processor and cache and 1.2 million transistors. Hewlett-Packard introduced the DeskJet printers.

1989 Microsoft's sales hit U.S. $1 billion.

1990 There were 100 million computers in use world-wide, and 100,000 hosts on the Internet. High Definition Television (HDTV) emerged. Compaq released battery-powered notebook computers and 486K computers are introduced. Grid introduced a laptop computer with a touch sensitive pad that recognized hand writing. Microsoft introduced Windows 3.0. IBM released System 390 (code name Summit) as its mainframe computer for the 1990's. Apple introduced low-end computers to compete with others, The Classic, LC and IISI. Sun Sparc station 2 emerged. Most PC vendors have laptop computers for sale.

1991 The computer world experienced payback. Many major companies once invincible, experienced quarterly or full year losses, including Compaq, DEC, IBM, Lotus and Unisys. Linus Torvalds, a Finnish university student made available on the Internet, a Linux kernel. Tim Berners-Lee introduced the World Wide Web – www.

1992 Wang Laboratories filed for chapter 11 protection, while Hewlett-Packard shipped out the LaserJet4 printer with 600 dots per inch resolution. But amidst this calamity, Tim Berners-Lee working at CERN in

Switzerland, posted the computer code HTML, Hyper Text Markup Language (HTML) on a newsgroup. IBM announced the Thinkpad computer.

1993 Micro-soft unveiled Windows NT and Intel shipped the 60 MHz Pentium chip with 64-bit bus and 3.2 million transistors, while Apple shipped the Newton Message Pad – its first personal digital assistant. .Compaq released the Presario, a computer for the PC family. IBM launched workstations. Novell, a networked operating system transferred the UNIX trademark to X/Open. IBM announced OS/2 for Windows.

1995 Microsoft released Windows 95, to be followed later by newer versions. Microsoft became a player in the software and operating systems manufacturers with Sybase, and SQL server.

CompuServe, AOL and Prodigy began Internet access and domain registration is no longer free. Sun Microsystems released Java, a high-level object-oriented programming language that's akin to a wonder drug for getting computers from different operating systems to work together. The hype is on to learn HTML, the basis to design web pages which can be downloaded from the Internet.

1996 The world's record for sending a terabit (a trillion bits) was broken, through transmission over looped glass wire.

1998 The iMac computer sent the competition reeling by defying PC consumerism with choice in aesthetics. The iMac is sold in five mouthwatering colors – blueberry, tangerine, mandarin, lime and grape. Sales are good. Who knows what's next?

1999 It's the last year before the Millenium, and Peter de Jager, the Y2K soothsayer mellowed out half way through the year, confusing followers with his comment that the millenium bug might be under control. The bionic bod has arrived and researchers have installed chips in their brains. Companies offering Internet services entice customers with free computers. Naked ladies promoting 3Com's palm pilot gets inked in the press, sparking acrimonious debates as to what's going on in the minds of computer marketing executives. The wife of Michael Coupland (Corel Draw president in Ottawa a.k.a. Silicon Valley North), a Pamela Anderson look-a-like makes national news for her $1-million lithe leather body suit and gold-plated breastplate studded by a humungous diamond nipple.

Microsoft bashing has reached epidemic proportions, and users seek other options. Posted for free on the Internet, Linux is one option. Both Extensible Mark Up Language (XML) and PERL, another programming language, became visible during the late 1990's.

By the late 1990's, corporations are trying to dramatically change the way they are thinking and doing business. Corporations are wild about the installation of ERP's (Enterprise Resource Planning) systems, like Baan or SAP, systems that streamline the logistics of the organization, facilitate communication, enhance efficiency and maximize productivity. Perhaps, altruistic to think that collaborative workplace environments can be created, but some companies who have moved in this direction, vouch improved productivity and profitability.

The Internet is also setting the stage for another r e v o l u t i o n . E-commerce has become the latest buzz.

In May 1999, Intel Corp. announced the Pentium III rated at 550 megahertz, enough amphetamine to jolt any home computer innards. Still, that's not enough speed and power for real computer geeks who eye Sun SPARC 5 workstations for personal use. Seniors are flocking to computers in droves, and are identified by mercenaries as the next market to be exploited.

Appendix II

Revenge of the Computer Widow Survey Questions

The detailed on-line survey is posted at www.geekculture.com/computerwidow

For those of you who do not have Internet access, here's a summary of the list of questions, which were asked after basic information like name, telephone, age, astrological sign, job title, marital status and number of children.

1. What are your personality strengths and weaknesses?
2. What's your favorite computer joke?
3. Given the three options of sex, computers or chocolate, and access to any of the three, what would you prefer.
4. Why do you enjoy working and playing on your computer?
5. What's the number of hours do you spend on your computer beyond the normal 8:00 a.m. to 5:00 p.m. Monday to Friday work week?
6. Do you play computer games? If so, do you play standalone and/or inter-active computer games?
7. Do you belong to chat groups? What's your experience with them like?
8. Do you belong to any computer user groups and if so, which ones?
9. Have you turned down a social invitation to spend time on the computer?

10. Do you take your computer/laptop on your vacations?
11. What are you doing when you're waiting to download?
11. What are your hobbies and interests?
12. Do you take holidays? If yes, what would you do?
13. In what year did you first learn how to use a mouse?
14. When you use the computer, do you prefer to use the mouse or the keyboard commands?
15. How old were you when you first learned how to use a computer?
16. Do you have any formal computer training or education?
17. How many meals per week do you spend eating in front of the computer?
18. How many hours per week do you spend shopping for new software and hardware?
19. In addition to computers at home, do you own the following items: stereo, VCR, television, electronic organizer, digital camera, cell phone, Harley Davidson, walkman radio or cassette recorder or laptop computer.
20. If you won a few thousand dollars, assuming that you were debt-free and you had to spend the money, what would you spend the money on?
21. Do you consider yourself to be an introvert or extrovert or a bit of both personality-wise?
22. What's your pet peeves about computers or life in general?
23. Why do you think some people have computer phobia?
24. What special names do you or your colleagues call individuals who are computer-illiterate?
25. What's your definition of a computer geek?
26. Do you consider yourself to be a computer geek?
27. If people called you a computer geek, does this term bother you?
28. How many computers do you have at home?
29. Relative to your home, where are the computers located?

30. Do you keep your computers on or off? If on, why?
31. Have you ever brought a laptop computer into bed with you?
32. How many phone lines do you have in your house?
33. Do you ever think of sex, when you're working on the computer?
34. Do you have any pets at home? How many? What are their names?
35. Do you own or rent a house or apartment or condo?
36. What kind of car do you drive or own?
37. What mode of transport would you take to get to work?
38. What's your favorite soft drink?
39. What would you order if you went into a coffee house, like Star Bucks?
40. Are you vegetarian?
41. What's your favorite take-out meal?
42. What's your favorite snack food?
43. Do you buy your clothes at one particular store or shop all over?
44. If you were to go drinking with your friends, what would you order?
45. Do you have any pierced body parts? If yes, where?
46. What kind of music do you enjoy listening to the most?
47. Do you play any musical instruments? If so, which ones?
48. What kind of books do you like reading?
49. Are you a Star Trek fan?
50. What's your favorite television sitcom?
51. What's your definition of success in life?
52. For guys, what style of underwear do you prefer?
53. For guys, do you wear Speedo style swimsuits or swim trunks?
54. For guys, do you have in your possession ties with cartoon characters on them?

55. For gals, what material is your underwear made of (cotton, polyester or silk)?
56. For gals, do you wear one-piece or two-piece swimsuits?
57. Do you believe in God?
58. Do you give to charitable organizations?
59. If somebody told you that they wanted to make big money, what advice would you give them?
60. If somebody told you that they wanted to make big money in the computer/high-tech industry, what advice would you give them?
61. For single persons, how would you describe yourself to another prospective date?
62. For single persons, have you tried on-line dating and what has your experience been like.

Please add any comments, feedback or e-mail addresses of friends/colleagues who don't take themselves too seriously to help. Your time and interest is appreciated. Thank you.

Appendix III

Salary Survey

All annual salaries were picked off charts published by *The Globe and Mail* in their weekly "Tech Jobs" section. The source for such data is compiled by Ottawa-based Personnel Systems, a consulting company, which conducts an Internet-based polling of more than 220 high-tech companies in Canada, and comprising 330 different jobs. Each week, *The Globe and Mail* features salaries for three different positions. Generally speaking, contract employees earn 20 to 30 per cent more than staff, but do not receive company benefits. Rates for contract employees can range from $20 per hour to over $200 per hour. Computer systems trainers and junior positions are at the low end of the pay scale, while IT executive and management, Java and C++ developers, certain types of computer consultants, and SAP implementation specialists command the higher end of the pay scale.

April 15, 1999
Integrated circuit engineering manager	$98,000
Marketing manager	$90,000
Software consulting manager	$87,000

April 29, 1999
Database analyst	$67,000
System design engineer	$63,000
Wireless software engineer	$56,000

MAY 6, 1999
- Integrated circuit engineer $75,000
- Software consultant $66,000
- Network administrator $50,000

MAY 20, 1999
- Customization programmer $67,000
- Software developer $63,000
- Graphics designer $54,000

MAY 27, 1999
- Strategic Alliance Manager $117,000
- Software development manager $113,000
- Network manager $87,000

JUNE 3, 1999
- Network architect $81,000
- Technical recruiter $66,000
- Webmaster $56,000

APPENDIX IV

Glossary of Terms

Abacus — bead and wire contraption used for calculations that works by shuffling beads back and forth, invented centuries ago, but still in use in certain parts of the world.

Adobe — name of a contemporary graphics software company, renowned for its programs, some of which enables users to do mind-boggling things with scanned photos and images. With Photoshop, for instance, you can take apart the components of a photo and change its color or shape.

Algorithm — the mathematical means to solve a problem.

American Micro Devices (AMD) — name of computer company that manufactures computer chips for graphics computers.

Apple — name of a personal computer company in a class by itself, also produces the iMac.

Applications software — programs written to tell a computer to carry out certain tasks, eg. word processing, spreadsheet analysis or accounting.

Architecture — structure on how the hardware and software systems are set up and managed.

ASCII — A Standard Code for Information Exchange, developed in 1963 to standardize the various brands of computers.

ASDL	Asynchronous Digital Subscriber Loop – high speed telecommunications line
Assembler	a program that translates a low-level programming language into machine code.
Boolean logic	part of algebraic principles developed by Irishman George Boole in 1854. Eg. If A > B and B>C, then A >C.
Cyrix	name of company that makes computer chips for entry level computers, eg. Commodore.
BASIC	simple computer language, without many features - easy to learn.
Backup	all computer users should make an extra copy of the files that they are working on to protect themselves from accidental file corruption or deletion. This extra copy is called backup.
Baud	unit of data transmission speed via telephone lines equal to one bit per second.
BHI	three letter acronym which translates to Better Human Interface, the stuff that computer widows and widowers see lacking in their significant others.
BINAC	Binary Automatic Computer, the first computer to operate in real-time, developed during the late 1940's.
Bit	is a component of a number system; with respect to computers where a binary system applies, there are two bits, either zero or one. Data in a computer is stored in bits.
Byte	is equivalent to eight bits. Byte is the unit referencing data storage in personal computers. A kilo-byte is 1,000 bytes. A mega-byte is one million bytes. A giga-byte is one billion bytes.

GLOSSERY OF TERMS   223

Bubble jet print
: type of commonly-used affordable printer that commonly has a resolution of 720 lines per inch (horizontal) by 360 lines per inch (vertical). Some bubble jet printers can produce the higher resolution of laser printers (1200 dots per inch by 1200 dpi) with the installation of photo cartridges.

C
: general all-purpose programming language adopted by the technical environment

Cache
: for PC's, the higher the cache, the quicker a machine responds. Cache is used for temporary storage of what's happening on your computer's desktop. Typically, PC's can be installed with two levels of cache, the size varies depending on the machine. Level 1 cache can be as little as 32K and Level 2 cache can be as big as 512K (mid-1999). When you're working on the Internet and you want to free up your cache, you can shut down all those windows hiding behind toolbars.

CD
: Compact Disk. One CD is capable of storing up to 650 megabytes of data. Compared to magnetic data storage, CD's are supposed to have more integrity. However, you should not leave your CD's lying around on your desk because they could get scratched and collect dust. Dust inside a computer is not nice.

CD burner/writer
: a external or internal hardware device that enables you to store data on CD's. Web sites like www.tripod.com has a MP3 player which enables visitors who pay, the privilege of downloading music onto their PC and then burn it onto a CD.

CD disk drive speed
: the speed at which the disk drive reads data from the CD, typically rated in bytes per second. Can get CD disk drives reading up to 50 bytes per second (mid-1999).

Commodore	name associated with popular 64K personal computers that could programmed in BASIC and were produced during the 1970's. Many computer geeks began their careers on Commodore computers for its ease of use.
Compaq	name of a contemporary computer company that manufacturers personal computers
Computer crash	when you are loading or running a program and your computer doesn't respond to keyboard or mouse commands. Your option is to abort the program or in the worst case scenario, shut the computer down entirely and start it up again (re-boot it.)
	Mainframe systems often crash less frequently than Windows.
Compiler	for some languages like C, Java, Fortan, the programmer source code has to be put through the compiler to convert it to machine code i.e. binary code.
COBOL	Common Business Oriented Language for developing business applications, eg. accounting and business reports
Corel Draw	name of another popular contemporary graphics program where you can manipulate images to its fullest; changing color, proportion, its dimensions, layering, etc.
Corporate fog	when vendors floor users with literature filled with 15 character words when two letter words would do.
Corruption of files (PC)	for some strange reason, files have not been accessed appropriately and the data gets all garbled up. Could be caused by improperly shutting down the computer, conflict of peripherals on your system, bad software, computer virus and other things that turns the GEEK red in the face.

Glossery of Terms 225

CPU — central processing unit – the hardware and software components, which process the software instructions. Typically, only one instruction can be run at a time.

Dot matrix printer
— old-fashioned type of printer common about 10 to 20 years ago, characters comprised of little dots visible to the eye, not much in use anymore.

Database — set of information, which needs to be stored, retrieved, archived and up-dated on a regular basis, often relevant to the corporate or institutional work environment. Some computer programs are designed specifically to the management of databases.

DEC — Digital Equipment Corp., company founded in 1957 and is well known for its mainframe computers.

Dell — manufacturer of a brand name of PC.

Desktop — machines by which users can view the data in a graphical friendly interface, i.e. computer that sits on your desk

Desktop publishing
— the means on from a PC, by which text and images are integrated for publishing documents, i.e. newsletters, books and other promotional items. QuarkExpress is the name of the desktop publishing software used widely in the print industry.

Diskette — hard plastic 3.25 inch rectangular disks used to store software programs and data.

Digital Video Disk (DVD)
— hold up to 3 gigabytes of data, used primarily for video data. DVD burners to be introduced to the PC marketplace early 2000 and will enable users to make their own DVD's.

DOAG   Daughter Of A Geek.

Dumb terminal
               monitor and keyboard that's connected to a computer in another room, user may think that this terminal is doing everything he or she wants.

E-commerce   buzz word referring to transactions that occur on the Internet, whether it be business to business or business to consumer.

EIS   Executive Information System, that was a promising concept a decade ago with inter-active computer monitor screens.

ERP   Enterprise Resource Planning System – used to streamline the logistics of an organization, facilitate communication, enhance efficiency and maximize productivity.

Ethernet   technology developed by Robert Metcalfe in the 1970's which enabled computers to communicate with each other.

Fiber optics   technology referring to the means by which data can be transmitted between computers at the rate of 10 to 30 megabits per second.

Floppy   originally referred to the 5.25 inch flexible magnetic disks used to store data. PC's would access this data via a floppy disk drive. Today, PC's have floppy disk drives for the 3.25 hard diskettes.

FORTRAN   computer programming language developed in 1954 by John Backus at IBM, is used mainly for scientific and engineering applications.

GEEK   husband of the lady who wrote this book.

GUI   acronym for Graphical User Interface, links what you see on the computer monitor and how you react with it, eg. Windows is a GUI, and includes scroll bars, buttons, icons and other graphical images.

GLOSSERY OF TERMS 227

Hacker	somebody who illegally accesses information on another person's computer, whether it be a mainframe or PC system and whether it involves de-coding a confidential password or creating a computer virus.
Hard Drive	hardware component usually built into the PC, and stores the operating system, programs and data.
Help Desk	the people you call when you're in trouble.
Hot mail	a web-based e-mail account, which can be procured for free off the Internet. Users only need to register with hot mail to qualify and the managers theoretically assure confidentiality. To retrieve e-mail via hot mail, you log on to the Internet and then to the hot mail web site. Then you key in your user password and check for your e-mail. Users do not need to have a personal computer to use hot mail but can access their e-mail from a computer in a cyber cafe or library.
Intel Corp.	world's producer of the most commonly-used microprocessor in 1999, the Pentium chip.
Intranet	collection of local area networks with restricted access to a single corporation.
Icq	personalized closed chat-instant messaging occurs between two computers and usually between two people who know each other, at least by their nicknames.
Internet	the world's biggest communications network, by which users can readily visit a gazillion web sites and talk with other computers and persons.
IBM	International Business Machines is the name of a computer company, which produces both hardware and software. IBM was established in 1924.
IBM clone	reference to personal computers that were designed to run on MS-DOS operating system.

IRC	multiple chat rooms, where people talk on-line to people whom they don't know from a hole in the ground.
ISDN	Integrated Signal Digital Network – high-speed telecommunications line.
Keyboard commands	a short string of symbolstyped by the keyboard, which can instruct the computer what to do.
Laser printer	high-quality printer used widely in the business environment, with a resolution of 1200 dpi x 1200 dpi.
Machine code	the code by which machines can execute a program, varies from one computer manufacturer to the next.
Macintosh	operating system of Apple Computers
Mainframe computer	large computers reserved for corporate and institutional users.
Microprocessor	another name for computer chip
Microsoft	name of the world's wealthiest computer software company which licensed out the operating system Windows to 90 per cent of the world's PC users and produces numerous other computer-related products.
Mini-computer	is the type of computer more commonly around a decade ago and filled the computing niche between mainframe and PC. DEC began producing mini-computers during the early 1960's.
MIS	Management Information System, used to analyze and format corporate data into pretty good looking reports for managers to review.

Modem	communications device that enables your computer to exchange data between other computers over a public telephone line. Most PC's sold during 1999 are equipped with 56K modems.
Motherboard	the electronic component found in the PC that contains the microprocessor and electronic circuitry, place you go to install computer hardware up-grades.
Mouse	the PC peripheral by which the user can interact with the computer.
MS-DOS	is an operating system that was commonly installed in PC's during the 1970's and was licensed by Microsoft. MS-DOS is a predecessor of the Windows operating system.
MUD	Multi-User Dungeons, on-line gaming activity where participants role play characters in real-time under assumed identifies. Various versions of MUD have acronyms that sound similar, MUSH, MUX, etc.
Network administrator	the techie who gets to the keep the corporate network going, re-booting it on days when the system crashes.
NEC	Japanese manufacturer of electronic computers and other electronic goods since the 1950's.
Nintendo	Japanese company established in 1949, which is responsible for the 1999 rage of GameBoy, a hand-held electronic game unit and game called Pokemon.
Operating system	the software, which acts as a messenger between the hardware and applications software.
OS/2	operating system developed by IBM and used in the financial services institutional environment, preferred system by many accountants.

PARC   Palto Alto Research Center founded by Xerox.

Palmtop computer
                 small computers, which weighed under two pounds and were introduced during the mid-1990's and have since been replaced by personal digital assistants.

Pentium chip   a microprocessor or computer chip installed in most PC's nowadays.

Personal computer (PC)
                 a computer that you can use at home. PC's have become popular since the late 1970's. Nobody thought they needed a computer at home, until the PC was invented.

PDA   Personal Digital Assistant – sophisticated electronic organizer, that can help you schedule and organize your daily personal affairs, eg. 3Com's Palm Pilot and Apple's Newton.

Peripheral   any hardware device that can be attached to your PC via a serial port connection, eg. printer, scanner, etc.

PERL   programming language, a multi-purposes scripting language, that doesn't require compiling.

Random Access Memory (RAM)
                 is a buffer space in the computer to hold programs currently running, and usually holds the files that you are working on. In a PC, the RAM is comprised of a chip.

Server   computer within a network of computers assigned to serving other computers. It could be a mainframe, PC or Unix machine. Servers often do the grunt work at one location before passing on the results to "client" computers.

Glossery of Terms 231

Slide Rule calculating device invented during the 17th Century, based on the fact that numbers could be multiplied and divided by the addition and subtraction of logarithms.

SOAG Son Of A Geek.

Source code code that programmers produce, can be written in any programming language being used. To make the source code executable, it has to be converted into machine code. Such a process is often two staged where first the source code is converted into machine code modules and then each module has to be linked together in an executable scheme.

Spam unsolicited e-mail, junk e-mail.

Structured query languages
fourth generation computer language to retrieve and present data that you can work with, converts data into bar or pie charts for final reports.

Sun Micro System
company which manufactures the workstation for the Unix-operating system.

Supercomputer
powerful mainframe computer capable of processing copious amounts of data to solve complex scientific equations, often used for modeling and simulations

Systems analysts
techies who put together and maintain the over all computing system requirements for a corporate or institutional environment.

Systems programmers
Back in the old days, systems programmers did a lot of assembler work. Nowadays, they work closely with the maintenance of a computer system with duties like installation of new software, organizing backups on the network, computer security, data input and apply remedial action when the computer crashes.

Texas Instruments	company known to produce electronic calculators and electronic components.
Utilities	programs required to run your PC system smoothly, eg. notepad, calculators, virus scanners, directory tools, dial-up software, etc.
UNIVAC	stands for Universal Automatic Computer developed during between 1946 and 1949, and slated for institutional use. Eventually 47 UNIVAC's were built.
UNIX	infamous operating system that started to take over small mainframe jobs during the 1960's and 1970's within government and university institutional environments, especially in engineering, physics, military and science departments. UNIX penetrated the corporate environment during the mid-1980's onwards for scientific applications, eg. petroleum industry.
Visual Basic	object-oriented programming language developed during the 1990's.
Workstation	definition changes from place to place. Sometimes synonymous with the UNIX desktop computer and sometimes, just the location where the user can access a computer, whether it be a mainframe or PC.
Virus	computer users dread at all cost. Can cause computer crashes and mortality.
Zippy disk	a diskette capable of storing up to 250 megabytes of data.

Twelve Reasons Why You Should Buy Revenge of the Computer Widow *for Your Friends, Family & Co-Workers*

1. If you are a computer widow(er), you will find out that you're not alone.

2. If you are looking for love and you are considering on-line dating, read this book.

3. Motivational material to develop your own ideas and interests independently of your significant other.

4. If you have never used a computer before, let this book show you the ropes without torturing you with a lot of three letter acronyms and jargon.

5. If you are a computer techie, this book will help you realize that maybe you're not so different after all, actually you're pretty much like everybody else.

6. Makes you think about getting a chip installed in your brain, for kicks.

7. If you are the boss of computer geeks, read this book.

8. If your customers are geeks, you need this book.

9. If you are studying computer science at university or college, or planning to, get this book to find out what the workplace may be like.

10. If you're planning a career switch into computers, at least find out who you may be working with.

11. If you're a modern-day gold digger, you should have this book memorized.

12. If you're an investor, get this book so you know at least what all the techies are talking about.

Reasons to Buy
Miracles for the Entrepreneur
*a must have funny book for anyone in business,
also by Nattalia Lea*

1. You want to laugh your way to the bank.

2. You're in business for yourself and you cannot afford healthcare.

3. You've been taken yourself too seriously.

4. You need a re-freshing outlook on business life to get you motivated.

5. You've had a real bad day at the office.

6. Cubicle life has gone too far and you're thinking of starting up your own business.

7. Here's what others had to say about the book:

   "For those entrepreneurs and friends who miss the humorous side of their business life, this book is a must read!"
   C.S. Roger Jarvis, President of Jarvis/Woodside Travel and Canadian Prairie Regional Entrepreneur of the Year 1995 (Services Division)

   "This book illuminates a lot of two bit situations in human affairs that we see every day. It isn't so much a humor book as a humorous book about business life."
   John A. Masters, President of Anschutz Exploration Corporation and former president of Canadian Hunter Exploration Ltd.

   "Move over Dilbert, here comes Joe Rat!"
   Leona Flim, Lethbridge Herald

Order These Books
for your friends, family & co-workers!
Show them that you care about them.

MIRACLES FOR THE ENTREPRENEUR
– a must have funny book for anyone in business

By Nattalia Lea
ISBN 0-86998-640-8 96 pages,
71 black and white cartoons.
Cheaper than Prozac with no long-term side effects,
let this book help laugh yourself to the bank!

REVENGE OF THE COMPUTER WIDOW
*– how to get what you want in life,
when computers are required*

By Nattalia Lea
ISBN 0-86998-641-6 256 pages, 11 tables $29.95
Includes comprehensive appendices
Over 250 pages of insights, pointers and anecdotes
to help you understand computer people,
introduce you to life in the Next Millenium
and educate you. Enjoyed by everybody
from computer newbies to power users!

Order Form

Your Name: _____

Your Address: _____

City: _____ Province/State: _____

Country: _____ Postal Code/Zip: _____

Your e-mail address: _____

ITEM	QTY.	PRICE	TOTAL
Revenge of the Computer Widow	x	$29.95	
Miracles for the Entrepreneur	x	$13.95	
Quality White Cool T-shirt *with silk-screened smashed computer image* (50% cotton/poly blend) (one size fits all)	x	$19.95	
Computer Widow Chocolate CD's (Canadian customers only) In re-usable CD coffee mug coaster	x	$9.95	
Shipping and Handling		$3.00	
Sub-total			
7 % G.S.T. (Canada only):subtotal		x .07	
Total Enclosed			

G.S.T. Registration No. R1330766   Prices are subject to Change

Please make check or money order payable to **Platypus Publishers, 2323E 3rd Ave. N.W., Calgary, AB. T2N 0K9 Canada**

International customers, please pay in U.S. funds.
American customers can also order by calling
Book Clearing House at **1-800-431-1579**
On-line orders accepted at www.geekculture.com

Please allow 2 to 6 weeks for delivery.
Visit: www.cadvision.com/eucalypt/platypus
For information on discounts for orders of five or more books,
  please call   (403) 283-0498 collect,
  fax: (403) 270-3023 or
  e-mail: platypus@cadvision.com